COMMON LISP
and
ARTIFICIAL
INTELLIGENCE

PATRICK R. HARRISON

United States Naval Academy

Prentice Hall
Englewood Cliffs, New Jersey 07632

Library of Congress Cataloging-in-Publication Data

Harrison, Patrick R., [date]
    Common Lisp and artificial intelligence / Patrick R. Harrison.
        p.   cm.
    Includes bibliographical references.
    ISBN 0–13–155243–0
        1. COMMON LISP (Computer program language) 2. Artificial
intelligence. I. Title.
QA76.73.C28H36 1990
006.3—dc20   89-23108
                                                              CIP

To Bruce Davidson, Vince Sigillito
and to my family,
Jackie, Kathy, Rob, and Charlie.

Editorial/production supervision and
    interior design: Fred Dahl and Rose Kernan
Cover design: Bruce Kenselaar
Manufacturing buyer: Ray Sintel

 © 1990 by Prentice-Hall, Inc.
A Division of Simon & Schuster
Englewood Cliffs, New Jersey 07632

Printed in the United States of America
10 9 8 7 6 5 4 3 2 1

ISBN 0-13-155243-0

Prentice-Hall International (UK) Limited, *London*
Prentice-Hall of Australia Pty. Limited, *Sydney*
Prentice-Hall Canada Inc., *Toronto*
Prentice-Hall Hispanoamericana, S.A., *Mexico*
Prentice-Hall of India Private Limited, *New Delhi*
Prentice-Hall of Japan, Inc., *Tokyo*
Simon & Schuster Asia Pte. Ltd., *Singapore*
Editora Prentice-Hall do Brasil, Ltda., *Rio de Janeiro*

Contents

CHAPTER 4

Elementary Functions, 64

CHAPTER 7

Program Development, 132

CHAPTER 8

State Space Search, 151

Preface

This book provides an introduction to Common Lisp and artificial intelligence programming for the computer science student or for the software engineer interested in artificial intelligence programming in Common Lisp. It can be used for a course in artificial intelligence programming, Common Lisp, expert system design, or as an adjunct resource or supplementary text for an introduction to artificial intelligence course. The presentation is clear and to-the-point, focusing the attention of the student on fundamental ideas. Any embellishments or additional ornamentation of basic algorithms is up to the instructor.

The underlying philosophy is that Lisp provides a natural and unencumbered means for expressing ideas about mind that can be subjected to experiments. The presentation tries to capture this naturalness without neglecting the basic principles of software design. The idea is to teach both areas without either one diminishing the other. A deeper philosophy is that Lisp is an artist's tool and can be used to express theories of mind in powerful and natural ways. The complexity and expressiveness of the symbol in Lisp, the *treeness* of the language, the concept of the Lisp environment, the creation of persistent side effects, and the concept of interpretation provide powerful constructs for expressing theories of cognitive function.

Structure of the Text

There is no clear starting point in Lisp. Therefore, it is necessary to *bootstrap* somewhat in getting started. Chapter 1 introduces enough detail to get the student started. The chapter describes the basic Lisp environment, introduces the concept of Lisp interpretation, discusses how to use the Lisp interpreter for problem solving, and teaches the basic syntax of the language. The chapter also discusses error recovery and basic input and output operations.

Chapters 2 and 3 introduce very basic Common Lisp primitives. The second chapter begins with *numbers* to start the student on familiar ground. It then moves to the more important topic of *symbols*. From symbols, *lists and primitives for manipulating list structures* are introduced in detail. The focus is on primitives that will be used later to express higher level abstractions. The material on lists builds naturally on an understanding of the Lisp symbol.

Chapter 4 gives the student the tools needed to write function definitions. By the end of the chapter, the student should be able to write simple programs. This chapter is crucial since it marks the transition from learning language primitives to using the language for expressing procedural abstractions.

Chapters 5 and 6 provide advanced tools for expressing procedural abstractions and for developing macro definitions. The focus is on learning to write macro definitions and on knowing how and when to use closures, arrays, hash tables, and DEFSTRUCTS in building good programs.

Chapter 7 puts it all together by discussing the organization of both small and large programs. It develops an example to show how the concepts might be implemented in an application. It also discusses compilation and efficiency.

Chapters 8, 9, and 10 progressively introduce the essential concepts in knowledge-based system design and implementation in Common Lisp. Chapter 8 focuses on problems associated with state space search and the control of search. This chapter also demonstrates the naturalness of object oriented design in Lisp programming. Chapter 9 focuses on unification, pattern directed inference, and deductive retrieval. The chapter implements a prototype system for pattern directed inference that can be scaled with ease into a much larger system. It also provides a dynamic facility for checking the internal consistency of entered rules. Finally, Chapter 10 introduces goal directed inference with multiple contexts and certainty factors. It also discusses techniques for the development of knowledge bases. A full application system is developed and a general approach to prototyping illustrated.

Acknowledgments

Program development and testing for this book was done using GOLDEN COMMON LISP ©™ developed by Gold Hill Computers, SUN™ COMMON LISP 2.1 a product of Sun Micro Systems, and VAX LISP 2.1 ©™ a version of Common Lisp developed by Digital Equipment Corporation: VAX and VAXLISP are trademarks of Digital Equipment Corporation.

The author wishes to thank these organizations for their cooperation during the development of this textbook and for granting permission to show example macro expansions in the chapter on using and writing macros. The Sun Common Lisp macro expansions shown in Chapter 5 were reproduced with the permission of Sun Microsystems, Inc., from Sun™ Common Lisp version 2.1, copyright © 1987 by

Sun Microsystems. Sun Common Lisp is a trademark of Sun Microsystems. Common Lisp is a product marketed by Lucid, Incorporated. The Golden Common Lisp macros shown in Chapter 5 were reproduced with permission of Gold Hill Computers, Inc., from Golden Common Lisp 3.0, copyright © 1988 by Gold Hill Computers. The VaxLisp macro expansions shown in Chapter 5 were reproduced with the permission of Digital Equipment Corporation, Inc., from VaxLisp version 2.2, copright © 1987 by Digital Equipment Corporation. A special thanks to Gold Hill Computers for providing excellent support for their Lisp products throughout this effort.

A special thanks to Dr. Ann Ratcliffe for reading the manuscript and spending many hours editing drafts and redrafts, testing problems and program code, and making numerous general suggestions that improved the clarity and quality of the manuscript. A special thanks also to my graduate students in the Whiting School of Engineering continuing education program at The Johns Hopkins University who provided valuable feedback, criticism, and suggestions during extended testing of the chapters. A special thanks to William A. Anderson and David Haupt whose evaluations and ideas were instrumental to the design of the final version of PDI.

1

The Magic of LISP

1.1 COMMON LISP

The formal development of Lisp started in the 1950s. This makes it relatively old, among the major languages, rivaled only by Fortran for seniority. It evolved as a language designed to facilitate the representation and manipulation of symbolic information. Lisp implements a universal symbol system and as such is sufficient to express intelligent action in procedural form (Newell, 1980). Common Lisp represents the current state of the evolution of Lisp. It was designed to provide a powerful, efficient and standard or common dialect of the Lisp language. Before Common Lisp, the numerous dialects of Lisp in use ensured a lack of portability and created a kind of "Tower of Babel" effect in communications between Lisp programmers and programs. The reference for this book and the specification for Common Lisp is Steele et al. (1984). The Steele book describes both the syntax and meaning of the basic primitive structures of the language. Any implementation that explicitly calls itself a Common Lisp implies by the use of that name that they have implemented the entire Common Lisp specification.

Figure 1.1 shows several of the major dialects of Lisp that have influenced the development of Common Lisp. Common Lisp is not a descendant of any one dialect of Lisp. It represents an amalgam of important concepts from a number of Lisp dialects as well as other Lisp-like languages that express programs as functions. From this point, when the word "Lisp" is used it will refer to Common Lisp. Sometimes the abbreviation CL will also be used.

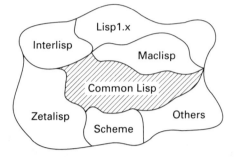

Figure 1.1   Some Dialects That Have Influenced Common Lisp.

1.2 THE BASIC OBJECTS OF THE LANGUAGE

The basic elements of Lisp are called *objects*. The basic objects discussed in this book are symbols, numbers, characters, lists, arrays, strings, functions, and structures. Figure 1.2 shows how these objects fit into the type organization of Common Lisp. In the early part of the text, focus will be on the use of symbols and lists. Strings and characters are used throughout the text since they serve a variety of purposes. More advanced or exotic object types will be introduced on an as-needed basis. The general way of referring to *any* Lisp object is as a symbolic expression.

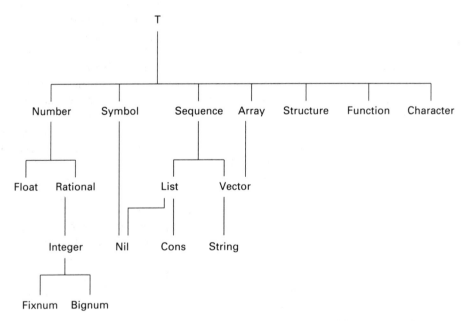

Figure 1.2   Partial Representation of the Type Organization of Common Lisp.*

*The basic organization of this figure from Simpson (1987). See back sheet of this reference for a complete type organization.

We will use the terms "object," "symbolic expression," or "expression" interchange-ably to refer to any legitimate Lisp object.

Names and Symbols

Traditionally, names are used to represent variables. In Pascal, for example, you might use names like Var1, Var2, or NumX. These names can then be given values using the standard assignment operator. For example, Var1:=10, Var2:= 345, and NumX:='A string'. In Lisp, names are translated into complex internal structures called *symbols*. Symbols can have values but can also serve other purposes. Names are input to Lisp as character strings. They are represented internally as symbols. The symbol is a complex internal data object that provides a powerful representa-tional structure. The term "symbol" will be used to refer to both the name and the internal structure that the name stands for. The distinction should be kept in mind when thinking about the representation of knowledge.

Lists

A well formed list is enclosed in an equal number of right and left parentheses (. . .). A left parenthesis indicates the beginning of a list and a right parenthesis the end of a list. The empty list is ( ) or NIL. NIL also stands for the boolean value false. It is convention to use ( ) to mean the empty list and '( ) to mean false. Elements of lists are separated by parentheses and spaces. Examples of lists are:

```
()                                       ;empty list
(a list of elements)                     ;simple list
(alistofelements)                        ;single element
(a,list,of,elements)                     ;illegal list
((a)(list)(of)(elements))                ;a list of lists
(((a))((list))((of))((elements)))        ;deeply nested
((a list of elements))                   ;single element
```

The first example is an empty list. The second example is a simple list with four elements. The third example is a list with one element with a rather complex looking print name. The fourth list is not "legal" syntax since it uses commas as separators. Commas have a special purpose and cannot be used as separators in Lisp. The fifth example is a list of lists with four elements, each of which is a list. The sixth example is another nested list with four elements, each of which is a list of lists. The final example is a list that contains only one element, which is a list.

Strings, Characters, and Comments

Strings are enclosed in double quotes. The string "hello there" illustrates. The empty string is "". Strings are used primarily for documentation and for printing.

The Common Lisp character set is the ASCII set and a newline character (#\newline). If you input the expression #\A to Lisp, A will be returned. The general form #\character returns character.

The semicolon (;) is used for commenting in Lisp. Anything to the right of a semicolon is ignored by Lisp as commentary or documentation. It is customary to precede comments with two or more semicolons (;;;) when documenting code outside of functions and a single semicolon when documenting within a function. For example:

```
;;Sample function call
(* 4 5)   ; everything after is ignored.
=> 20
```

1.3 WHAT IS LISP?

Lisp is an environment developed for interactive symbolic computing. When we type the command LISP, CLISP, GCLISP, CL, or whatever command signals the operating system that we are ready to compute with Lisp, the Lisp environment is loaded and initialized, and a listener is invoked. The listener provides a means for using the Lisp environment to do computations. It provides an interface between the Lisp environment and the programmer. The listener you invoke when you activate Lisp is called the TOP LEVEL LISTENER to distinguish it from any other listener you activate while computing.

The Listener

The *listener* is defined as a loop that prompts (usually *, >, or ->) for a Lisp expression, evaluates the input expression, and prints the results of the evaluation back to the user. It then prompts (listens) for the next expression. This process continues until the computational process is stopped by the programmer—usually by the explicit expression (EXIT), which terminates the interactive session. There is nothing sacred about the listener, and it could be written in many ways and could take on many forms. If, for example, you input a nonstandard expression that signals an error, a listener called a *debugger* is activated. This is another listener that provides a view of the computational state at the time the error occurred. It also makes additional tools available for debugging the error. It provides a different view of the Lisp environment than the listener you were using before the error occurred. Any number of debug listeners can be activated if you continue to compound the initial error. These listeners are usually distinguished by numbered prompts (1>, 2>, 3> . . .).

The Very Basic Nomenclature

The examples in this section illustrate the basic nomenclature needed to describe an interactive session. No prompt will be used in the text as illustrated by the expression (* 3 4). The symbol => indicates that whatever immediately follows is the *value* of the computed expression. The value 12 is returned in the example. When no result need be returned or none is returned, the symbol => will be followed by nothing. When the result returned is implementation dependent, the dependency will be explicitly noted.

```
(* 3 4)
=> 12
```

The format of output and the prompt used will differ from implementation to implementation. Implementation-dependent features of interest will be noted when pertinent. In some cases, functions will both return values and print text. The printed text is a side effect of the execution of a function and is not the same as a returned value. By definition, a function should only return values. The print function shows an example of this:

```
(PRINT 'HELLO)
HELLO
=>HELLO
```

First the print command is executed and hello is printed. This is one kind of side effect in a function. Notice the symbol => does not precede the side effect. Secondly, the value of the object HELLO is returned. This is indicated by the => preceding the result. Since Lisp functions can compute by side effects as well as by returning values, the terms "function" and "procedure" are often used interchangeably when describing Lisp definitions. The term "function" focuses one's attention on returned values. The term "procedure" focuses one's attention on computing by side effect.

Evaluation and Extensibility

The fundamental idea in Lisp is that expressions are *interpreted* by the *listener* with reference to the *Lisp environment* and the value of the *interpreted* expression is returned. In some cases, the process of interpreting an expression produces a change, called a *side effect,* to the internal Lisp environment. For example, the previous computation might have created a new symbol with a value. If this symbol is available in the Lisp environment after the computation has completed, it is a side effect because it has changed the Lisp environment and therefore the environment in which the next computation will take place. This is why the Lisp environment is called *extensible.* In the process of computing, the environment can be extended by creating side effects. You might say that one definition of a Lisp program is that it is an extended Lisp environment. In my own work with Lisp, I like to go one step further and consider the extended environments as theories of mind! This keeps my own use of Lisp centered on the ultimate value of the language as a symbol system for expressing intelligent behavior.

EVAL and Forms

The heart of the interpretive process is evaluation. Evaluation is defined by a
complex function EVAL, which really defines the semantics of the interpreter. The
basic rule is simple, with few exceptions Lisp evaluates everything, and the course
of the evaluation process is determined by the definition of the EVAL function.

A FORM is a Lisp expression that is meant to be evaluated. Most of what you
input to the interpreter are forms or composite forms. There are basically three
kinds of forms in Lisp: self-evaluating forms, variable forms, and list forms. A
number is a self-evaluating form; it evaluates to itself. A variable evaluates to
whatever value it has at the time of evaluation. List forms are more complex. The
way they are evaluated depends on the name following the left parenthesis in the
list. For the time, assume that, if the name following the left parenthesis is not a
special name indicating that a definition (DEF . . .) will follow (DEFUN,
DEFMACRO, . . .), then consider it the name of a definition to be accessed and
applied to whatever arguments follow.

```
23 => 23
12.12345678987654321 => 12.12345678  ;may vary
VAR1 => (A LIST OF STUFF)            ;value of VAR1
(* 23 34) => 782
(+ (* 3 4) (/ 10 2)) => 17
```

The first example is a number that evaluates to itself. The second example shows
the same concept but suggests the realities of precision and rounding errors. The
third example shows that, when you input a name, the value associated with the
name is returned. The fourth example is a list form. The name after the left
parenthesis is the multiplication symbol. The definition associated with the *
symbol is applied to the evaluated arguments 23 and 34. The final example shows
a nested expression. For the addition to be carried out, it is necessary that the two
inner (nested) expressions be evaluated first. This is exactly how Lisp works.
Evaluation proceeds from left to right, with each left parenthesis causing an
iteration of the basic computational loop producing levels of computation. In this
manner, nested expressions return values to outer expressions that need the evaluated arguments to complete the computation. Only the value of the top level
expression is returned and *only the last value computed by the top level form is
returned*.

Primitives of the Language

Notice that function names such as *, +, and / preceded their arguments. These
symbols name predefined Lisp functions that multiply, add, and divide the values of
their arguments or operands. We will adopt the convention of calling all such
predefined procedures *primitives*. The primitive (*) is applied to the arguments 23

and 34 after they have been evaluated. Since numbers are self-evaluating forms, 23 evaluates to 23, and 34 evaluates to 34. The resulting value, 782, is returned.

Cambridge Polish Notation

Notation with the function name preceding the arguments is a prefix notation called Cambridge Polish. It is the standard form for a procedure call. Everything is evaluated from left to right. So any name following a left parenthesis in any Lisp form will have special significance to Lisp (EVAL . . .). Thereafter, will follow information that is used according to the definition of the first term.

Interpretation and Compilation

It should be noted that the expression being interpreted may be *compiled*. This is true of the functions (called *primitives*) that are made available with the Common Lisp implementation. This is sometimes confused with the notion of *interpretation*. The interpretive loop performs the process on both compiled and uncompiled expressions. The purpose of compilation in Lisp is to improve the efficiency of computation.

Type

Lisp is called a *latently* typed language. This is because every object carries type information with it (has type information as a property), and every object is embedded in a type hierarchy. Each type in Lisp can be thought of as a set of Lisp objects. This is because a Lisp object can be a member of more than one type. For example, an integer 10 is in the set T, COMMON, ATOM, NUMBER, RATIONAL, INTEGER, and FIXNUM in increasingly restrictive order.

The practical consequence of this is that we are not required to declare a variable of a particular type before assigning it a value, and a variable is not restricted to being assigned one type of object. Since the value of a variable carries type information with it, a variable can take any object as its value.

A Pointer World

Lisp has driven much of the complexity of the language below the surface. Lisp is a pointer world, with all the headaches that explicit pointer manipulation and management can cause. Most computations in Lisp involve the manipulation of pointers rather than actual data. However, Lisp manages the pointer world, freeing the programmer to focus attention at a higher level of composition and abstraction. The term *cell* will be used in text to refer to pointer locations.

The consequence of the relaxation of the strong typing constraint is that memory must be allocated and deallocated during run time. This process creates garbage in the form of memory cells that are no longer in use. Lisp maintains a garbage collection facility to reclaim memory that is no longer in use and reallocate it as available for use again. If you see the letters GC light up in a corner of your screen or you notice computation slow down or stop occasionally, it is probably your garbage collector at work.

Programs as Data

One of the strengths of Lisp is that programs and data are represented in the same way. The list (* 6 7) can be used as the value of a variable or as an executable expression that returns the value of the multiplication operation. The semantics of any expression are defined by the evaluation process in Lisp. The rule is that Lisp tries to evaluate everything. In the form (* 6 7) Lisp evaluates (*), 6 and 7. Then (*) is applied to the evaluated arguments. To use (* 6 7) as a data object, stop the evaluation process by quoting the list. For example:

```
(*  6  7)  =>  42
'(*  6  7)  =>  (*  6  7)
(QUOTE  (*  6  7))  =>  (*  6  7)
```

By inputting (* 6 7) to Lisp, the value 42 will be returned. By inputting '(* 6 7) or (QUOTE (* 6 7)), the expression within the quote '(. . .) or (QUOTE . . .) will not be evaluated and the expression itself is returned. Note, for the time being, that (') can be used to stop evaluation of an expression. Remember that any Lisp object can serve as data.

1.4 NOTATION

When learning a new language, it is important to spend some time on the relatively uninteresting task of mastering the basic notation used in the language specification. You will learn more quickly and understand more fully everything that follows if you do this. This section introduces the basic notation used throughout the book. Steele et al. (1984) is the specification for Common Lisp and should be considered the reference document for any question of syntax or semantics. The notation used in this text is consistent with that used by Steele but varies in the following ways. The names of primitives are capitalized and in bold print for emphasis. The first letter of arguments that are not evaluated are capitalized. Lambda list keywords, such as &OPTIONAL and &REST, are capitalized to distinguish them from following arguments.

Notation for the Language Primitives

The name of any definition is capitalized and in bold print. All argument forms that are evaluated appear in lower case italics. If the argument form is not evaluated, the first letter is capitalized. Two examples for the arbitrary definition FUNC, which takes two arguments, are shown in the definition box.

FUNC *arg1 arg2*
FUNC *Arg1 arg2*

In the example, the first version of FUNC has two arguments, both of which are evaluated. In the second version, the first argument is not evaluated. All definitions from the Common Lisp specification will be defined using standard syntax and will be boxed in text. For the more complex definitions, an informal definition will also be provided. An alphabetical index of these definitions with page number references is provided in Appendix A.

Two primitives that have already been introduced briefly are shown next. These two forms will be examined in more detail later. For now, only their syntax is of interest. EVAL takes a form. The lower case first letter on form indicates that *form* is evaluated. In the second example, *Object* is not evaluated.

EVAL *form*
QUOTE *Object*

Lambda List Keywords

Some definitions contain lambda list keywords indicating special features of the argument list for that function. The most common of these are &OPTIONAL, &REST, and &KEY.

The &OPTIONAL keyword indicates that an optional argument may be supplied. If it is not supplied, a default value is used. The nature of the default is dependent upon what the definition computes. The &REST keyword indicates that the primitive can take a variable number of arguments. The &KEY keyword precedes keywords of the form :name. The use of these lambda list keywords in definitions is shown in the examples. Lambda list keywords will be shown in normal typeface and uppercase. Keywords following the &KEY lambda list keyword will have a colon followed by normal type face and lower case.

FUNC1 &REST *numbers*
FUNC2 *integer1 integer2* &OPTIONAL (*integer3* 10)
FUNC3 &KEY :name1 :name2

In the first example, the function FUNC1 can take any number of arguments. The arguments must be numbers. In the second example, the function FUNC2 takes two required arguments, followed by an optional third argument. If no value is specified in a call to FUNC, integer3 gets the default value 10. All arguments must be integers. FUNC3 takes two arguments name1 and name2. A call to this function could look like this (FUNC3 :NAME1 'BILL :NAME2 'JANE) or like this (FUNC3 :NAME2 'JANE :NAME1 'BILL).

System Variables

When you initialize Lisp, a number of systems variables are set to default values. It is possible to modify these while you are computing by reassigning values or by building a user initialization file that is loaded whenever you activate the interpreter. The basic form of a system variable is *variable-name*. Systems variables will be discussed on an as-needed basis.

```
*STANDARD-INPUT*
=> TERMINAL-IO-STREAM ;syntax may vary
```

More Syntax and Conventions

Whenever braces {} occur in a definition, it implies that repetitions of the argument set within the braces may occur zero or more times { . . . }* or one or more times { . . . }+. When brackets [] occur in an expression, they indicate that whatever is within them is optional.

The symbol <=> indicates that two forms are equivalent in the sense that they return the same values and create the same side effects in the Lisp environment. For example, (QUOTE HELLO) <=> 'HELLO.

1.5 HOW DO I GET STARTED?

Using the Interpreter

To get started, activate the interpreter using whatever command your operating system recognizes (SYS> is the system prompt we will use). Then start an interactive session by inputting valid expressions. The basic arithmetic functions +, *, /, and − might provide a starting place. They are defined as follows:

```
+ &REST numbers
* &REST numbers
− number &REST more-numbers
/ number &REST more-numbers
```

In addition, you might experiment with the utilities shown in the following sample interaction (definitions follow). They provide basic program development tools for the Lisp programmer.

```
SYS> LISP

WELCOME TO COMMON LISP VERSION ...
(* 10 20)
=> 200
(+ 2 3 4 5)
=> 14
(TIME (+ 2 3 4 5))
TIMING DATA...
=> 14
(DESCRIBE '+)        ;Implementation dependent
   + is a symbol
It has no value
Its function definition is #<COMPILED FUNCTION>
Its property list is empty
=>
(DRIBBLE "SCR")
=>
(* 2 3)
=> 6
(* (+ 3 4) (LOG 100))
=> 32.2362
(DRIBBLE)
=>
(EXIT)

SYS> list scr

(* 2 3)
6
(* (+ 3 4)(LOG 100))
32.2362
(DRIBBLE)
```

The example shows several utility functions being used during an interactive computing session. Each simple calculation returns a value (=> value) or nothing (=>). The DESCRIBE utility can be used to list the bindings associated with any symbol. It is particularly useful in looking at the symbols you create. It returns no value but it prints a description of the symbol as a side effect. The content and format of this description is implementation-dependent. The symbols +, *, and LOG name precompiled primitive functions in Common Lisp.

The DRIBBLE facility allows you to "dribble" your interactive session into a file. This facility continues to operate until you enter (DRIBBLE) with no arguments. This closes the file you have been sending the interactive session to. Later, when you finish computing (EXIT) or (QUIT), you can review what you did by looking at the dribble file.

The function TIME allows you to time the execution of an expression. The format and content of the output are implementation-dependent. It is important to know what a "tick" means on your machine in order to use the TIME function effectively.

The function DOCUMENTATION accesses documentation associated with the named symbol. The second argument, *doc-type*, specifies the kind of documentation wanted with reference to the symbol. Normally, this would have the value *function*, indicating that documentation is wanted for the named function or named macro.

TIME *form*
DESCRIBE *object*
DRIBBLE &OPTIONAL *pathname*
DOCUMENTATION *symbol doc-type*

In addition, the APROPOS function can be used to do searches. APROPOS takes a string as an argument and returns all symbols that have that string as a substring. What do you think this would return? The answer is all symbols in all packages since the empty string is a subset of every string or name.

```
(APROPOS "")
```

If your Lisp implementation comes with a resident editor (most have one), the ED function can be used to call it. Normally a filename or pathname is the argument to ED. Once the file is loaded, using ED without arguments returns you to the editor environment in the same state you left it. Most Lisp editors, EMACS for example, come with a number of commands that facilitate movement between the Lisp environment and the editor environment.

Any saved file that you have built can be loaded using the LOAD primitive. The LOAD function takes a filename such as "MYFILE.LSP" as an argument and can take additional keyword arguments that specify options you may want to exercise. The VERBOSE keyword is either set to true (T) or false (NIL). If true, a message is printed when the file is loaded. Usually this message indicates the full pathname of the file loaded and other useful information. The PRINT keyword, when set to true, causes the value of each expression to be printed to *standard-output* (default is the terminal) as the file is processed. The final keyword IF-DOES-NOT-EXIST, can be used to determine whether or not an error is signaled if the file being loaded does not exist or can not be found. If specified and set to NIL, NIL is returned and no error is signaled.

APROPOS *string* &OPTIONAL *package*
ED &OPTIONAL *x*
LOAD *filename* &KEY :verbose :print :if-does-not-exist

1.6 READING, PRINTING, AND FORMATTING

Reading

The functions READ and READ-LINE are the most commonly used functions for reading input. The INPUT-STREAM refers to the source for input. The rest of the arguments will be discussed later. Examples of the use of these functions are shown next. READ-LINE returns a string terminated by a newline. NIL is also returned if the string was terminated normally.

READ &OPTIONAL *input-stream eof-error-p eof-value recursive-p*
READ-LINE &OPTIONAL *input-stream eof-error-p eof-value recursive-p*

```
(READ)hello
=>HELLO
(READ)(THIS IS A TEST)
=>(THIS IS A TEST)
(READ)'HELLO
=>(QUOTE HELLO)
(READ-LINE) The light became brighter and brighter
=>"The light became brighter and brighter" ; NIL
```

Printing

The primary printing functions are PRINT, PRINC, and PRIN1. PRINT produces a newline character before printing the object that is its argument. PRINC and PRIN1 print without the newline character. PRINC is similar to PRIN1 but acts differently for certain types. For example, it prints strings without quotes whereas PRIN1 would print the string with quotes. PRIN1 produces output that can be read back in by READ. PRINC makes no such guarantee. The function TERPRI can be used to output a newline. Examples of the basic print functions are shown with both the value printed (the side effect) and the value returned (the second value).

```
(PRINC (PRINC (PRINC "hello")))
hellohellohello
=>"hello"

(PRINT (PRINT (PRINT "hello")))
"hello"
"hello"
"hello"
 =>"hello"

(PRIN1 (PRIN1 (PRIN1 "hello")))
"hello""hello""hello"
=>"hello"
```

PRINT *object* &OPTIONAL *output-stream*
PRINC *object* &OPTIONAL *output-stream*
PRIN1 *object* &OPTIONAL *output-stream*
TERPRI &OPTIONAL *output-stream*

Formatting

Common Lisp has a powerful language for formatting printed output. Formatting can be used with the various print function or alone. The first argument to FORMAT is called "DESTINATION." This could be the name of an output stream or the symbols NIL or T. For now it suffices to discuss the use of T and NIL as destinations.

If the value of destination is NIL, a string is created containing the output. This is returned as the value of FORMAT. If the value of the destination is T, the output is printed as a side effect and NIL is returned. The default destination in both cases is *STANDARD-OUTPUT* which is normally the terminal.

FORMAT *destination control-string* &REST *arguments*

The second argument to FORMAT is the control string. This can be exceedingly complex, and only the very basic ideas are presented at this point. The control string contains directives that determine how the *arguments* are formatted. The most basic directives are shown in Figure 1.3 and demonstrated in the following examples:

```
(FORMAT () "a test")
=> "a test"

(FORMAT () "~% a test")
=> "
   a test"

(FORMAT NIL "~% a test")
=>"
 a test"

(FORMAT T "~% a test")
a test
=>NIL

(FORMAT NIL "~A" (QUOTE (A LIST OF STUFF)))
=>"(A LIST OF STUFF)"

(FORMAT T "~A" (QUOTE (A LIST OF STUFF)))
(A LIST OF STUFF)
=>NIL

(FORMAT NIL "~S" (QUOTE (A LIST OF STUFF)))
=>"(A LIST OF STUFF)"

(FORMAT T "~D" 1234)
 1234
=>NIL

(FORMAT NIL "~D and ~D" 1234 34567)
=>"1234 and 34567"

(FORMAT NIL "~F and ~D" 1234 34567)
=>"1234.0 and 34567"
```

A tilde (~) indicates that a directive follows. The directive ~% produces a newline. The directive ~5% produces 5 newlines. The directive ~10T tabs 10 spaces. The directive ~A prints the corresponding argument in ASCII without

FORMAT *destination control-string* &REST *arguments*

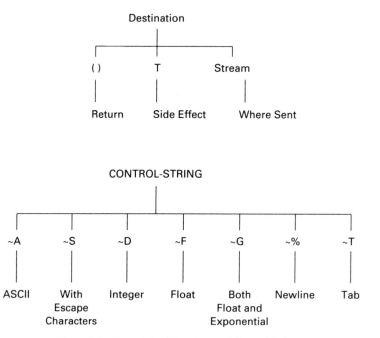

Figure 1.3   Formatting Directives and Control Strings.

escape characters. The directive ~S prints expressions with escape characters. The directives ~D, ~F, and ~E are used to print integers, fixed-format floating, and exponential form floating-point numbers. The G directive prints either fixed or exponential forms as necessary.

Y-OR-N-P &OPTIONAL *format-string* &REST *arguments*
YES-OR-NO-P &OPTIONAL *format-string* &REST *arguments*

Y-OR-N-P and YES-OR-NO-P can be used with format strings to send messages that require a Y/N or YES/NO answer. First the message is printed, and then a (Y or N) or (YES or NO) prompt is printed requiring the user to respond with one of the two responses. An affirmative response returns T and a negative response returns NIL.

1.7 DEALING WITH ERRORS

A useful thing to know at the outset is what to do if you produce an error. If you type in an expression that creates an error condition, you will get an error message of some kind. Often this takes the form of a new kind of prompt, such as 1>. If you continue and make another error, the prompt changes to 2>. This can continue for a very long time. The handling of error conditions and the debugging environment for fixing bugs in programs is implementation-dependent. There is no one standard. There are, however, standard debugging functions that are part of the Common Lisp specification. Two are particularly useful and are introduced now, TRACE and STEP.

TRACE {*Function-name*}*
UNTRACE {*Function-name*}*
STEP *form*

The TRACE function provides a trace of the arguments passed to and the values returned from calls to the functions named as arguments. Any number of functions may be traced simultaneously. The UNTRACE function can be used to stop the tracing process. If UNTRACE is called without arguments, tracing is stopped on all functions being traced. If (UNTRACE FOO) is called, then only FOO is no longer traced. The example assumes we have a recursive function, called FACT, that computes a factorial. The format of the trace will vary with the implementation.

```
(TRACE FACT)
=>T
(FACT 3)
(1 ENT FACT = 3)
  (2 ENT FACT = 2)
    (3 ENT FACT = 1)
      (4 ENT FACT = 0)
      (4 EXIT FACT = 1)
    (3 EXIT FACT = 1)
  (2 EXIT FACT = 2)
(1 EXIT FACT = 6)
=> 6
(UNTRACE)
(FACT 3)
=> 6
```

The STEP primitive allows the programmer to single-step through the evaluation of any form. This primitive provides a useful learning tool when you are trying to understand evaluation. It is also useful when debugging forms to determine the step in which an error occurred.

```
(STEP (* 23 34))
23 evaluates to 23
34 evaluates to 34
(* 23 34) evaluates to 782
=>782
```

A final thing you need to know at the outset is how to reset the listener to the top level after an error has occurred. This will normally be one of several alternative actions the debugger provides when an error has occurred. However, most Lisp implementations streamline this process by providing additional tools.

1.8 SUMMARY

This chapter introduced enough information to get you started using Lisp. We had to bootstrap to a degree, introducing concepts and terms that you will not fully understand until you have finished the first half of the text. It is recommended that you work interactively with the textbook and the implementation of Common Lisp you have available. Remember:

1. Normally everything is evaluated.
2. Evaluation is from left to right.
3. Quoted objects are not evaluated.
4. When nested expressions are evaluated, the results are returned to the previous level.
5. Top level is normally where a computation starts and finishes.
6. EXIT or QUIT usually terminates a session.

1.9 PROBLEMS

1.1 Describe two kinds of side effects that can occur in Common Lisp.

1.2 Would this work? What would it return if given the string "THIS IS THE TIME"?
```
(PRINC (READ))
```

1.3 In what order would the objects in the following expressions be evaluated?
  a. `(FUNC1 X (FUNC2 Y Z))`
  b. `'(A LIST OF LOVELY COCONUTS)`
  c. `(A B C)`

1.4 Of what types is the expression VAR a member?

1.5 Is (+) a valid expression?

1.6 Explain the difference between the definitions for * and /? What does the expression (/ 10 20 30) mean?

1.7 Common Lisp definitions provide for a great deal of flexibility. For example, a function call may allow for a variable number of data objects using &REST or for some data objects to be optional using &OPTIONAL with default values if no value is input in the expression. Show *all* the various forms of legal calls that could be made using each of the following arbitrary function definitions. The calls should illustrate fully the flexibility of the function definition.
a. FUNC1 *Arg1 arg2* &REST *stuff*
b. FUNC2 *num* &OPTIONAL (*base 20*)
c. FUNC3 &KEY *numerator Denominator*

1.8 What do the following system variables control? Note: To answer this question you must refer to the Steele book. What is the initial value of each in your Common Lisp implementation?
a. *PRINT-LENGTH*
b. *READ-BASE*
c. *PRINT-BASE*
d. *TRACE-OUTPUT*
e. *PACKAGE*

1.9 Name two primitives in your version of Common Lisp that are implementation-dependent.

1.10 The usefulness of the TIME function is enhanced if a "tick" is defined for your system. What is the value of a tick for your system?

2

Symbols and Numbers

2.1 INTRODUCTION

Symbols, and to a lesser degree numbers, make up the basic atomic objects out of which Lisp structures and definitions are composed. We start by looking at a variety of primitives used to compute with numbers since this most clearly draws on your experience with other programming languages and allows you to move gently towards symbolic computing at a lower level of abstraction. A mythology has been sustained that Lisp is not suitable for numeric computing. Though this was probably true for older Lisp dialects, Common Lisp has considerable power for numeric computing and offers a very flexible environment for that purpose.

2.2 KINDS OF NUMBERS

Figure 2.1 shows the basic kinds of number objects in Lisp and their place in the type hierarchy for numbers. An *integer* is defined as a whole number. In Common Lisp, an integer can have a decimal point but will never have any digits following it. A real number is a floating-point number (2364.85) with a decimal part or an exponent part if in scientific notation (23.6485×10^2). The ratio form for numbers allows you to express a rational number in an exact way. Lisp recognizes the ratio 1/3 as a legitimate form and would return 1/3. We will focus on integers and real numbers but will occasionally use other number types in problems or examples. Complex numbers will not be discussed.

Numbers are self-evaluating forms. Remember that a form is a symbolic

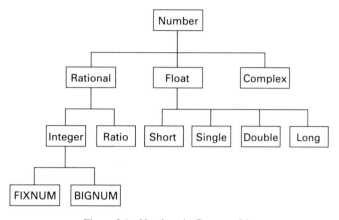

Figure 2.1   Numbers in Common Lisp.

expression that is meant to be evaluated. A self-evaluating form evaluates to itself. So, if we input a number, the number is returned.

```
234 => 234                      ;fixnum
2345678765432234 => 2345678765432234 ;bignum
23e3 => 23000.0                 ;single-float
3.3456d12 => 3.456d12           ;double-float
4E2 => 400.0                    ;single-float
23.4 => 23.4                    ;single-float
#b100 => 4                      ;fixnum in binary notation
#xa => 10                       ;fixnum in hexadecimal
#xA => 10                       ;shows case has no effect
#o12 => 10                      ;fixnum in octal
#2R100 => 4                     ;general radix notation
2/3 => 2/3                      ;a ratio
2/4 => 1/2                      ;notice simplification
4/2 => 2                        ;rational canonicalization
```

The example shows some of the variety of number types and notations used to represent numbers in Common Lisp. The notation #x, #o, and #b refers to hexadecimal, octal, and binary representations, respectively. In general, any radix greater than or equal to 2 and less than or equal to 36 can be used. The format is #nnRdddd where n is the radix, R or r indicates radix notation, and dddd is the number being represented. So #2R100 would be equivalent to #b100. The default in Common Lisp is radix 10.

   Real numbers can be represented in decimal (400.0) or scientific (4E2) notation. The representation of floating point numbers involves implementation-dependent issues, so we will only note that both double (line 4 of the previous example) and single precision (lines 3,5 and 6) are available. The reader is referred to Steele et al. (1984) for a detailed discussion of floating point numbers.

Contagion and Coercion

The concept of floating-point contagion is important in thinking about numbers. The general idea is to coerce type changes in function arguments or results when both rational (integer or ratio) and reals are represented to retain as much precision as possible in the result. In a numeric function, if integer or ratio arguments are mixed with floating-point arguments, the result is represented as a floating-point number. This is referred to as *floating-point contagion*. It is accomplished by the use of implicit coercions.

COERCE *object result-type*

Coercion can also be done explicitly using the function COERCE. This is a general purpose function that can be used with numbers as well as other object types. It takes an object and the specification of a result-type. If the coercion can be performed, the object is returned as result-type. If the coercion cannot be performed, an error is signaled. In terms of numbers, basically two kinds of coercions can be done. Any noncomplex number can be transformed into a floating-point number or any number can be transformed into a complex number. Examples of simple coercions are;

```
(COERCE 234 'FLOAT) => 234.0      ;integer to real
(COERCE 2/3 'FLOAT) => 0.666667   ;ratio to real
```

2.3 NUMBER PREDICATES

Recognizers

NUMBERP *object*
INTEGERP *object*
FLOATP *object*

The predicates NUMBERP, INTEGERP, and FLOATP can be used to recognize integer and floating-point numbers. If a number is a member of the type indicated by the function name, true is returned; otherwise nil is returned. All numbers are of type NUMBER. Integers come in two varieties, FIXNUM and BIGNUM. The distinction is implementation-dependent. BIGNUM, as the name implies, refers to very large integers of arbitrary precision.

Attribute Recognizers

ZEROP *number*
PLUSP *number*
MINUSP *number*
ODDP *integer*
EVENP *integer*

A number of predicate functions make a test on a property of an individual number. These predicates return a boolean value if given a number of the specified type. It is an error to call them with an object of other than the specified type. ZEROP takes any number as an argument. PLUSP and MINUSP take any non-complex number as an argument. These functions return T if the number is zero, strictly greater than zero and strictly less than zero, respectively. Two others EVENP and ODDP take integers as arguments and test whether the integer is even or odd, respectively. It should be noted that, because it is an error to give functions certain types, this does not imply that an error will be signaled. So be aware of how your system deals with error cases such as those noted for these predicates. The next example shows some interesting examples of the use of these predicates.

```
(ZEROP -0.0) => T           ;minus zero is zero
(ZEROP #B-100) => NIL       ;minus 4 is not zero
(PLUSP +0) => NIL           ;plus zero is zero
(PLUSP 0.000001) => T       ;a fraction greater
(PLUSP #B100) => T          ;plus 4 is greater
(MINUSP -0.0) => NIL        ;minus zero is zero
(MINUSP -8) => T            ;minus 8 is less
(ODDP 23) => T              ;23 is an odd number
(ODDP 0 ) => NIL            ;zero is even
(EVENP 0) => T              ;zero is even
(EVENP -234) => T           ;negative but even
```

2.4 NUMBER COMPARATORS

=*number* &REST *more-numbers*
MAX *number* &REST *more-numbers*
MIN *number* &REST *more-numbers*

The comparator functions available for numbers include the standard boolean functions; the same (=), greater than (>), greater than or the same (>=), less than (<), less than or the same (<=), all different (/=), the most positive value (MAX), and the minimum value (MIN). The syntax for these is the same, except that (=) and (/=) can take complex arguments whereas the rest require noncomplex arguments. The &REST portion of the definition indicates that these functions can take any number of arguments. The example illustrates these functions:

```
(= 3 3.0 #b11) => T                ;mixed representations
(= -0.0 0.0) => T                  ;- and + zero are <=>
(= 12) => T                        ;trivial case
(< 3 #B100 #XA #XB #19R18) => T ;3<4<10<11<27
(> 0 -10) => T                     ;0 is greater
(> -10 -1000000) => T              ;-10 is greater
(< -1000 -10000000) => NIL         ;-1000 is not less
(<= 0.0 0) => T                    ;zero equals zero
(>= 23 4 3 2 2 1 1) => T           ;evaluate from left
(>= 23 4 3 2 2 1 2) => NIL         ;1 is not >= 2
(/= 2 3 4) => T                    ;numbers are not equal
(/= 2 2.0) => NIL                  ;2 = 2.0
(MAX 12 234 2E30) => 2.0e30        ;floating-point contagion
(MIN 2e3 4 45.6 -23) => -23        ;mixed types
(MAX 12e10 12d10) => 1.2e11        ;12e10 = 12d10
```

The examples show various notations and mixed types as valid arguments for these functions. All can accept multiple arguments. Evaluation of the boolean occurs from left to right. This means that (< 2 3 4 5) first does the test 2<3, then the test 3<4, and finally the test 4<5. There is no distinction between (−0.0) and (0.0). MAX and MIN may use implicit coercion but it is not required.

2.5 ARITHMETIC OPERATIONS

```
   + &REST numbers
1+ number
1- number
MOD number divisor
REM number divisor
```

The definitions for the basic arithmetic operations; addition (+), subtraction (−), division (/), and multiplication (*) were shown in Chapter 1. All of the basic operations will work with any type of number. Coercion will occur if mixed types are given to any of these functions. To be clear on how these functions operate with more than two arguments, make the assumption that the primitive (*, /, +, or −, for example) is being applied to the first two arguments, then the result of that evaluation with the third argument, and so on until all arguments have been exhausted. So (/ 400 2 10 4) would first do (/ 400 2), then (/ 200.0 10.0), and finally (/ 20.0 4.0). Make sure that there is at least one space between the function name and the first argument. The form (*8 9) produces an error because *8 is evaluated as a symbol rather than a number. The function 1+ and 1− are equivalent to (+ number 1) and (− number 1) respectively. They are convenient for incrementing values.

MOD and REM accept two arguments: a number and a divisor. The arguments can be of type integer or floating-point, though both functions are typically used with integer arguments. The value of MOD is the modulo of the first argument divided by the second. The value of REM is the remainder of the result of dividing the first argument by the second. A definition of MOD using the FLOOR function is shown when the FLOOR function is introduced. A small sampling of arithmetic operations is shown in the next example.

```
(+ 23/7 2e3 23.4 #b100) => 2030.685  ;floating-point
(+) => 0                     ;identity
(- 5) => -5                  ;returns the negative
(/ 400 2 10 4) => 5          ;result is fixnum
(/ 400 2 10 4.0) => 5.0      ;result is single-float
(/ 400 2 11 4) => 50/11      ;result is ratio
(/ 2) => 1/2                 ;reciprocal
(* -300 2 4 -5) => 12000     ;integer multiplication
(1+ 10) => 11                ;incrementing a number
(1- 10) => 9                 ;decrementing a number
```

```
(MOD 22 6) => 4            ;modulo 6
(MOD -22 6) => 2           ;negative number
(MOD -22 -6) => -4         ;negative number & divisor
(MOD 22 -6) => -2          ;negative divisor
(REM 22 6) => 4            ;remainder
(REM -22 6) => -4          ;negative number
(REM -22 -6) => -4         ;negative number & divisor
(REM 22 -6) =>  4          ;negative divisor
```

2.6 EXPONENTIAL, LOGARITHMIC, AND TRIGONOMIC FUNCTIONS

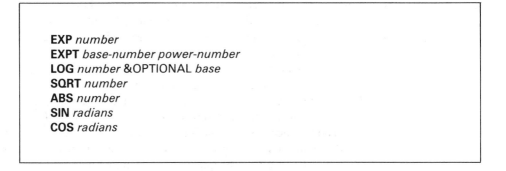

EXP *number*
EXPT *base-number power-number*
LOG *number* &OPTIONAL *base*
SQRT *number*
ABS *number*
SIN *radians*
COS *radians*

The function EXP can be given any number as an argument, and it returns the value of raising the base for the natural logarithm *e* to the power indicated by the *number*. EXPT is a more generalized version of this function where *base-number* is raised to the *power-number* power. The reader is referred to Steele for a detailed description of the handling of this function. Several examples of the use of these functions are:

```
(EXP 1) => 2.718281828     ;e raised to the first power
(EXP 0) => 1.0             ;e raised to zero power
(EXP 0.0) => 1.0           ;floating-point version
(EXP #b100) => 54.59814    ;using binary notation
(EXPT 2 3) => 8            ;2 cubed
(EXPT 2. 3.) => 8          ;2. and 3. are integers
(EXPT 2.0 3.0) => 8.0      ;note the approximation
(EXPT 10 2.0) => 100.0     ;another example
(EXPT 10.0 2) => 100.0     ;compare to previous
```

The function LOG will return the logarithm of any number to the base *e*. The default base *e* can be changed using the optional argument to specify any base.

SQRT returns the square root of any number. ABS returns the absolute value of any number. Several examples of these functions are;

```
(LOG 20) => 2.995732274          ;coercion
(LOG 200 10) => 2.301029995      ;base is 10
(LOG 200.0 10.0 ) => 2.301029995 ;base is 10.0
(SQRT 3/2) => 1.224744871        ;ratio argument
(ABS -23) => 23                  ;absolute value
```

The trigonometric functions, such as SIN and COS, expect the argument to be in radians. Some implementations also have a constant called *PI*, which when used as an argument has the value of the mathematical constant *PI*. The example illustrates.

```
PI => 3.141...            ;PI radians is 180 degrees
(SIN PI) => <some small negative number>
(SIN 0) => 0.0           ;SIN of 0 degrees is 0.0
(COS 0) => 1.0           ;COS of 0 degrees is 1.0
(COS PI) => -1.0         ;COS of 180 degrees -1.0
```

2.7 NUMBER MODIFIERS

FLOAT *number* &OPTIONAL *other*
FLOOR *number* &OPTIONAL *divisor*
CEILING *number* &OPTIONAL *divisor*
TRUNCATE *number* &OPTIONAL *divisor*
ROUND *number* &OPTIONAL *divisor*

We finish this section by discussing several functions useful for the modification of numbers. All of these functions can take any noncomplex argument. The function FLOAT is used to convert any number other than a complex number into a floating-point number. The optional second argument can be used to specify the format the coercion is to have. The second argument, if used, must be a floating-point number. The first argument will then be converted into a floating-point number just like the optional argument.

The function FLOOR returns an integer result that is the largest integer not larger than the argument. If given two arguments, it returns the floor and the remainder. The function CEILING, which has the same syntax as FLOOR, returns an integer result that is the smallest possible integer larger than the argument.

TRUNCATE returns only the integer portion of any argument it is given. ROUND rounds the value to the nearest integer. If the argument has a fractional part equal to exactly 0.5, then the number is rounded to the even integer. The optional second argument allows you to specify a value that will be used as a divisor before the function is applied. So (TRUNCATE 23.6 3.0) would be the same as applying TRUNCATE to the results of dividing 23.6 by 3.0.

```
(FLOAT 2) => 2.0                    ;conversion to float
(FLOAT 3/2) => 1.5                  ;rational argument
(FLOOR 3.4) => 3 ; 0.4             ;largest integer < number
(FLOOR -3/2) => -2 ; 1/2           ;notice direction of change
(FLOOR 22 6) => 3 ; 4              ;3 is floor 4 is remainder
(+ (* 3 6) 4) => 22                ;defines floor
(MOD 22 6) => 4
(- 22 (* 6 (FLOOR 22 6))) => 4  ;MOD using floor
(CEILING 3.4) => 4 ; -0.6         ;smallest integer > number
(CEILING -3/2) => -1 ; -1/2       ;notice direction of change
(TRUNCATE 2.5) => 2 ; 0.5         ;remove decimal portion
(TRUNCATE 0.5) => 0 ; 0.5         ;remove decimal portion
(ROUND 2.5) => 2 ; 0.5            ;round to even integer
(ROUND 3.5) => 4 ; -0.5           ;round to even integer
```

2.8 INTRODUCTION TO SYMBOLS

Names are used to reference things such as variables, definitions, and property lists. To understand symbols in Lisp, it is important to make a distinction between the string of characters you input from the terminal, called a *print-name* or *name,* and the internal representation of that string of characters called a symbol. When you input a Lisp expression, a collection of functions, called the *reader,* reads the expression in a character at a time and converts it into an internal representation. The term "symbol" refers to the internal representation.

Print Names of Symbols

Print-names are constructed from letters, numbers, and any combination of the characters +−*/@$%^&\<>~._ (Steele et al., 1984). Numbers cannot be used as names. From the programmer's point of view, Lisp is case-insensitive to the letters in print-names. The print-names atm and ATM are considered to be the same internal symbol. Internally, case makes a difference. This is handled by converting all letters in print-names input to upper case before conversion to internal representation. If you want to use a print-name containing a character that has special meaning in Lisp, such as a comma (,) or sharp sign (#), preceding it with the escape character (\) tells Lisp to treat the character that follows as an ordinary character. The print-names in the example would generate legal symbols in Common Lisp.

```
var1<->VAR1<->VaR1          ;all VAR1 internally
123a<->123A                 ;123A internally
hello-there-i-am-a-symbol   ;any length can be used
&rest                       ;name is used in arguments
CONS                        ;name of a primitive
:keyword                    ;keywords preceded by (:)
```

Special Symbols NIL and T

The symbols NIL and T are constants. This means their value cannot be altered. They are self-evaluating forms. So T => T and NIL => NIL. NIL can also be written as ().

The symbol T is used to signal the value "true." NIL is used both to signal the value "false" and to represent the empty list. The predicates ATOM and LISTP are used to illustrate these ideas.

ATOM *object*
LISTP *object*

```
NIL => NIL          ;NIL is a self-evaluating form
T => T              ;T or t is also
(ATOM T) => T       ;T is an atom
(ATOM ()) => T      ;NIL is an atom
(ATOM NIL) => T     ;the same as ()
(LISTP T) => NIL    ;T is not a list
(LISTP NIL) => T    ;NIL is the empty list
(LISTP ()) => T     ;use () when referring to the
                    ;empty list
```

Symbols as Data Objects

There are times when we might want to use a symbol as a data object. In this case, we would want to stop the normal process of evaluation. The special form QUOTE is used to stop the evaluation process.

QUOTE *object*

Any Lisp object, given as the argument to QUOTE, is simply returned. Since QUOTE is used so often to stop the evaluation process, the single quote (') can be used in its place. Internally, QUOTE and (') are identical. This is an example of what is called *syntactic sugaring*. The expression 'VAR is expanded to (QUOTE VAR) by the READ function. The use of (') simplifies the syntax of complex expressions by cutting down on the number of left and right parentheses required. Examples of the use of QUOTE and (') are shown in the example. Self-evaluating forms do not need to be quoted.

```
HELLO => value          ;value of symbol returned
(QUOTE HELLO) => HELLO   ;return argument
'HELLO => HELLO          ;same as QUOTE
123 => 123               ;self-evaluating
'123 => 123              ;quote not needed
(QUOTE 123) => 123       ;quote not needed
```

2.9 COMPONENTS OF A SYMBOL

Associated with each symbol in Common Lisp is a set of components that can either be empty or contain symbol component information. Figure 2.2 shows a representation of this important idea. The figure emphasizes that the print name you use is what you see above the "surface," but the symbol represented below the surface is quite complex. Each time Lisp creates a symbol, it creates a pointer location for each of the components shown in the picture: print-name, value, definition, package, and property list. This means that Lisp symbols are complex objects that can be used in more than one way. Figure 2.3 shows a summary of the accessor functions that can be used to access any of these five components of a symbol.

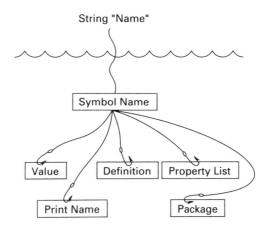

Figure 2.2   The Relationship Between a Print-Name and a Symbol.

```
SYMBOL-NAME sym = > print-name
SYMBOL-PACKAGE sym = > package or nil
SYMBOL-FUNCTION sym = > definition or <error>
SYMBOL-PLIST sym = > property-list or nil
SYMBOL-VALUE sym = > value or <error>
```

Figure 2.3   Accessor Functions for Symbol Components.

Symbol Print-Name Component

Each symbol has a component called its *print-name* or *pname*. This is the symbol's external representation. When you print a symbol, you print the pname. The print-name represents an interface between the external and the internal representations of a symbol. It is what you see on the surface.

SYMBOL-NAME *sym*

The function SYMBOL-NAME is used to return the print-name of a symbol. Notice the case of each symbol in the following example:

```
(SYMBOL-NAME 'VAR1) => "VAR1"   ;upper case internally
(SYMBOL-NAME 'var1) => "VAR1"   ;conversion
(SYMBOL-NAME 'VaR1) => "VAR1"   ;conversion
```

Symbol Value Component

The value cell contains the value of the symbol. It is referenced when the symbol is being used as a variable. If we input a print-name, Lisp will access the value cell for the derivative symbol and return the object that is the symbol's value. If the value cell of the symbol is empty, the symbol is said to be *unbound*. Any attempt to return the symbol's value will signal an error if the symbol is unbound.

If X has the value 3 and Y has the value 4, then the expression (+ X Y) would return 7. X would evaluate to 3, the value contained in its value component, and Y would evaluate to 4, the value contained in its value component. Then 3 and 4 would be added together and the result would be returned. The function SYMBOL-VALUE can be used to access the value of a symbol.

SYMBOL-VALUE *symbol*
BOUNDP *symbol*

```
(SYMBOL-VALUE 'X) => 3
(SYMBOL-VALUE 'Y) => 4
(+ X Y) => 7
(+ (SYMBOL-VALUE 'X) (SYMBOL-VALUE 'Y)) => 7
(BOUNDP 'X) => T
(BOUNDP 'Z) => NIL
```

Symbol Definition Component

The definition cell can contain a function definition, a macro definition, or a special form with symbol (name) as its name. Consider the form (+ X Y), which we have already seen. Lisp converted the name in the first position of this form into a symbol, accessed the definition cell, and applied the definition to the value of the arguments. The function FBOUNDP can be used to see if a symbol has a definition. The following example illustrates:

SYMBOL-FUNCTION *symbol*
FBOUNDP *symbol*

```
(SYMBOL-FUNCTION '+) => implementation dependent
  but a pointer to the definition of +
(SYMBOL-FUNCTION 'X) => <error>
(FBOUNDP '+) => T
(FBOUNDP 'SYMBOL-FUNCTION) => T
(FBOUNDP 'X) => NIL
```

Symbol Property List Component

The property cell contains a list of pairs in which the first element of each pair is a property and the second element is a property value. Suppose we have a symbol BILL (we will assume at this point that you understand the distinction between a print-name and a symbol), and it has a property list (HEIGHT 68 WEIGHT 200 AGE 22 EDUCATION BS). The first property is HEIGHT with the value 68. The second property is WEIGHT with the value 200. The third is AGE with the value 22. The last property is EDUCATION with the value BS. The function SYMBOL-PLIST will return the property list of a symbol.

SYMBOL-PLIST *symbol*

Symbol Package Component

The package cell contains the name of the home package for the symbol. A package can be thought of as a catalog, table, or name space that indexes all symbols defined (interned) in the package. Common Lisp requires a minimum of four packages: lisp, keyword, system, and user packages. Normally an implementation will have many more than these, since a package is an excellent way to encapsulate a conceptually distinct entity. We are only interested in the user package at present. The user package is the default package when you activate Lisp. It is the current value of the system variable *PACKAGE*. It is the name space you normally work in, and it contains all of the symbols you define in an interactive computing session.

The central concept in this discussion of packages is that, if a symbol is defined (interned) in a package (called its *home package*), it is represented uniquely in that package. The package component for that symbol points to the package it belongs to. Any reference to a symbol in a package is always to the same symbol. At the same time, symbols with the same print-name may be interned in more than one package. A symbol's definition either implicitly or explicitly includes reference to its home package. This is an important software engineering idea, because it allows the use of the same names in more than one package without the problem of name conflicts. The value of the variable *PACKAGE* is the current package. The function LIST-ALL-PACKAGES can be used to find out what packages have been defined in your implementation of Lisp. The function SYMBOL-PACKAGE, which takes a symbol as an argument, returns the contents of the package component for the symbol or NIL if the symbol has no package.

LIST-ALL-PACKAGES
SYMBOL-PACKAGE *sym*

```
(SYMBOL-PACKAGE 'X) => USER    ;returns the package of
                                the symbol. Implementation
                                dependent form.

(SYMBOL-PACKAGE '+) => <LISP or GLOBAL, for example>
```

Figure 2.4 summarizes the relationship between the concept of interned and bound symbols. An uninterned symbol cannot be bound. On the other hand, an interned symbol may or may not be bound; that is, it may or may not have a current top-level value.

Equality of Symbols

Symbols with the same print-name that reside in the same package, the home package, are EQ, which means that they are equivalent. This is a powerful idea. It means that the symbol A that you have entered and the A in the list (A LIST OF STUFF) that you entered later, in the *same package*, are the same A. They have the same underlying complex symbol structure available for use. It also means that modification of A in either context potentially affects every other context that contains the symbol A. For example, suppose the name A refers to a symbol that has already been created in your current package. You input the name A, *which automatically creates the symbol associated with the name A*, and you give it the value (GRADE A). The symbol structure underlying the name A can be accessed directly from the name A or from the A being used as part of the value (GRADE A). In the second case, a function would be needed to access the name, and then a second accessor function could be used to access any symbol cell of the associated symbol. The point is that any instance of A in the same package—whether used as the name of a definition, variable, or data element—can, when given the right accessor function, be treated as the *symbol* associated with the name. Since symbols are EQ in their home package, the same name references the same symbol structure. Figure 2.5 provides a graphical representation of this idea.

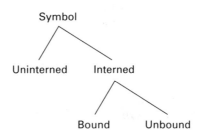

Figure 2.4   Relationship Between Interned and Bound Symbols.

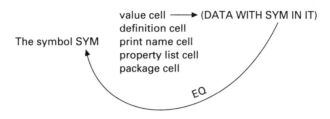

Figure 2.5   Symbols Are EQ in the Same Package.

Using the Describe Function

The DESCRIBE function was defined briefly in Chapter 1. It returns no value but, when given a Lisp object as an argument, it prints a description of the object. If DESCRIBE is given a symbol as an argument, a description of the symbol value, property list, definition, and maybe the package components are printed as a side effect. Remember that the form and content of the description are implementation-dependent, so that the following example may be different from what you will see with the implementation of Common Lisp you are using. Suppose the symbol X has the value 23 and the property list (NAME BILL AGE 23 HEIGHT 72 WEIGHT 200). The example shows what DESCRIBE might print in this case. The definition component was not printed in this case since X did not have a definition.

```
(DESCRIBE 'X)
Symbol X is in the USER package.
The value if X is 23.
X has property WEIGHT: 200
X has property HEIGHT: 72
X has property AGE: 23
X has property NAME: BILL
```

2.10 CREATING SYMBOLS

Normally, symbols are created automatically by the reader. This is done during the read part of the read-evaluate-print loop. The functions GENSYM, GENTEMP, and MAKE-SYMBOL can also be used to create new symbols. For GENSYM and MAKE-SYMBOL, the newly created symbols will be uninterned. That means the symbol has no home package. You cannot give a value or a definition to an uninterned symbol. Normally, GENSYM is used to generate internal symbols and is transparent to the user. However, in later chapters GENSYM will be used extensively for building certain kinds of definitions. An internally generated symbol might also be needed to store properties or information until the name of the owner of those properties can be identified.

GENSYM returns an uninterned symbol with a prefix and a number portion. The number portion is incremented each time GENSYM is called to ensure that each created symbol is unique. It can be called with no arguments. It can also be called with either a non-negative integer or a string as an argument. If the argument is a number, the number is incremented and returned. Each time GENSYM is called, the previous number is incremented by one until you make a change by introducing a new number argument. So if we input (GENSYM) without an argument, an uninterned symbol such as #G321 will be returned. The number used depends on how many times it was called before. If GENSYM is called again, the symbol #G322 will be returned. If you call GENSYM using (GENSYM 0), then #G0 will be returned. In this case, the number argument was used as a means of initializing the counter used by GENSYM. GENSYM can also take a string as an argument. In this case, the string is used as the prefix for GENSYM. This new prefix will be used until it is changed again. The call (GENSYM "rule-") would return RULE-1. The syntax for internally generated symbols varies from implementation to implementation. However, the # sign at the beginning of the name indicates the symbol is not interned. The following example demonstrates the behavior of these functions:

GENTEMP &OPTIONAL *prefix package*
GENSYM &OPTIONAL *x*
INTERN *string* &OPTIONAL *package*
MAKE-SYMBOL *print-name*

GENTEMP creates and interns a new symbol. It can be assigned a value like any interned symbol. Since it is interned in a package, the function gives you the option of specifying the package. If one is not specified, the current package is used by default.

```
(GENSYM 0) => #G0              ;implementation dependent
(GENSYM "RULE-") => #RULE-1 ;prefix is added
(GENSYM) => #RULE-2            ;prefix appears until changed
(GENSYM "CRAB-NUMBER-")        ;a new prefix
=> #CRAB-NUMBER-3
(SYMBOL-PACKAGE (GENSYM)) => NIL ;uninterned symbol
(SYMBOL-PACKAGE (GENTEMP))  ;returns current package
=> USER                        ;or current package
```

2.11 THE ASSIGNMENT OF VALUE

When a symbol is used as a variable, the value component is accessed. The current value of a variable can be any Lisp object. Two of the basic operations on variables are assigning value to a variable and accessing that value when needed. If we input a symbol to Lisp, the evaluator accesses the value component of the symbol as noted earlier and returns the value. In the form (+ X Y), the value components of X and Y are accessed and the values of X and Y are returned. The primitive + is then applied to the values.

One way a variable can take on a value is through explicit assignment. Called SETting the value, this is done using either SETQ a special form, SET a function, or SETF a macro. We will use SETF throughout this book and will use SETQ and SET only under special circumstances. These forms both return a value and create a *side effect*. The side effect is that the value component of the symbol is assigned the value given in the SETting expression. This side effect remains as the global value of the symbol until another SETting operation occurs on the symbol.

SETQ {*Var form*}*
SET *symbol value*
SETF {*place newvalue*}*
VALUES &REST *args*

SETQ is the traditional assignment statement used in most dialects of Lisp. SETQ can take any number of argument pairs in which the first element of the pair is a variable name and the second element is any form. The variable is assigned the value of the form. Note that SETQ is a special form since the first argument in each pair is not evaluated. SETQ returns the last value assigned.

SET takes only one pair. The first element is a symbol and the second a value. Both arguments are evaluated and the value of the second argument is returned.

SETF is the generalized form of SETQ. It is a macro. Like SETQ, it allows for multiple argument pairs. Unlike SETQ, the first argument in SETF is a place rather than a variable name. When the first argument to SETF is a variable name, place refers to the value component of the variable. It accesses the same location as SETQ. What makes SETF more general than SETQ is that place can refer to locations other than the value cell of the variable. SETF returns the last value assigned. Examples of SETQ, SET, and SETF are shown in the next example. The function VALUES is also shown in this example. It returns the value of each argument, in order. If VALUES is given no arguments, it returns nothing.

```
(SETQ X 23) => 23                       ;X assigned 23
(SETQ X 23 Y 10) => 10                  ;Multiple assignments
X => 23                                 ;Access value of X
Y => 10                                 ;Access value of Y
(VALUES X Y) => 23 10                   ;returns value of each
(SETF A 100) => 100                     ;A is assigned 100
(SETF B 200 C 300 D 400) => 400         ;Multiple assignments
(VALUES A B C D) => 100 200 300 400     ;Values of A,B,C,D
(SETF A 'B) => B                        ;A assigned symbol B
A => B                                  ;Value of A is B
B => 200                                ;B has value 200
(SET A 999) => 999                      ;Arguments evaluated
(VALUES A B C D) => B 999 300 400       ;Note change in B
(SETF A 100) => 100                     ;Does not evaluate A
(VALUES A B C D) => 100 999 300 400     ;Note change to A
(SETF B A) => 100                       ;B is not evaluated
(VALUES A B C D) => 100 100 300 400
(SETF X (+ A B)) => 200                 ;The nested form
                                        ;is evaluated first
X => 200                                ;X assigned result
(SETF Y (* 1 2 3 A)) => 600             ;* returns 600 which
                                        ;is assigned to Y
(VALUES) => <returns nothing>
```

2.12 SUMMARY

The first part of this chapter provided a quick introduction to a variety of Lisp primitives for recognizing, computing, comparing, and modifying numbers. Numbers were introduced first because they should be most familiar to you, making the adjustment to the syntax of Lisp minimal. The examples illustrate the flexibility of the language for numeric computing. Expressions that compute can contain multiple object types and bases. Implicit coercion takes care of the mixed types. Expressions can have mixed radices or bases. Some arithmetic primitives take a variable number of arguments. Precedence for arithmetic operators and boolean operators is explicit. Order of evaluation is controlled by the programmer using parentheses. Finally, the language offers a great amount of precision for floating-point numbers and unique features with ratios and "bignums."

The second part of this chapter focused on the definition and basic components of symbols in Lisp. A Lisp symbol is a complex data object that can serve multiple purposes. How it is used depends upon which component of the symbol is being accessed. Primitives were introduced that are useful in accessing, creating, and manipulating symbols. The concept of SETting the value component of a symbol was introduced showing the use of symbols as variables. The effect of SETting is that the value component of the symbol is assigned a value. This is considered a side effect because the effect of the assignment remains after the expression has been computed.

In general, assignment to any symbol component produces a modification to the Lisp environment that remains until another assignment to the same component occurs. Once, for example, a symbol is given a value, that value may be accessed without using any further SETting operations.

Assignment allows us to give symbols powerful representational forms. These forms are of value because they provide building blocks for the development of higher-level abstractions. We will come back to the more important primitives such as SETF many times as we develop and deepen our understanding of Lisp and its representational power.

2.13 PROBLEMS

2.1   Is 43. a member of type REAL?

2.2   What would the following s-expressions return?

a. `2/4 =>`
b. `4/2 =>`
c. `#16RA =>`
d. `(COERCE 4/3 'FLOAT) =>`

2.3   What would these return?

a. `(ODDP #B-100) =>`
b. `(EVENP 23.6) =>`
c. `(INTEGERP 0.) =>`

2.4   What would each of these return?

a. `(= 2 2.0 #B10 #x2) =>`
b. `(MAX 2e2 2 2.0 2d2) =>`
c. `(MAX 2 2.0 2e2) =>`

2.5.   What would each of the following return?

a. `(/8 2) =>`
b. `(1+ -1) =>`
c. `(1- -1) =>`
d. `(- 1 10) =>`

2.6   Which of the following would produce the same result?

a. `(MOD 10 7) <=> (REM 10 7)?`
b. `(MOD -10 7) <=> (REM -10 7)?`
c. `(MOD 10 -7) <=> (REM 10 -7)?`
d. `(MOD -10 -7) <=> (REM -10 -7)?`

2.7   What is the value of each of these function calls?

a. `(ABS -0) =>`
b. `(SQRT -5.0) =>`
c. `(EXP 1) =>`
d. `(LOG 0) =>`
e. `(LOG 1) =>`

2.8 Does an implicit coercion occur in any of the forms in Problem 2.7?

2.9 What value is returned by each of these functions?
   a. `(FLOOR 3/2)` =>
   b. `(CEILING 3/2)` =>
   c. `(FLOOR -3/2)` =>
   d. `(CEILING -3/2)` =>

2.10 What will each of these s-expressions return?
   a. `(/ (/ (/ 400 2) 10) 4)` =>
   b. `(LOG (EXP 1))` =>
   c. `(SQRT (EXPT 10 2))` =>
   d. `(= (TRUNCATE -2.5) (FLOOR -2.5))` =>
   e. `(= (FLOAT (FLOOR -3.4)) (ROUND -3.5))` =>

2.11 What would each of these s-expressions return?
   a. `(SIN (/ PI 2))` =>
   b. `(COS (/ PI 2))` =>
   c. `(= (/ (log 5 10) (log 2 10)) (log 5 2))` =>

2.12 Write a nested expression that computes (REM 22 7) without using the function REM.

2.13 Are these legal symbols?
   a. `123`
   b. `^%$+`
   c. `VAR128-3`
   d. `:hello`
   e. `new var 1`
   f. `#sym`

2.14 What would these expressions return?
   a. `''123` =>
   b. `(QUOTE (QUOTE HELLO))` =>
   c. `'()`
   d. `123t`

2.15 What packages are defined in your implementation of Common Lisp?

2.16 What would these expressions return?
   a. `(SYMBOL-PACKAGE (GENSYM "a-variable"))` =>
   b. `(SYMBOL-PACKAGE (GENTEMP))` =>

2.17 Assuming the following expressions are evaluated in order from a to d, what would each return?
   a. `(GENSYM 1)` =>
   b. `(GENSYM "RULE-")` =>
   c. `(GENSYM 10)` =>
   d. `(GENSYM "")` =>

2.18 What would each of these return assuming they are evaluated in order from a to f?
   a. `VAR1` =>
   b. `(SETF VAR1 100)` =>
   c. `(SETF VAR2 VAR1)` =>
   d. `(VALUES VAR1 VAR2)` =>

e. (SETF A 10 B 20 C B) =>

f. (VALUES A B C) =>

2.19 Suppose that, after each session using Lisp, Lisp would automatically save the total Lisp environment. The next time you signed on, you would be able to start where you left off the last time. What would be the advantages and disadvantages of this?

2.20 What would each of the following return?

a. (SETF A 'B C 'D) =>

b. (SET A 100) =>

c. A =>

d. B =>

2.21 Could the symbol X have more than one value at a time? Explain.

3

Lists

3.1 INTRODUCTION

A *list* is any collection of Lisp elements contained within a balanced number of left and right parentheses. The parentheses define the extent of the list. Each item in a list is called an *element* of the list. An element can be any Lisp object. The content of the list could be a collection of data elements or it might contain a function call or function definition. There is no requirement that the elements of a list be of one type. The empty list is (), which is equivalent to NIL. An example of a simple list would be a list of names and phone numbers:

```
(BILL 2343456 KAREN 7366650 SAM 2223451 JOSH 2683465)
```

A *nested* list contains at least one other list as an element. An example of a nested list is

```
((A B C)(1 2 3)(YES (NO OKAY)(MAYBE 3 $)
(HELLO GOODBYE 4) ATM1)
```

In both examples, the number of left and right parentheses match, the elements of the list are separated by parentheses or spaces, and more than one kind of object is represented as an element in each list. In the first example, each name and each number, BILL 2343456 KAREN 73666500 and so on, are elements of the list. In the second case, the first element of the list is (A B C), the second element is (1 2 3), the third element is (YES (NO OKAY)(MAYBE 3 $)), the fourth is (HELLO GOODBYE 4), and the last element is the object ATM1.

42

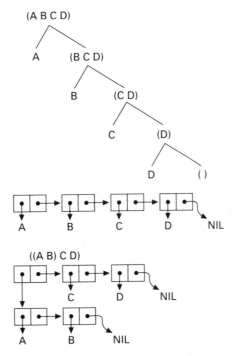

Figure 3.1   Representation of Lists as CONSes.

3.2 LISTS AS TREES

Any list can be represented as a tree structure with lists as interior nodes and atomic objects as leaves. The left branch of each list node points to the first element in the list, and the right branch points to the rest of the list. Figure 3.1 shows a representation of several lists using this scheme. For example, the list (A B C D) is broken down into two pieces; the first element on the list, which is the atom A, and the rest of the list, which is the list (B C D). The sublist (B C D) is then broken down in the same fashion, with B being the first element and the list (C D) being the rest of the sublist. This continues until all leaves of the tree contain atoms. Note that at each level in the tree the left branch points to the first element of the list represented at that level and the right branch points to the rest of the list. At the next level down, if the element is still a list, the left branch points to the first element of the list at that level, and the right branch points to the rest of the list. This idea is applied until we have leaves that are atoms. NIL is both an ATOM and a LIST.

Elements and Levels

Thinking of a list in terms of its "treeness" helps us understand the concept of the elements of a list. If we start with the top node in the tree, the left branch points to the first *element* in the list. If we then follow the right branch to the second node,

the left branch of the second node points to the second element of the list. If we
then follow the right branch to the third node, the left branch of the third node
points to the third element. This continues until we get to the last node in the tree.
The left branch points to an element in the tree. If the right branch points to NIL,
the left branch points to the last element in the list. However, if the right branch
points to an atom, then the right branch points to the last element in the list. This
later case can cause problems when processing lists. So, in general, we will construct lists that have the final right branch pointing to NIL.

Box Notation

Figure 3.1 also shows an alternate representation for lists that is closer to how lists
are represented in Lisp. This representation shows each level in the tree as a box
with two storage locations, called *pointer cells,* a left pointer cell and a right pointer
cell. Looking at the box representation for the list (A B C D), you can see that it
captures the same information as the tree drawing just discussed. In the first box,
the left pointer cell contains a pointer to the first element of the list, in this case, A.
The right pointer cell contains a pointer to the rest of the list. If we follow the right
pointer to the second box, again the left cell contains a pointer to the first element
of the list (B C D), and the right storage location contains a pointer to the rest of the
list. The bottom panel of Figure 3.1 shows the same idea for a list containing an
element that is a list. The idea that we applied to the right side of the tree in the
previous example applies to the left side of the tree when the left pointer cell
contains a pointer to an element that is a list.

3.3 BASIC LIST CONSTRUCTORS

The fundamental list operation is defined by the following axiom:

```
(CONS (CAR LIS) (CDR LIS)) => LIS
or
(CONS (FIRST LIS) (REST LIS)) => LIS
```

This says that a list is a CONS with a CAR or FIRST element and a CDR that is the
REST of the list. Referring back to Figure 3.1, the boxes represent CONS cells, and
the list is represented in all its "treeness" as a series of these CONS cells connected
by pointers. The list can now be defined as a series of CONSes that are linked
together. All pointers eventually lead to atoms, atoms being the termination points
or leaves of the tree representation. Figure 3.2 shows a representation of a CONS
cell.

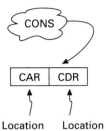

Figure 3.2   A CONS Cell Representation.

CONS *x y*
LIST &REST *args*
APPEND &REST *lists*
NCONC &REST *lists*

CONSing

The basic constructor function in Lisp is CONS. CONS takes two arguments and "CONSes" them together. The arguments can be any Lisp object, though normally the second object should be a list, such that (LISTP y) => T. In the notation CONS × y, if y is not a list, then a dotted pair results. A true list is defined as a CONS with a CAR that can be any object, and a CDR that is either a CONS or NIL. A dotted pair is not a true list since it has a CDR that is an atom other than NIL. For example:

```
(CONS 'A '(LIS)) =>(A LIS)        ;a true list
(CONS 'A 'B) => (A . B)           ;a dotted pair
(CONS '(A) '(LIS)) => ((A) LIS)   ;a true list
```

Figure 3.3 shows a representation of how CONS works using box notation. A CONS cell is created and then the appropriate pointers are put into the CAR and

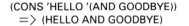

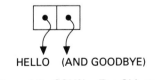

Figure 3.3   CONSing Two Objects.

CDR pointer locations. While you are becoming familiar with this idea, it is helpful to liken the effect of CONS to taking the left parenthesis from the object y and moving it to the left of the object x. Figure 3.4 shows this idea for the expression (CONS 'A '(B C)).

(CONS 'A '((B C))
=> (A B C)

Figure 3.4   CONS Puts Objects Together.

LIST, APPEND, and NCONC

LIST and APPEND are other commonly used constructor functions. LIST can take any number of Lisp objects as arguments (&REST) and creates a list of them. APPEND can also take any number of arguments, but the arguments should be lists. APPEND concatenates lists. The effect of APPEND is to remove the inner parentheses between lists being APPENDed. This is shown in Figure 3.5.

NCONC also concatenates lists, but it is a destructive function. This means that, rather than copying top-level elements such as APPEND, it actually changes pointer cell values of any lists given as arguments. This creates side effects, but it also generates fewer CONS cells. Examples of the use of APPEND, NCONC, and LIST are:

```
(SETF L1 '(A B C D)) => (A B C D)
(SETF L2 '(X Y Z)) => (X Y Z)
(CONS L1 L1) => ((A B C D) A B C D)
(APPEND L1 L1) => (A B C D A B C D)
(LIST L1 L1) => ((A B C D)(A B C D))
(APPEND L1 L2) => (A B C D X Y Z)
L1 => (A B C D)
(NCONC L1 L2) => (A B C D X Y Z)
L1 => (A B C D X Y Z)   ;notice side-effect
L2 => (X Y Z)
```

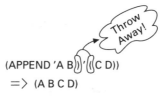

(APPEND 'A B))'((C D))
=> (A B C D)

Figure 3.5   APPEND Illustrated.

3.4 LIST SELECTORS

> **CAR** *list*
> **FIRST** *list*
> **CDR** *list*
> **REST** *list*

The fundamental selector functions are CAR and CDR. The purpose of selector functions is to access whatever part of a list structure you would like to use for a given purpose. The CAR function takes a list as an argument and returns the first element of the list. The CDR function takes a list as an argument and returns a list with the first element removed. So, given the list (A B C D), the CAR would be A and the CDR would be (B C D). Since the names CAR and CDR are not very mnemonic, FIRST and REST were made part of the Common Lisp specification. FIRST is equivalent to CAR and REST is equivalent to CDR. Examples of the use of these functions are:

```
(SETF L1 '(A B C D)) => (A B C D)
(CAR L1) => A
(CDR L1) => (B C D)
(FIRST L1) => A
(REST L1) => (B C D)
(CAR (CDR L1)) => B
(CAR (CDR (CDR L1))) => C
```

Walking down a list a CDR at a time, looking at each CAR, is called *looking at the elements* or *top-level elements of a list*. The top-level elements of a list refers to the respective CARs while walking down the CDRs.

Extensions of CAR and CDR

The functions CAR and CDR are extended in most implementations so that combinations of CAR and CDR are available as primitives. Figure 3.6 shows several examples of the syntax of these combined forms. Because these combinations of CAR and CDR are used so often to access different parts of a list, having these extended forms available can improve efficiency.

There are also other accessor functions that can be used to access the same elements as CAR and CDR. Figures 3.7, 3.8, and 3.9 show examples of these functions. The functions NTH can be used to access any *element* of a list. The CAR

(SETF L '((A B)(C D) E))

FORM IS C . . . R WHERE . . . IS A COMBINATION OF THE LETTERS A AND D

(cAr L) = > (A B)
(cAAr L) = > A
(cADr L) = > (C D)
(cADDr L) = > E

Figure 3.6 Combinations of CAR and CDR Forms.

or first element of a list would be accessed using (NTH 0 LIS). The second element would be (NTH 1 LIS). Likewise, NTHCDR can be used to access any CDR of a list. The expression (NTHCDR 1 LIS) would access the CDR of the list.

NTH *n list*
NTHCDR *n list*
SECOND *list*
THIRD *list*
LAST *list*
BUTLAST *list* &OPTIONAL *n*

The function LAST takes a list as an argument and returns a list with only the last element on it. The function BUTLAST returns a list comprised of all but the last element. So the LAST of the list (A B C) would be (C) and the LAST of ((A B)(C D)) would be ((C D)). BUTLAST of (A B C) would return (A B) and ((A B)) for the

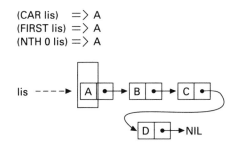

Figure 3.7 Comparable Functions for Accessing the First Element of a List.

(SECOND lis) $=\rangle$ B
(NTH 1 lis) $=\rangle$ B
(CADR lis) $=\rangle$ B

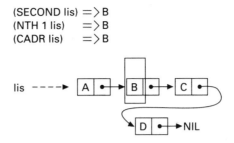

Figure 3.8   Comparable Functions for Accessing the Second Element of a List.

(CDR lis) $=\rangle$ (BCD)
(REST lis) $=\rangle$ (BCD)
(NTHCDR 1 lis) $=\rangle$ (BCD)

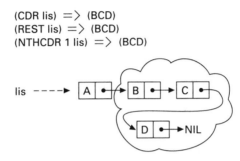

Figure 3.9   Comparable Functions for Accessing the CDR of a List.

previous lists. The optional argument N allows you to specify more than just the last item for exclusion. The last example shows this:

```
(SECOND '((A B)(C D))) => (C D)
(LAST '((A B)(C D))) => ((C D))
(BUTLAST '((A B)(C D))) => ((A B))
(THIRD '(A B C D E)) => C
(CADDR '(A B C D E)) => C
(NTH 2 '(A B C D E)) => C
(BUTLAST '(A B C D) 2) => (A B)
```

Top-Level Functions

Some of the list processing functions are called *top-level list functions,* because they process *only* the top-level elements of the list. CAR and CDR are examples. They return the top-level elements of a list no matter how complex they might be.

3.5 EQUALITY OF LISTS

Lists are EQUAL if they have the same CARs and CDRs. So (EQUAL '(A B C) '(A B C)) returns true (T). Lists are EQ if they are the same list (the same pointer). EQL acts the same way as EQ for lists. The importance of equality in manipulating lists is shown in two examples. The first example illustrates the difference between EQ and EQUAL in comparing lists:

```
(SETF L1 '(A B C D)) => (A B C D)
(SETF L2 L1) =>(A B C D)
(SETF L3 '(A B C D)) => (A B C D)
(EQUAL L1 L2) => T
(EQUAL L1 L3) => T
(EQ L1 L2) => T
(EQ L1 L3) => NIL
(EQL L1 L2) => T
(SETF (CAR L1) 'XXX) => XXX
L1 => (XXX B C D)
L2 => (XXX B C D)
(EQ L1 L2) => T
(SETF L1 (CDR L1)) => (B C D)
(EQ L1 L2) => NIL
(EQ L1 (CDR L2)) => T
```

In the example, L1 is given a list as a value, and L2 is given the same value as L1, which means that L1 and L2 are pointing to the same list. L3 has a list as a value that has the same CARs and CDRs as L1 but is not the same list. So L1 and L2 are EQ but L1 and L3 are not. Since L1 and L2 are EQ and therefore EQL, they must be pointing to the same thing. The expression (SETF (CAR L1) 'XXX) accesses the CAR of the list L1 and destructively changes it to XXX. Since L1 and L2 are pointers to the same list, in changing the CAR of L1, we also changed the CAR of L2. They are still EQ. However, if we change the value of L1 to the CDR of L1, L1 and L2 are no longer EQ. However, the pointer L1 and the pointer to the CDR of L2 are still identical, and L1 and the CDR of L2 are EQ. Figure 3.10 shows several visual examples of equality tests on lists using box notation.

Figure 3.11 shows a graphical representation of the concept of equality. Stated simply, two lists are EQ if they are the same pointer, that is, two names with a pointer to the same CONS or NIL. Two lists are EQL and EQUAL if they are EQ. EQUAL lists have the same structure. They have the same CARs and CDRs. The figure shows the concept of equality as a pyramid to emphasize the hierarchical nature of equality. The most restrictive concept of equality is EQ. Two objects that are EQ will also be EQL and EQUAL. If two objects are EQL, they are also EQUAL.

EQ *x y*
EQL *x y*
EQUAL *x y*

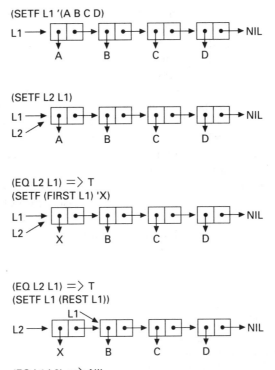

Figure 3.10   EQ and EQUAL Illustrated.

3.6 LIST AS SEQUENCES

In Common Lisp a *sequence* refers to an ordered list or a vector. Presently, we are interested in sequences as ordered lists, such as a list of finishers in the Tour De France bicycle race or a list used as a queue or stack. There are a number of functions intended for use with sequences. LENGTH is a function that

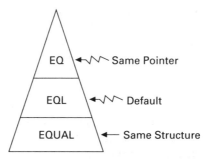

Figure 3.11   EQ, EQL, and EQUAL.

returns the number of top-level elements on a list. So (LENGTH '(A B C)) and (LENGTH '((A B C)(D E F)(G H I))) would both return 3. REVERSE returns the sequence with all the top-level elements in reverse order. So (REVERSE '(A B C)) would return (C B A), and (REVERSE '((A B)(C D)(E F))) would return ((E F)(C D)(A B)). The function SUBSEQ, given a starting position in the sequence and an optional end position, returns a subsequence of the list from start to end where END defaults to the end of the sequence. So (SUBSEQ '(A B C D A B) 2) would return (C D A B) and (SUBSEQ '(A B C D A B) 2 4) would return (C D). The function SORT takes a sequence and a predicate, and sorts the items on the list according to the order defined by the predicate. SORT is not stable, meaning that the original order of elements that are equal according to the predicate is not guaranteed after the sort. So the expression (SORT '(2.9 2.8 2.7 2.6 2.55) #'<) returns (2.55 2.6 2.7 2.8 2.9), and the expression (SORT '(2.9 2.8 2.7 2.6 2.55) #'< :KEY #'TRUNCATE) returns (2.9 2.8 2.7 2.6 2.55) since the application of the key TRUNCATE to each item before it is tested results in all items being equal to 2. SORT is a destructive function.

LENGTH *sequence*
REVERSE *sequence*
SUBSEQ *sequence start* &OPTIONAL *end*
SORT *sequence predicate* &KEY *:key*

The function REMOVE is one of several functions used to remove items from sequences. It requires that each element of the sequence be tested against the item being removed. The success of the REMOVE function in deleting items from a sequence is determined by whether EQ, EQUAL, or EQL is used for testing. The example shows how a problem could occur using equality in testing:

```
(SETF L1 '(A B C A D)) => (A B C A D)
(SETF L2 '((A B)(C D)(A B)(A B))) => ((A B)(C D)(A B)(A B))
(REMOVE 'A L1) => (B C D)
(REMOVE 'A L2) => ((A B)(C D)(A B)(A B))
(REMOVE '(A B) L2) => ((A B)(C D)(A B)(A B))
(REMOVE '(A B) L2 :TEST #'EQUAL) => ((C D))
```

The default test used by REMOVE is EQL, so (A B) will not be EQL to the occurrences of (A B) in the sequence. The keyword :TEST, followed by EQUAL as the specified test, works since (A B) is EQUAL to (A B) and the occurrences of (A B) in the sequence are removed.

REMOVE *item sequence* &KEY :from-end :test :test-not
                            :start :end :count :key

TEST, TEST-NOT, AND KEY

The terminology :TEST, :TEST-NOT, and :KEY will be used in a number of functions that follow. These are keywords that follow &KEY in the argument list. This means they can be used in any order, and they have default values if you do not choose to use them. For example, the default :TEST is usually EQL. If you want the test to be EQUAL, you include in your expression :TEST #'EQUAL indicating that the test is to be EQUAL. The keyword :TEST-NOT indicates that the complement of the test is to be used. For example, :TEST-NOT #'EQUAL would imply true if the item was not EQUAL to whatever it was being compared to. So (REMOVE '(A B) '((A B)(C D)) :TEST-NOT #'EQUAL) would return (A B). The keyword :KEY is used to specify a function that is applied to each item on the list before it is tested.

A variation on the REMOVE function is REMOVE-IF. This function allows us to REMOVE any item from a sequence *if* it satisfies the specified test. For example:

```
(REMOVE-IF #'CONSP '((A B) X Z (S D F))) => (X Z)
(REMOVE-IF #'NUMBERP '(A S 3 4 R F 6 G 7 H))
=> (A S R F G H)
(REMOVE-IF #'FLOATP '(1 2 3 4 32)) => (1 2 3 4 32)
(REMOVE-IF #'FLOATP '(1 2 3 4 32) :KEY #'FLOAT) => NIL
(REMOVE-IF #'FLOATP '(1 2 3 4 32) :KEY #'FLOAT :COUNT 2)
=>(3 4 32)
(REMOVE-IF #'NUMBERP '(A B C 1 2 3 4) :COUNT 3)
=> (A B C 4)
```

In the first case, the predicate CONSP is tested against each element of the list. If the element is a CONS, it is removed. In the second case, numbers are removed from a list using NUMBERP. The next three cases illustrate the use of KEY and COUNT. The keyword KEY is followed by the function FLOAT that is applied to each argument before it is tested. FLOAT converts each number into floating-point format before it is tested. The keyword COUNT specifies an upper bound on the *number of items that can be removed*. In the first example using COUNT, the upper bound is set to two so that the last three items are returned. In the last example, the COUNT value is 3; so the number 4 is still part of the returned list. The function DELETE-IF is the destructive counterpart of REMOVE-IF.

REMOVE-IF *test sequence* &KEY :from-end :start :end :count :key
DELETE-IF *test sequence* &KEY :from-end :start :end :count :key

---

3.7 MODIFYING LIST STRUCTURES

We have looked at several functions that destructively modify lists. In this section, we look more deeply into list modification, focusing on the generality of SETF for this purpose.

Using SETF to Modify Lists

Generally, lists are modified by using the macro SETF. Remember that the first argument of each argument/value pair in SETF is a *place*. So the expression (SETF (CAR LIS) 'NEW-VALUE) puts the new value in the *place* CAR LIS. Table 3.1 is a summary of the functions defining *place* that are discussed in this chapter. These include all of the CAR and CDR combinations, the symbol component accessor functions, accessors starting with GET, and several others. A complete list is found in Steele.

Suppose we have (SETF LIS1 '((A (B C)) (D E))), and we want to copy this list as the value of LIS2. We could use the function COPY-LIST or the function COPY-TREE. The function COPY-LIST copies only the top level elements of the list, whereas the COPY-TREE function copies all CONS of the list being copied. In the first case, if we modified the value of the CAR of LIS1, which is a top level element, we would not modify the value of the CAR of LIS2:

```
(SETF LIS1 '((A (B C))(D E))) => ((A (B C))(D E))
(SETF LIS2 (COPY-LIST LIS1)) => ((A (B C))(D E))
(SETF (CAR LIS1) 'AN-ATM) => AN-ATM
LIS1 => (AN-ATM (D E))
LIS2 => ((A (B C))(D E))
```

TABLE 3.1 SUMMARY OF VALID PLACES FOR THE PLACE
ARGUMENT TO SETF.

---

1. Combinations of Car, Cdr that access locations
2. First, Second, Third . . .
3. Nth
3. Functions that start with get . . .
4. Symbol cell accessors symbol-value, symbol-function, and symbol-plist

---

The reason is that we copied all the top level elements of LIS1, and the CAR of a list is a top level element. So we modified a copied element.

Now suppose we modify the list component (B C) in LIS1, which is not a top level element. Since it has not been copied, we would expect that modifying it would affect both lists:

```
(SETF LIS1 '((A (B C))(D E))) => ((A (B C)(D E))
(SETF LIS2 (COPY-LIST LIS1)) => ((A (B C))(D E))
(SETF (CADAR LIS1) 'THE-BIG-TEST) => THE-BIG-TEST
LIS1 => ((A THE-BIG-TEST)(D E))
LIS2 => ((A THE-BIG-TEST)(D E))
```

The example shows that this is the case. The deeper levels of the list LIS1 were not copied and were therefore shared by LIS1 and LIS2. The expression (EQ (CADAR LIS1)(CADAR LIS2)) is true, whereas the expression (EQ LIS1 LIS2) is not. Figure 3.12 shows this graphically.

Now suppose we do the following:

```
(SETF LIS1 '((A (B C))(D E))) => ((A (B C))(D E))
(SETF LIS2 (COPY-TREE LIS1)) => ((A (B C))(D E))
(SETF (CADAR LIS1) 'ANOTHER-TEST) => ANOTHER-TEST
LIS1 => ((A ANOTHER-TEST)(D E))
LIS2 => ((A (B C))(D E))
```

In this case, we have used COPY-TREE, which copies every CONS in the list, so modifying the component (B C) in LIS1 does not affect the same component in LIS2.

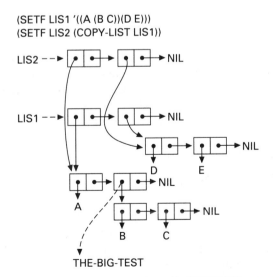

Figure 3.12 Copyings Lists with COPY-LIST.

The components are EQUAL but not EQ. The function COPY-LIST moves down the list following the CDR pointers while copying the top level CAR and CDR cell pointer. COPY-TREE moves down each CAR and CDR pointer in the list copying pointers in the CAR and CDR components for all the CONS cells in the list.

COPY-LIST *list*
COPY-TREE *object*

SETF Replaces RPLACA and RPLACD

The functions RPLACA and RPLACD both take a CONS (*x* in the boxed definition) and an object (*y* in the boxed definition) as arguments. The function RPLACA replaces the CAR of the CONS with the object. So (RPLACA '(A B C) 'X) would replace A with X and return (X B C). The change is destructive. The function RPLACD does the same thing but to the CDR of the list. So the expression (RPLACD '(A B C) '(X)) would replace (B C) with (X) and return (A X).

RPLACA *x y*
RPLACD *x y*

SETF can be used to accomplish the same thing. (SETF (CAR '(A B C)) 'X) will replace A with X returning X, and (SETF (CDR '(A B C)) '(Y)) will replace (B C) with '(Y) returning (Y). Note that the value returned using SETF is different from the value returned using RPLACA and RPLACD. This is typically not important since, in both cases, the functions are used for the side effects they produce.

Stack Operations on Lists

Common Lisp has the basic stack macro functions PUSH, POP, and PUSHNEW as primitives. These macros destructively modify lists viewed as stacks. A *stack* is a data structure with the property that the last thing you put on it is the first thing you can access. To access an item deep within the stack, you have to remove (called POP) all the items on top of it. It is like a stack of plates. When you store plates, you stack them on top of the existing stack of plates. When you want a plate, you take it from the top of the stack.

Suppose we have a list called FRUITSTACK with the value (APPLES PEARS PEACHES CHERRIES). The expression (POP FRUITSTACK) would return APPLES and make the value of FRUITSTACK equal to (PEARS PEACHES CHERRIES). The expression (PUSH 'ORANGE FRUITSTACK) would CONS, ORANGE onto FRUITSTACK changing its value to (ORANGE PEARS PEACHES CHERRIES). The macro PUSHNEW accomplishes the same thing as PUSH but only pushes the item onto the stack if it is not already on the stack. You can also define what test determines equality (EQL, EQUAL,EQ) for PUSHNEW using :TEST or :TEST-NOT. :KEY is used to specify a function to be applied to each argument before it is processed by PUSHNEW.

PUSH *item place*
PUSHNEW *item place* &KEY :test :test-not :key
POP *place*

3.8 PROPERTY AND ASSOCIATION LISTS

Property lists were introduced in the chapter on symbols. Each symbol has a property list component that can be accessed to construct a property list. The purpose of such a list is to provide a place for the storage of property-symbol and property-value information about the symbol. A *property list* is a list of pairs in which the first object defines a property-symbol, and the second the value associated with the property-symbol. Since initially the property list of a symbol is NIL, any attempt to access it to check for the value of a property symbol will return NIL. This is the default value. The value of a property-symbol can be any Lisp object. However, only one object can be the value of a property-symbol at a time. The macro SETF is used to add properties and values to the symbol's property list. The function GET is used to access the property list to look for a property/value pair. The function SYMBOL-PLIST discussed in the chapter on symbols will return the entire property list. The examples illustrate:

```
(SETF VAR 'A-VALUE) => A-VALUE
(SYMBOL-PLIST 'VAR) => NIL
(GET 'VAR 'PROP1)   => NIL
(SETF (GET 'VAR 'PROP1) 'RED) => RED
(GET 'VAR 'PROP1) => RED
(SETF (GET 'VAR 'PROP2) 'GREEN) => GREEN
(SYMBOL-PLIST 'VAR) => (PROP2 GREEN PROP1 RED)
(SETF (GET 'VAR 'PROP2) NIL) => NIL
(SYMBOL-PLIST 'VAR) => (PROP2 NIL PROP1 RED)
```

GET is used to access the property list component of the symbol. The macro SETF is used with GET to modify the property list. Note that SETF is used in conjunction with GET to add or delete a value from the property list.

GET *symbol indicator* &OPTIONAL *default*

Association Lists

Association lists are similiar to property lists except that an association list is a list of lists where every nested list is a pair. Each pair consists of a key and a value. For example, the list ((BALL RED)(HOUSE GREEN)(CAR BLACK)(DOG BROWN)) could be made into an association list. The function ASSOC is used to access KEY/DATUM pairs on an association list. The function ACONS is the constructor function. Normally ASSOC lists are maintained as dotted pairs as shown in the example.

```
(SETF ALIST NIL)
=>NIL
(SETF ALIST (ACONS (QUOTE V1) 100 ALIST))
=>((V1 . 100))
(SETF ALIST (ACONS (QUOTE V2) 200 ALIST))
=>((V2 . 200) (V1 . 100))
(SETF ALIST (ACONS (QUOTE V3) 300 ALIST))
=>((V3 . 300) (V2 . 200) (V1 . 100))
(ASSOC (QUOTE V2) ALIST)
=>(V2 . 200)
ALIST
=>((V3 . 300) (V2 . 200) (V1 . 100))
```

ACONS *key datum a-list*
ASSOC *item a-list* &KEY :test :test-not :key

3.9 LISTS AS SETS

Lists can be used to represent sets. The basic set operations for testing set member-ship, union, intersection, and difference are all available as primitives. The function MEMBER is used to determine whether an item is a member of a list of items. The concepts we studied earlier concerning EQ versus EQUAL when testing items that are lists is important here as well. The expression (MEMBER 'A '(X Y S A D F)) will return (A D F). MEMBER returns a list starting with the list member that matches the item or NIL if there is no match. The expression (MEMBER '(A) '((A)(B)(C))) would return NIL, but the expression (MEMBER '(A) '((A)(B)(C)) :TEST #'EQUAL) would return ((A)(B)(C)).

MEMBER *item list* &KEY :test :test-not :key
UNION *list1 list2* &KEY :test :test-not :key
INTERSECTION *list1 list2* &KEY :test :test-not :key
SET-DIFFERENCE *list1 list2* &KEY :test :test-not :key

3.10 PREDICATES ON LISTS

A number of predicates are useful in testing properties of list structures. The functions LISTP and CONSP both test whether an object is a list. They differ, however, since (CONSP NIL) is NIL and (LISTP NIL) is true. NIL is not a CONS but it is considered a list—the empty list. The function NULL can be used to test for an empty list. The only member of type NULL is NIL, so (NULL NIL) is true. NULL anything else is NIL or false. ENDP is also used to test the end of a list. It is the preferred way to test the end of a list since ENDP is NIL for CONS, TRUE for NIL, and it signals an error for all other objects. NULL and ENDP are used to terminate recursive and iterative processing of lists.

NULL *object*
ENDP *object*
LISTP *object*
CONSP *object*

3.11 SUMMARY

In this chapter we introduced basic functions and macros for creating, accessing, and modifying lists. CONS, APPEND, and LIST are the basic list building functions. CAR and CDR are the fundamental accessor functions. Mutators or modifiers are more numerous. SETF can be used with accessor functions to modify lists.

There are also a number of both destructive (the change is permanent) and nondestructive functions available.

Representation of lists in Lisp was also discussed. A *true list* was defined as a series of CONSes connected by the CDR component with the end of the list containing NIL. A *dotted pair* was defined as a list with a non-nil final CDR component. In understanding the underlying structure of Lisp, it was useful to consider the "treeness" of list structures.

The concept of EQ and EQUAL lists is important because it is a common source of errors in using list functions. Lists are only EQ when they are the same list, that is, when the value of the name of the lists is the same pointer. Lists are EQUAL when they have the same CAR and CDR components.

Finally, the chapter introduced a number of useful functions that will be used in building functions and programs in later chapters. These included predicate, association list, and set functions.

3.12 PROBLEMS

3.1   Which of the following are Lisp lists?
    a. (((( )))
    b. (A (B (C (D))))
    c. (((A B)) (C) ((((D))))))
    d. (1 2 3 45 HELLO ())
    e. ((A   )C D)
    f. (A (B C D)
    g. (A
       B)
    h. (A . B)
    i. (A B . C D)

3.2   What are the top level elements of the list ((A B) (C (D) (E F (G))))?

3.3   Using box notation, draw a representation of the list ((A B) (C) D ((E))).

3.4   Draw a box representation for the list (((A)) (B C (D))).

3.5   What list does this box drawing represent?

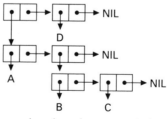

3.6   Assume the following expressions have been executed:

<pre>
        (SETF L1 '(A B C D))
        (SETF L2 '(X Y Z))
        (SETF L3 '((M N)(O P)))
</pre>

What would be returned by each of the following expressions?

a. `(LIST L1 L2 L3)  =>`
b. `(CONS 'A 'B)  =>`
c. `(CONS 'A '(B))  =>`
d. `(CONS 'A (LIST 'B))  =>`
e. `(APPEND '(A) '(B))  =>`
f. `(APPEND (CONS 'A ()) (LIST 'B))  =>`

3.7 Could CONS be used to accomplish the same thing as APPEND? Illustrate with the expression `(APPEND '(B C) '(D E))`.

3.8 The predicate function CONSP is used to test whether an object is a CONS. The predicate function LISTP is used to test whether an object is a list. Use these predicates to demonstrate the difference between a list and a CONS.

3.9 Suppose you want the last item on a list returned but not as a list. You want the element returned. How would you accomplish this using the functions in this section?

3.10 What does each of the following functions return when given the empty list as an argument?

a. CAR
b. CDR
c. CADR
d. SECOND
e. CDDDR

3.11 Is the function LAST a top level function?

3.12 Draw a box representation of the following sequence of operations:

a. `(SETF LIS-A '(A B C D))`
b. `(SETF LIS-B LIS-A)`
c. `(SETF LIS-A (CONS 'XXX LIS-A))`

3.13 Assuming that L1 has the value (A B C D) and L1 and L2 are EQ, which of the following are EQ?

a. `(EQ (CDR L1)(CDR L2))  =>`
b. After `(SETF L1 (CDDR L1))`
`(EQ L1 L2)  =>`
`(EQ (CDDR L2) L1)  =>`
c. After `(SETF L1 (CONS 'A L1))`
`(EQ (CAR L1) (FIRST L2))  =>`

3.14 What does the expression (REMOVE NIL '(A () B C NIL S ())) return? Since (LISTP NIL) => T, why does this work correctly even though the test is EQL rather than EQUAL?

3.15 Write a nested expression using REVERSE that would return the last element of a list as a list.

3.16 Suppose you have a list of names and for each name you have a value that is the estimated wealth of each. For example, suppose you have the following list of names and values:

```
(SETF LIS '(MARSH SUE BILL HUFF KIM))
(SETF MARSH 100 SUE 20 BILL 20000 HUFF 10 KIM 100000)
```

Write an expression using SORT that would rearrange the list in ascending order by wealth.

3.17 Suppose you have the following:

```
(SETF L '(A B C))
(PRINT (SETF (CDR L) L))
```

What does this print? Draw a representation of what happened using box notation.

3.18 Suppose the following expressions had been executed:

```
(SETF LIS1'(A B C D)) => (A B C D)
(SETF LIS2 LIS1) => (A B C D)
```

What would be the effect of (RPLACD LIS1 'BOOM) on LIS1 and LIS2?

3.19 Suppose we had the following:

```
(SETF LIS1 '(A LIST OF STUFF)) => (A LIST OF STUFF)
```

What would be the effect of (SETF (SYMBOL-VALUE 'LIS2) LIS1) on LIS2? Would LIS1 and LIS2 be EQ?

3.20 Suppose I have a stack called S1 with items (A B), (C D), and (E F) on it. What would be the effect of (PUSHNEW '(A B) S1) on S1?

3.21 Suppose we have the list L with the value ((TIME . 1000)(PLACE . PARIS)(YEAR . 99)). What would each of the following expressions return?
a. (ASSOC 'AGE L) =>?
b. (ACONS 'TIME 1200 L) =>?
c. (ACONS 'TIME 0800 L) =>?
d. (ASSOC 'PLACE L) =>

3.22 Given the following assignment, (SETF S1 '(A B C) S2 '(B C D)), what would each of these expressions return?
a. (UNION S1 S2) =>?
b. (INTERSECTION S1 S2) =>
c. (SET-DIFFERENCE S1 S2) =>
d. (SET-DIFFERENCE S2 S1) =>

3.23 Given two rules (IF A & B & C THEN D) and (IF B & A THEN D), use set operations to show that one of the rules is contained in the other.

3.24 Write the expression using the MEMBER function that would successfully test that '(A B) is a member of the list '((A B)(C D)).

3.25 Bill has a collection of stamps. Each stamp has a set of properties he would like to catalog including the country the stamp was minted in, year of mint, value, condition, and a list of the names of any previous owners of the stamp. Demonstrate how property lists could be used to store this information.

3.26 Show the operations shown below using box notation.

```
(SETF L1 '((A B)(C D)))
(SETF L2 (COPY-LIST L1))
(SETF (FIRST 11) 'GONE)
```

3.27 What would each of the following return? Think it through using a box diagram.

    a. `(SETF L1 '((A B)(C D)))   =>`
    b. `(SETF L2 (COPY-LIST L1)) =>`
    c. `(EQ L1 L2) =>`
    d. `(EQ (FIRST L1)(FIRST L2)) =>`
    e. `(EQ (CAAR L1)(CAAR L2)) =>`
    f. `(EQ (REST L1) (REST L2)) =>`

4

Elementary Functions

4.1 BASIC ASSUMPTIONS

In this chapter, we begin to see the beauty and expressive power of Common Lisp for composing functions and programs. Lisp lends itself to the development of layered abstractions with complexity relegated to a very low level. This makes Lisp a natural vehicle for expressing very high level abstractions. Think of the function as the basic unit of composition.

Top Down Design

Lisp programs are naturally designed top down and constructed bottom up. Top level functions provide overall control for the program and describe the overall goal of the program. They are, in effect, a description of the program. These top level functions are then decomposed into smaller subprograms. This process of analysis and decomposition continues until the lowest levels of description call for functions that are immediately composable and testable. The process of building the program moves bottom up with the developing and testing of increasingly inclusive portions of the final product.

Lisp environments also lend themselves to fast prototyping. That is, you develop a simplified version of what you want first. You get the prototype up and running and use it to test the validity of your original concepts. You then "grow complexity" as you develop and elaborate your initial software specification.

The Basic Building Block

The function is the basic building block for developing Lisp programs. The term *function* will be assumed to refer to all Lisp procedures regardless of whether or not they produce side effects. This is so because, when we are composing Lisp programs, we are really thinking about functions and the values they return rather than procedures and their side effects. This is not to imply that side effects are not important. Side effects are necessary and sometimes their use improves the efficiency of the program.

   User defined functions can be thought of as abstractions. They are abstractions, because they are composed using primitives provided by the Lisp language and previously constructed user defined Lisp functions. These abstractions, in turn, can be used to develop additional layers of abstraction. We will also think in terms of data abstractions since we want to generalize functions to work with classes of objects. The expression (* X Y) describes a data abstraction since any number can be substituted for X or Y.

4.2 DEFINITION OF A FUNCTION

The simplest way to describe a function definition is to use a lambda expression. As you can see from the boxed definition, the syntax of a lambda expression can be quite complex. The focus will be on working with simplified versions of the lambda expression for the present.

LAMBDA ({*var*}* &OPTIONAL {*var* |(*var* [*initform*[*svar*]])}*]
    [&REST *var*]
    [&KEY {*var* |({*var* |(*keyword var*)}
      [*initform* [*svar*]])}* [&ALLOW-OTHER-KEYS]]
    [&AUX {*var* |(*var*[*initform*])}*])
    {*declaration* | *documentation-string*}*
    {*form*}*)

Lambda Expressions

The basic form for computations in Lisp is (form1 additional-forms). Form1 can be a name referencing a definition, or it can be a lambda expression that is a definition. The lambda expression can therefore be used directly as the first argument in a function call. Form1, be it name or lambda expression, is then followed by argu-

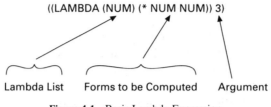

Figure 4.1   Basic Lambda Expression.

ments as needed. So one basic computational form is (LAMBDA-EXPRESSION ARGUMENTS). Figure 4.1 shows an example of the simple computation of the square of a number using this idea. The lambda expression is a list that itself is the first element in the call. The expression starts with the word LAMBDA. It is followed by an argument list called the *lambda list*, and the body of the expression consisting of the forms to be computed. Finally, the arguments to the lambda expression that are bound to the variables in the lambda list are specified in the expression. Each component of this expression is noted in the figure. The lambda expression is evaluated as are the following arguments. The values of the arguments in the function call are bound in order to the arguments on the lambda list, and the computed value of the last form in the body of the lambda expression is returned. The following two examples illustrate these two points.

```
((LAMBDA (X Y) (* X Y)) 30 40)
=>1200
((LAMBDA (X Y) (* X Y)()) 20 30)
=> NIL
```

In the first case, 30 is bound to X and 40 is bound to Y. The values of Y and then X are multiplied, and the last value computed is returned. In the second case, the value of (* X Y) is computed but never returned. The last value computed is NIL so NIL is returned.

Lambda List Keywords

The lambda list portion of the lambda expression is a list of parameters. Normally this list contains the variable names used in the body of the function. Values are bound to these names when a function call is made, and the function is executed using the bound values. A set of lambda list keywords that start with the ampersand (&) are provided to allow additional flexibility in defining parameters. The use of lambda list keywords in function calls was introduced in Chapter 1. Now the question is how do you use them in building your own functions.

The basic lambda list keywords are listed in the order in which they should be used regardless of what combination of them might be in a particular definition.

REGULAR PARAMETERS
&OPTIONAL
&REST
&KEY

The option called &OPTIONAL allows optional parameters to be defined with default values. Note in the following examples that, if objects are passed as arguments, their values become the values of X and Y. If not, the default value 0 is assumed. If no default is provided, NIL becomes the default value.

```
((LAMBDA (&OPTIONAL X Y)
    (LIST X Y)))
=>(NIL NIL)
((LAMBDA (&OPTIONAL X Y)
    (LIST X Y)) 10 20)
=> (10 20)
((LAMBDA (&OPTIONAL X Y)
    (LIST X Y)) 10)
=> (10 NIL)
((LAMBDA (&OPTIONAL (X 0)(Y 0))
    (LIST X Y)) 2 3)
=> (2 3)
((LAMBDA (&OPTIONAL (X 0)(Y 0))
    (LIST X Y)))
=> (0 0)
((LAMBDA (&OPTIONAL (X 0)(Y 0))
    (LIST X Y)) 2)
=> (2 0)
```

The option called &REST allows for a variable number of parameters in the lambda list. In the first example, &REST is used alone in the lambda list. All argument values are made into a list that is bound to the variable LIS. If no arguments are supplied in the function call, the value of LIS becomes NIL.

```
((LAMBDA (&REST LIS)
    LIS) 1 2 3 4)
=> (1 2 3 4)
((LAMBDA (&REST LIS)
    LIS))
=> NIL
((LAMBDA (&REST LIS) LIS) 'A 'B '(C D E))
=>(A B (C D E))
```

The &KEY option allows you to violate the order of the variable/binding relationship. You specify which value goes with which variable by supplying key-

words. Note in the example that NIL is the default value for a variable if no value
is supplied. Also note that defaults can be supplied using the same syntax as
&OPTIONAL.

```
((LAMBDA (&KEY X Y)
     (LIST X Y)) :X 10 :Y 20)
=> (10 20)
((LAMBDA (&KEY X Y)
     (LIST X Y)) :Y 20 :X 10)
=> (10 20)
((LAMBDA (&KEY X Y)
     (LIST X Y)))
=> (NIL NIL)
((LAMBDA (&KEY X (Y 30) Z)
     (LIST X Y Z)))
=> (NIL 30 NIL)
```

APPLY and FUNCALL

The APPLY and FUNCALL functions can be used to explicitly invoke a function
application. The syntax for FUNCALL and APPLY are shown in the boxed definitions. When a lambda expression is the first argument, the syntax #' or FUNC-
TION is used to indicate that the expression is to be interpreted as a definition. The
syntax #' is another version of FUNCTION that simplifies syntax.

```
(SETF X 2 Y 3) => 3
(APPLY #'+ '(2 3)) => 5
(FUNCALL #'+ 2 3) => 5
(FUNCALL #'(LAMBDA (X) (* X X)) 3) => 9
(FUNCALL #'(LAMBDA (X) (* X X)) X) => 4
(APPLY (FUNCTION +) '(2 3)) => 5
```

The examples point out some of the features of APPLY and FUNCALL. The
function argument to each can be a symbol, in which case the global functional
value of that symbol is used or it can be the read macro #', FUNCTION primitive,
or a LAMBDA expression. Notice that, when X is given as the argument to the
third FUNCALL example, it evaluates to the assigned value 2. FUNCALL makes
all arguments into a list as in example 3. APPLY will accept a single argument or a
single argument with all additional arguments made into a list. It should be noted
that in all cases the functional argument to either FUNCALL or APPLY cannot be
a macro or special form.

> **FUNCALL** *fn* &REST *arguments*
> **APPLY** *function arg* &REST *more-args*
> **FUNCTION** *fn*

The DEFUN Macro

On occasion, using lambda expressions directly in computations is useful. One example is when the computation is going to be done only once in a program. More often, however, it is useful to define a function once but be able to refer to it whenever it is needed for future computations. Future computations require only that the referenced name be supplied as the first element of the function call. The DEFUN macro is provided for this purpose. A macro is first expanded into another form and then executed. The DEFUN macro not only produces a globally available reference name for the function being defined, it also simplifies the syntax of the definition by taking care of certain constructions during macro expansion. So you need only provide those components that cannot be supplied by the operation of the macro. This is a powerful feature of Lisp that simplifies programming by taking care of complexity internally and simplifying the programmer's view. We will refer to these internally supplied forms as implicit forms, and we will discuss some of them later. They are useful in understanding how Lisp computes functions.

The syntax of the DEFUN macro is shown in the box below. A globally named function definition consists of the word DEFUN, which is mnemonic for *define the function*, a symbol that is the name of the function and a lambda expression. The syntax of the lambda-list expression has a rather complex syntax (as was noted), but allows great flexibility in handling parameters (arguments) and parameter values (bindings) in functions. The pointer to the function definition is attached to the definition component of the symbol used as the function name. Figure 4.2 shows the function definition for squaring a number using the DEFUN macro. Note that the lambda expression is identical. To use the function, simply provide the reference name and argument (SQUARE 3) => 9.

> **DEFUN** *name lambda-list {declaration|doc-string}* {form}**

```
(DEFUN SQUARE (NUM)
  (* NUM NUM))
```

Figure 4.2   Simple Function Definition.

4.3 BUILDING ELEMENTARY ABSTRACTIONS

Suppose we want to build a function that is given a number as an input and is to return the cube of that number as an output. The only precondition for the computation is that the input must be a number. The resulting function is shown in the following example:

```
(DEFUN CUBE (NUMBER)
  (* NUMBER NUMBER NUMBER))
```

The name of the function is CUBE. It takes one argument called NUMBER and returns the result of the computation (* NUMBER NUMBER NUMBER). We have *composed* a simple functional abstraction in the Lisp environment and have provided a data abstraction since X stands for any number. The function CUBE is now available until the definition cell for the symbol CUBE is redefined. CUBE has been added to the current Lisp environment. To use it, call CUBE with the proper argument:

```
(CUBE 10) => 1000
(CUBE 2) => 8
```

Branching

One of the powerful features of the Lisp language is the flexibility of the control macro COND. COND, meaning conditional, is the general macro for branching. The syntax for the conditionals COND and the special form IF are shown in the boxed definition. The IF form provides a clearer syntax when only one condition is being tested and will be used when possible for this reason.

COND {(*test* {*form**})}*
IF *test then* [*else*]

Going back to our previous example, we wanted to calculate the cube of a number. The precondition was that the value of the parameter of the function was a number. Now the previous function can be changed by adding a guard to ensure that the input is a number.

```
(DEFUN CUBE (N)
   (IF (NUMBERP N) (* N N N) "Input has to be a number"))
=>CUBE
(CUBE 3) => 27
(CUBE 'N) => "Input has to be a number"
```

This version reads as follows. IF N is a number THEN (* N N N) is computed ELSE the string "Input has to be a number" is returned. In the general form (IF TEST RETURN1 RETURN2), the RETURN2 part is optional. If it is not specified and the test fails, NIL is returned.

The more general form of conditional is COND. The function CUBE with the guard NUMBERP would be written using COND as follows:

```
(DEFUN CUBE (N)
   (COND ((NUMBERP N) (* N N N))
         (T "Input has to be a number")))
```

The basic form is:

```
(COND ((TEST1) (EXP1)(EXP2)...)
      ((TEST2) (EXP1)(EXP2)...)
      (T (EXP1)(EXP2)...))
```

Each test condition is queried in order from TEST1 to TEST2 to T. IF TEST1 is not NIL then the expressions to the right of TEST1 are computed and the result of the last computation is returned. If TEST1 is NIL then TEST2 is evaluated. If TEST2 does not evaluate to NIL, then the expressions to the right of TEST2 are computed and the result of the last expression is returned. Finally, if TEST1 and TEST2 both evaluate to NIL, then the unconditional clause T evaluates to T and the expressions to the right of T are computed and the result of the last is returned.

Note two things. Any number of expressions could be to the right of a test condition. Second, there is no intrinsic limit on how many tests can be used in a conditional. The form is very flexible. It was one of the original conceptions of John McCarthy who is considered the inventor of the Lisp language. Figure 4.3 shows the conceptual relationship between the logical flow of IF-THEN-ELSE thinking and the logical flow through the conditionals IF and COND.

The boolean functions are often used in test forms. All booleans are short circuit in Common Lisp. This means that they return a value as soon as the result is determined.

```
(COND
  ((= N 0) 0)
  ((= N 1) (+ N 2))
  ((= N 2) (+ N 4))
  (T (* N N)))

IF N = 0 THEN RETURN 0
ELSE
IF N = 1 THEN RETURN N + 2
ELSE
IF N = 2 THEN RETURN N + 4
ELSE
RETURN N * N
```

Figure 4.3   The Basic Concept of COND.

AND {*form*}*
OR {*form*}*
NOT x

```
(AND T T T (QUOTE A))
=>A

(AND T T T NIL (QUOTE A))
=>NIL

(OR (QUOTE A) (QUOTE B))
=>A

(OR NIL (QUOTE A))
=>A

(NOT T)
=>NIL

(NOT NIL)
=>T
```

Defining Local Variables

Local variables are defined using the LET and LET* special forms. The syntax for a
LET is shown in the boxed definition. LET and LET* have the same syntax. They
differ in how they handle binding within the LET. The scope of a local reference is

determined by the extent of the LET form. It is (LET. . . . .). Outside of the LET form used to produce a temporary binding for a variable, the local variable cannot be referenced. A simple example shows this idea:

```
(DEFUN LET-EXAMPLE (X)
    (LET ((X 999))
        (PRINT X)) X)

=>LET-EXAMPLE
(LET-EXAMPLE 'HELLO)
999
=>HELLO
```

When LET-EXAMPLE is called with HELLO as an argument, HELLO is bound to X. Subsequently, X is redefined locally and 999 is bound to X. When the PRINT function is executed within the LET, the value 999 is printed. The last form to be evaluated in the function, however, is X. This reference to X is outside the LET; so LET-EXAMPLE returns the value HELLO.

A second example shows the use of LET as a top level expression. In the LET, the value 2 is temporarily bound to the systems variable *PRINT-BASE*. When PRINT is computed, the value 1111100111 is printed. This is the binary equivalent of 999. Finally, 999 is returned. Why?

```
(LET ((*PRINT-BASE* 2))
    (PRINT 999))
1111100111
=> 999
```

LET ({*var* |(*var value*)}*) {*declaration*}* {*form*}*
LET* ({*var* |(*var value*)}*) {*declaration*}* {*form*}*

The bindings of values in the LET form are assumed to occur in parallel. For this reason, the following would cause an error:

```
(LET ((X 1)
      (Y X))
    (LIST X Y))
=>The variable X is unbound
```

X takes the value 1 in the LET. In parallel with this, Y takes the value of X. But the value of this X is not 1 but rather whatever value X had before the LET was evaluated. This is a common source of coding errors. The side effect of a prior SETF masks an error that is not detected until the next computing session when the side effect is no longer present. The next example shows this:

```
(SETF X 100) => 100
(LET ((X 1)
      (Y X))
  (LIST X Y))
=> (1 100)
```

The value of X before entering the LET was bound to Y. LET* performs the bindings of variables sequentially. So, in the preceding example, if the LET were changed to LET*, then you would get:

```
(SETF X 100) => 100
(LET* ((X 1)
       (Y X))
  (LIST X Y))
=> (1 1)
```

Since the bindings are done sequentially, X takes the value 1 and then Y takes the current value of X, which is 1 rather than 100.

Suppose that we wanted the function CUBE to be interactive. We want to be able to activate it and have it query the user for a number to be cubed. This is an application where a local variable would be handy. CUBE has already been defined and there is no need to modify it since it has been tested and does what it is supposed to do. We need an additional function that administrates the interface with the user. The input and output specification has not changed. We simply want it to work interactively. By using the previous version of CUBE in this new composition, we can take advantage of the correctness of CUBE that has already been established. The following example shows two ways this could be composed:

```
(DEFUN INTERACTIVE-CUBE ()
   (PRINT "Enter A Number")
   (LET ((N (READ)))
      (CUBE N)))

=>INTERACTIVE-CUBE
(INTERACTIVE-CUBE)
"Enter A Number" 3
=> 27
```

Actually this could be streamlined by supplying the value directly to CUBE. The example shows the code for this version.

```
(DEFUN STREAMLINED-INTERACTIVE-CUBE ()
   (PRINT "Input A Number")
   (CUBE (READ)))
```

What happens if N is bound to 4 and then N is given after the prompt in this version? It fails because READ does not evaluate N. CUBE, however, is still guarding the input, so it would return "Input has to be a number."

4.4 RECURSIVE FUNCTIONS

Recursion provides a means of concisely composing functions that solve a problem by reducing the problem to immediately solvable subproblems or subgoals. Once an immediately solvable problem is defined by the recursive process, it is solved and the results are propagated back to the top level. Figure 4.4 shows the decomposition of the problem of computing a factorial, in this example, factorial 5. The decomposition is shown as a tree. The arches connecting the branches of the tree indicates that all subproblems must be solved in order to solve the factorial problem. The tree is called an AND/OR tree. In this case, all branches are ANDed.

Figure 4.5 shows an input/output specification for the factorial. The input

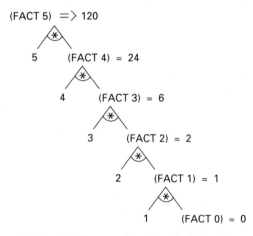

Figure 4.4   Decomposition Tree for Factorial.

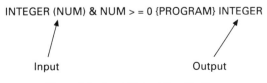

Figure 4.5   Input Output Specification.

must be an integer greater than or equal to 0, the output is an integer. The problem can be decomposed by noting the following facts: factorial (0) = 1 and factorial (X) = X * factorial (X−1), where X is an integer greater or equal to 0. Here are two ways the factorial can be expressed using a recursive Lisp function:

```
(DEFUN FACT (INT)
    (IF (= INT 0)
        1
        (* INT (FACT (1- INT))))))

(DEFUN FACT (INT)
    (COND ((= INT 0) 1)
          (T (* INT (FACT (1- INT)))))))
```

Since there is an additional requirement that INT is an integer greater than or equal to zero, a guard should be defined as well.

```
(DEFUN FACTORIAL (INT)
    (COND ((AND (INTEGERP INT) (>= INT 0)) (FACT INT))
          (T (PRINT "Input must be >= 0. Try again ")
             (FACTORIAL (READ)))))
```

Figure 4.6 shows a TRACE of the execution of (FACTORIAL 5). Note the correspondence between the decomposition tree in Figure 4.4 and the trace of the execution of the function in Figure 4.6.

```
(FACT 5)
(1 IN FACT 5)
   (2 IN FACT 4)
      (3 IN FACT 3)
         (4 IN FACT 2)
            (5 IN FACT 1)
               (6 IN FACT 0)
               (6 EX FACT 1)
            (5 EX FACT 1)
         (4 EX FACT 2)
      (3 EX FACT 6)
   (2 EX FACT 24)
(1 EX FACT 120)
=> 120
```

Figure 4.6   Trace of Factorial.

Using Recursion to Analyze Lists

Assume we have a variable LIS that has the value ((A B C)(D E F)(G H I)). This is a nested list with three top level elements (A B C)(D E F) and (G H I). Suppose we wanted to compose a recursive function to count the elements on this list. The input to the function is a list and the output of the function is an integer. The function should signal an error if a nonlist object is given as an argument. Count = 0 for the empty list and count = 1 + count (REST lis) otherwise.

```
(DEFUN LIST-ELEMENT-COUNTER (LIS)
   (IF (NULL LIS)
       0
       (+ 1 (LIST-ELEMENT-COUNTER (CDR LIS))))))
```

A trace of list counter for the sample list is shown in Figure 4.7. Suppose that we call LIST-ELEMENT-COUNTER with the argument (A . B) a dotted pair or a nonlist object. There is no guarantee as to what will happen. The function can either be generalized to include these possibilities or they can be guarded against. In fact, an error will be signaled if a dotted pair is given to the current version of the function. One could assume therefore that this provides an adequate guard. The following changes would generalize the function to include dotted pairs and atoms:

```
(DEFUN LIST-ELEMENT-COUNTER (LIS)
   (COND ((NULL LIS) 0)
         ((ATOM LIS) 1)
         (T (+ 1 (LIST-ELEMENT-COUNTER (CDR LIS))))))
```

Notice that what was done in the previous example was CDR down the list until the trivial case was satisfied, NULL LIS = T. The fact that we CDRed down the list in this fashion means we did a top level analysis of the list. Suppose now we wanted to count every atom contained in the list. That is, we wanted to go deeply into the list. In this case, we want to analyze all nested lists completely.

The input to this new counter is a list and the output is an integer count of all

```
(LIST-ELEMENT-COUNTER '((A B C)(D E F)(G H I)))

(1 IN LIST-ELEMENT-COUNTER ((A B C)(D E F)(G H I)))
   (2 IN LIST-ELEMENT-COUNTER ((D E F)(G H I)))
      (3 IN LIST-ELEMENT-COUNTER ((G H I)))
         (4 IN LIST-ELEMENT-COUNTER ())
         (4 EX LIST-ELEMENT COUNTER 0)
      (3 EX LIST-ELEMENT-COUNTER 1)
   (2 EX LIST-ELEMENT-COUNTER 2)
(1 EX-LIST-ELEMENT-COUNTER 3)
```

Figure 4.7   Trace of List Element Counter.

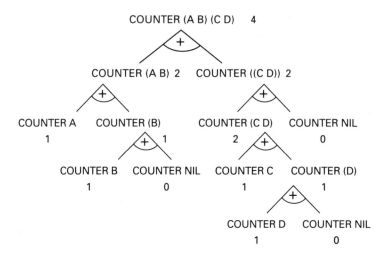

Figure 4.8 Decomposition Tree for Counter.

atoms in the list. In our example, the list contains nine atoms. We can start by noting the following cases:

NULL LIS $->$ OBJ = 0
ATOM LIS $->$ OBJ = 1
ELSE COUNT = COUNT (CAR LIS) + COUNT (CDR LIS)

Figure 4.8 shows the decomposition tree for the list ((A B)(C D)). The resulting function would be:

```
(DEFUN COUNTER (LIS)
   (COND ((NULL LIS) 0)
         ((ATOM LIS) 1)
         (T (+ (COUNTER (CAR LIS)) (COUNTER (CDR LIS))))))
```

A trace of the execution of this function for the the list ((A B)(C D)) is shown in Figure 4.9.

4.5 ITERATION

The DO macro is the basic way iteration is performed. The DO macro and several other iteration forms are defined in the boxed definition.

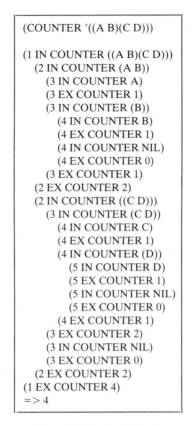

Figure 4.9   Trace of Counter.

```
DO ({(Var[init [step]])}*)
   (end-test {result}*){declaration}*
   {tag | statement}*
DOLIST (Var listform [resultform])
   {declaration}* {tag | statement}*
DOTIMES (Var countform [resultform])
   {declaration}* {tag | statement}*
```

Figure 4.10 shows an informal definition of the DO macro that might be more useful in initially learning to use the DO macro. It should be noted that DO* (which

```
(DO ((VAR1 INITIAL-VALUE (ITERATION FORM))
      VAR2 INITIAL-VALUE (THIS PART IS OPTIONAL)
      VAR3
       .
       .
      .)

    ((TERMINATION TEST) VALUE TO BE RETURNED)

   BODY)

(DO ((VAR1 '(A B C D) (REST VAR1))
     (VAR2))
    ((NULL VAR1) VAR2)
  (PRINT VAR1))

(A B C D)
(B C D)
(C D)
(D)
=> NIL
```

Figure 4.10   Informal Definition of DO Macro.

is not shown) has the same syntax as DO. DO is to DO* as LET is to LET*. That is, they differ in the way in which they bind local variables.

In the section on recursive techniques, a function was developed to compute factorials. It will now be rewritten using iteration.

```
(DEFUN FACT (N)
   (DO ((RESULT 1)
        (I 1 (1+ I)))
       ((> I N) RESULT)
     (SETF RESULT (* RESULT I)))))
```

The DO is entered and a variable RESULT is initialized to 1. The DO can recognize that RESULT is not incremented in the loop. The variable I is initialized to 1 and then incremented by 1 each time the loop is executed. The termination test is I greater than N. When the termination test is true, RESULT is returned. Otherwise, the new value of RESULT becomes the product of I and the previous value of RESULT. I is then incremented by 1 and tested for termination and so on until I is greater than N. This is an iterative version of factorial. Notice that the guard need not be changed. From the point of view of the user, it is of no consequence whether factorial is implemented in a recursive or iterative fashion. In general, recursive functions are more concise and easier to write (once you get used to them). However, they are sometimes not as efficient as iteration. In the case of the factorial, iterative forms tend to be faster than recursive forms. The following version of iterative factorial should be faster for large factorials than the previous version:

```
(DEFUN FACT (N)
    (DO* ((I 1 (1+ I))
          (RESULT 1 (* RESULT I)))
         ((= I N) RESULT)))
```

In this version, the computation is done in the incrementing part of the DO* by taking advantage of the sequential binding strategy used with DO*. I is initialized to 1 and RESULT to 1. When I is equal to N, RESULT is returned. With each step, the new value of RESULT becomes the product of the old value of RESULT and the new value of I.

DOTIMES is useful executing a specific number iterations. A simple example shows its basic operation.

```
(DOTIMES (X 5 T) (PRINT X))
0
1
2
3
4
=> T
```

Notice that X acts as an index that is incremented 5 times. It takes on consecutively the values 0, 1, 2, 3, 4. The value returned is the result-form T. The body (PRINT X) simply prints the value of the index X with each iteration. A useful way to employ DOTIMES is when timing the execution of functions. Suppose the efficiencies of the interpreted and compiled versions of iterative FACT are compared. Interpreted FACT could be timed. FACT could then be compiled using the function COMPILE and the tests repeated. Using the iterative version shown earlier, the average execution time was significantly smaller for the compiled version. Compilation will be discussed more in the chapter on program development.

COMPILE *name* &OPTIONAL *definition*

```
(DOTIMES (I 20 ()) (TIME (FACT 100)))
evaluation of FACT took 280000 microseconds

evaluation of FACT took 286790 microseconds
```

The evaluation line would have been printed 20 times for the 20 executions of DOTIMES. The granularity of the timing and the format of the printed timing message would be implementation-dependent.

The DOLIST macro can be used to iterate through a list an element at a time. Suppose we have the list (A (B C) D) and want to print each element that is an atom. This can be easily done with the DOLIST macro.

```
(SETF LIS '(A (B C) D)) => (A (B C) D)
(DOLIST (ELEMENT LIS 'DONE)
    (IF (ATOM ELEMENT) (PRINT ELEMENT)))
A
D
=> DONE
```

Iteration Using Map Functions

Iteration over list can be accomplished using MAP functions. For the time being only three mapping functions will be discussed: MAPCAR, MAPC, and MAPLIST.

MAPCAR *function list* &REST *more-lists*
MAPC *function list* &REST *more-lists*
MAPLIST *function list* &REST *more-lists*

Both MAPCAR and MAPLIST apply the function to the list or lists that follow. If multiple lists follow, the iteration continues until one of the lists is exhausted. Special forms and macro cannot be used as *function* arguments to MAP functions. They must be functions.

MAPCAR applies the function to the successive CARs of the following list or lists. MAPCAR returns a list of the results of each call. MAPC works in the same fashion as MAPCAR except it does not return a list of the results. MAPLIST applies the function to the successive CDRs that follow. The result is a LIST of the results of the successive applications. The following examples show the basic operation of these three functions:

```
(SETF A 1 B 2 C 3) => 3

(MAPCAR #'EVAL '(A B C)) => (1 2 3)
(MAPC #'EVAL '(A B C)) => (A B C)

(MAPCAR #'+ '(1 2 3) '( 1 2 3))
=> (2 4 6)
```

```
(MAPCAR #'(LAMBDA (ELEMENT)(IF (ATOM ELEMENT) 'ATOM 'CONS))
'(A (B C) D)) => (ATOM CONS ATOM)

(MAPLIST #'APPEND '( X Y) '(A B)) => ((X Y A B)(Y B))
(MAPLIST #'(LAMBDA (LIS)
                (IF (ATOM (CAR LIS)) 'ATOM 'CONS))
   '(A B (C) D))
=>(ATOM ATOM CONS ATOM)
```

The first two examples of mapping functions illustrate the difference between MAPCAR and MAPC. The third example shows that MAPCAR can use multiple lists. In this example, two lists of numbers are added a CAR at a time. The fourth example defines a lambda expression directly and uses it to return the word ATOM if an element of the argument list is an atom and the word CONS otherwise. The first MAPLIST example simply APPENDs the successive CDRs of two lists. The final MAPLIST example returns either ATOM or CONS depending on the structure of the CAR of the successive CDRs. In all cases, the results are returned as a list.

4.6 ENCAPSULATING FUNCTIONS

Every function defined using the DEFUN macro is visible at top level. The following example illustrates this point:

```
(DEFUN FOO (X)
    (DEFUN BAR (Y)
        (* Y Y Y))
    (* X X))

(FOO 10) => 100
(BAR 10) => 1000
```

For this reason, nesting DEFUNs would serve no useful purpose. Lisp provides two primitives for defining local functions. They are FLET and LABELS. They have identical syntax except that LABELS allows you to define a locally recursive function whereas FLET does not.

FLET ({(*name lambda-list* {*declarations* | *doc-string*}*
                    {*form*}*)}*) {*form*}*
LABELS ({(*name lambda-list* {*declarations* | *doc-string*}*
                    {*form*}*)}*) {*form*}*

Using labels, factorial can be redefined as follows;

```
(DEFUN FACT (N)
   (LABELS ((FAC-REC (N)
                (IF (= N 0)
                    1
                    (* N (FAC-REC (1- N)))))))
      (IF (AND (INTEGERP N) (>= N 0))
          (FAC-REC N))))
```

The recursive function FAC-REC is completely contained within the body of FACT and is only available to FACT. We gain the ability to encapsulate function definitions. At the same time, debugging becomes more difficult. FAC-REC cannot be traced using the TRACE function.

Destructive Functions

Using a specification from Mason (1986), an implementation of the function RE-VERSE+ would be:

```
(DEFUN REVERSE+ (LIS)
   (LABELS ((REV-REC (OLD NEW)
                (IF OLD
                    (REV-REC (REST OLD)
                             (CONS (FIRST OLD) NEW))
                    NEW)))
      (REV-REC LIS NIL)))
```

Of note is the fact that the function creates CONS cells proportional to the length of the list being reversed. A second version uses destructive modification of CDR cells rather than creating and copying into new CONS cells.

```
(DEFUN REVERSE+ (LIS)
   (LABELS ((REV-REC (OLD NEW)
                (IF OLD
                    (REV-REC (REST OLD)
                             (RPLACD OLD NEW))
                    NEW)))
      (REV-REC LIS NIL)))
```

In this version, RPLACD destructively modifies pointer cells. Much less garbage has been created, but the original list has been modified in the process. It is sometimes desirable to minimize CONSing and to use destructive functions. There is typically a gain in efficiency.

Taking Advantage of Tail Recursion

Notice that recursive computations are typically done by creating a chain of recursive calls until a halting condition occurs and then the computation is done as the recursion unwraps or returns levels. Suppose, instead, the computation was done on the way down. In this case, when the halting condition is reached, it would save computation time if no returns were necessary. When the simplifying conditions were met, the result would simply be handed to the next computation. The last example could be made even faster by taking advantage of this idea. Suppose the reversed list is needed for the following computation:

```
#'(LAMBDA (REVERSED-LIST)
        (DO-STUFF REVERSED-LIST))
```

The previous example is already tail recursive, it is only necessary to modify it so that it computes on the way down the recursive chain. Rewriting the previous function:

```
(DEFUN REVERSE+ (LIS -C-)
   (LABELS ((REV-TAIL (OLD NEW -C-)
               (IF OLD
                     (REV-TAIL (REST OLD)(RPLACD OLD NEW) -C-)
                     (FUNCALL -C- NEW)))))
   (REV-TAIL LIS NIL -C-)))
```

The call would now be:

```
(REVERSE+ LIS #'(LAMBDA (REVERSED-LIST)
                      (DO-STUFF REVERSED-LIST)))
```

This style of programming is called continuation style. It can make computations more efficient but is much harder to read.

4.7 THE BEHAVIOR OF FUNCTIONS

In this section, we explore in more detail several concepts that are central to understanding the behavior of functions:

- The order of evaluation of arguments.
- The order of evaluation of expressions in the body of a function definition.
- The use of PROG forms to alter normal returns.
- The explicit use of APPLY and FUNCALL.
- Forms used for nonstandard exit and entry from/to functions.

Order of Evaluation of Expressions Using PROGN, PROG1, and PROG2

Simple sequencing is accomplished using PROG forms. The body of a function executes forms sequentially as an implicit PROGN. This means that normally the forms in a function definition are executed one at a time in order of appearance in the sequence and, more importantly, that the side effects produced by a previous execution are part of the environment for the execution of the next form in the sequence. Several compound statements (such as DO, LET, and COND) use implicit PROGN structures to allow for multiple arguments at different points in the syntax of the form, to control execution, and to control which value is returned. These forms may be used explicitly to alter the return from a sequence of expressions. PROGN is a special form that sequentially evaluates forms returning the last value. An implicit PROGN is the standard. PROG1 and PROG2 are macros that sequentially evaluate forms returning the value of the first form and second form, respectively.

PROGN {*form*}*
PROG1 *first* {*form*}*
PROG2 *first second* {*form*}*

The following examples of the use of these PROG forms illustrate their behavior:

```
(PROGN (* 3 4) (- 3 4) (+ 3 4)) => 7
(PROG1 (* 3 4) (- 3 4) (+ 3 4)) => 12
(PROG2 (* 3 4) (- 3 4) (+ 3 4)) => -1
(SETF LIS '(FIRST SECOND THIRD)) => (FIRST SECOND THIRD)
(PROG1 (CAR LIS)(SETF LIS (CDR LIS))) => FIRST
LIS => (SECOND THIRD)
```

In the first example, the results of (* 3 4), (− 3 4) are discarded and the result of (+ 3 4) is returned. In the second example, the results of the first form evaluated (* 3 4) is returned and the results of (− 3 4) and (+ 3 4) are discarded. In the third example, the second argument is returned. The fourth example creates a list and then shows the use of PROG1 to return the first element or CAR of the list LIS while creating the side effect of assigning the LIS the CDR of the original list.

BLOCK and RETURN-FROM

BLOCK *name {form}**
RETURN-FROM *Name* [*result*]
RETURN [*result*]

When you define a function, an implicit block is created with the same name as the function. The expressions in the block body are executed sequentially returning the last value. The special form RETURN-FROM allows you to return immediately from any textual location within the named block. This feature allows you flexibility in controlling exits. The following example illustrates this:

```
(DEFUN TEST (CRITICAL-VALUE)
    (LABELS ((MONITOR ()
                (LET ((TEST-VAL (GET-TEST-VALUE)))
                    (IF (>= TEST-VAL CRITICAL-VALUE)
                        (RETURN-FROM TEST 'ALARM))
                    (RECORD TEST-VAL)
                    (RESET-TESTSET))))
        (MONITOR)))
=> TEST

(TEST 130) => ALARM
```

In the example, CRITICAL-VALUE is assigned some value that is being monitored. The value used in the example is 130. The function TEST calls the local recursion MONITOR that conducts a test using GET-TEST-VALUE. If the value of TEST-VAL is greater than or equal to CRITICAL-VALUE, then the function returns immediately the ALARM. If TEST-VAL is less than CRITICAL-VALUE, it proceeds to evaluate the rest of the forms recording test data (RECORD TEST-VAL) and resetting the test set (RESET-TESTSET). MONITOR continues to execute a recursive loop until an alarm condition is found. Note that the name used in RETURN-FROM is the function name and is not quoted.

LOOP *{form}**

We can also combine RETURN and RETURN-FROM with any iterative structure to provide for nonstandard exits. An example would be using the LOOP function, which will simply execute a nonterminating loop. Combined with RE-TURN, it provides a means of building iterative structures. Here is FACT using LOOP:

```
(DEFUN LOOPY-FACT (N)
   (LET ((RESULT 1)
         (I 1))
      (LOOP
        (IF (> I N) (RETURN-FROM LOOPY-FACT RESULT))
        (SETF RESULT (* I RESULT))
        (INCF I)))))
```

Later the LOOP function will be used to build macros that will extend the basic iterative structures. The macro INCF in LOOPY-FACT increments I destructively. The argument *delta* in INCF determines the increment. The default value is 1.

INCF *place* [*delta*]

4.8 SCOPE AND EXTENT

Scope and *extent* are concepts used to describe where and when a Lisp object may be referenced. It helps to envision a simple Lisp program when learning about these concepts. Figure 4.11 shows such a program.

```
(DEFUN FIR (X)
  (SEC) X)

(DEFUN SEC ()
  (SETF X 9999))

(DEFUN FIR-DYN (X)
  (DECLARE (SPECIAL X))
  (SEC) X)

(FIR 10) = > 10

(FIR-DYN 10) = > 9999
```

Figure 4.11 An Illustration of Dynamic Variables.

Lexical scope refers to the textual region in the program in which a Lisp object can be referenced. This region is specified by the definition environment. For example, the variable X is a parameter in the definition FIR. The binding to the location X can be referenced within the block FIR. X is lexically scoped. The body of the defining function FIR is the textual region or implicit block within which X may be referenced. So when (FIR 10) is called, the value 10 is returned rather than the value 9999.

Lexical objects have indefinite extent. That is, the object continues to exist as long as a possible reference to it remains. Dynamic objects, which are called *SPECIAL objects,* have indefinite scope. They can be referenced anywhere if their binding is still in effect. In the function FIR-DYN, X is declared to be a dynamic variable. The reference to X is now to the most recent binding to X. When X is changed to 9999 in SEC, the function FIR-DYN has not finished executing. Therefore, the dynamic binding to X is changed and FIR returns 9999. This is because X was DECLAREd to be SPECIAL or dynamic in function FIR.

Dynamic objects have finite extent. They exist only as long as their binding is in effect. If the dynamic object is defined at the top level, then it acts as a global reference and is available throughout the program.

Masking

Suppose that a function SEC-FUN, was written as follows:

```
(SETF Y 9999)

(DEFUN SEC-FUN (X)
   (LET ((Y 100))
      (IF (> X Y)
          (RETURN-FROM SEC-FUN Y))
   )
  Y)
```

This function would return the value of the local variable Y when X is greater than Y but the value of the nonlocal Y when X is less than or equal to local Y. The local variable masks the binding of nonlocal reference within the LET under certain circumstances.

Declarations

If you look at the syntax of DEFUN in Section 4.2, you will see that directly following the lambda list is an option to include declarations. Many Lisp forms, such as LET and DO, make this provision. The special form DECLARE is used to make local declarations within other forms such as DEFUN. In Figure 4.11, for example, the variable X was declared special using the declaration (DECLARE (SPECIAL X)). For the present, we will only consider two declaration specifiers that can be used with

DECLARE. These are SPECIAL, which is used to specify a dynamic variable, and TYPE, which is used to declare the type of a variable. SPECIAL has the form (SPECIAL var1 var2 . . .) and TYPE is of the form (TYPE type var1 var2 . . .). In the next example, the use of SPECIAL is illustrated.

SPECIAL
TYPE

```
(DEFUN FOO1 (X Y Z)
   (DECLARE (SPECIAL X Y))
   (FOO2 Z)
   (LIST X Y Z))
=> FOO1

(DEFUN FOO2 (Z)
   (SETF X 99 Y 99 Z 99))
=> FOO2

(FOO1 10 10 10) => (99 99 10)
```

Variables X and Y are declared special in FOO1. When FOO2 is called, it makes nonlocal references to the current dynamic bindings of X and Y. When SETF is used to reassign the variables, the dynamic bindings are changed and the current value of both X and Y become 99. Note that, even though the value of Z is changed in FOO2, the change was local to FOO2. When FOO1 returns the value of the last executed form, the lexical binding of Z in FOO1 is restored. Not so with the special variables X and Y, they evaluate to their current dynamic bindings that occurred in FOO2.

The PROCLAIM function is used for global declarations. We will opt for using global variable and constant forms rather than PROCLAIM for global declarations. These are described in the next section.

A more important use of declarations is in declaring parameters and local variables in functions. For example, in the iterative version of factorial:

```
(DEFUN FACT-ITER (N)
   (DECLARE (TYPE FIXNUM N))
   (DO* ((I 1 (1+ I))
         (R 1 (* I R)))
        ((>= I N) R)
     (DECLARE (TYPE FIXNUM I))))
```

Using type declarations, when possible, can have a significant impact on the efficiency of the compiled Lisp code. The impact depends on the quality of the compiler and the environment in which the computing is done. One could expect the use of declarations to have less of an impact on Lisp machines, for example.

DECLARE {*decl-spec*}*
PROCLAIM *decl-spec*

Global Variables and Constants

The macros DEFVAR and DEFPARAMETER are used to declare global variables. DEFCONSTANT is used to define global constants. DEFPARAMETER always requires an initial value for the declared variable but DEFVAR does not. DEFVAR, when given an initial value for a declared variable, will only bind the initial value if the variable is unbound at the time of declaration. The constant declared by DEFCONSTANT cannot be changed in the program without redefining the constant. If the constant is redefined, any functions that refer to that constant must be recompiled since the value of the constant rather than the constant name may be in the compiled code. The following examples illustrate the use of these macros. Note that all three provide a means for documentation. Global declarations should always be documented.

```
(DEFVAR V 20) => V
V => 20
(DEFVAR V 30) => V
V => 20
(DEFPARAMETER V 99) => V
V => 99
(DEFCONSTANT C 10) => C
C => 10
(DEFVAR SCALE1 10 "Initial value of scale is 1")
=> SCALE1
(DOCUMENTATION 'SCALE1 'VARIABLE)
=> "Initial value of scale is 1"
```

In the first example, the variable V is initialized to 20. Example two shows that DEFVAR will not change the binding of a bound variable. Example three shows that DEFPARAMETER will always bind the initial value to the variable. Example four creates a constant that cannot be changed in the body of the program. The final example shows how to use the documentation string for a global declaration.

> **DEFVAR** *name* [*initial-value* [*documentation*]]
> **DEFPARAMETER** *name* *initial-value* [*documentation*]
> **DEFCONSTANT** *name* *initial-value* [*documentation*]

ASSERT

Common Lisp has a primitive macro called ASSERT. ASSERT is part of the
Common Lisp specification and can be used to build a guard in a function. As long
as the input satisfies the test expression in the ASSERT function, the ASSERT
macro has no effect on the computation. If, however, the ASSERTion given to the
ASSERT macro is violated, a specified ACTION is taken by ASSERT. This could
be the activation of an error routine. The expression in ASSERT could be viewed
as an invariant that should always be true if the function is to compute in a correct
way. During program development, this is a useful way to control the correctness of
data flow through the program.

> **ASSERT** *test-form* [({*place*}*)[*string* {*arg*}*]]

The place argument to ASSERT allows you to specify a list of *places* to be evaluated
if an error is signaled. These names allow you to modify and continue from a
signaled error. If you do continue, ASSERT is called again after the fixes have been
accomplished. ASSERT is used throughout the later chapters.

4.9 SUMMARY

This chapter introduced the basic concepts required to compose functional abstractions in Common Lisp. The concept of specification was introduced to provide an
accepted approach to building correct abstractions. Simple input/output specifications were used to write functional specifications for function input and output. The
proper use of specifications and guards on input provides a partial verification of
the abstraction as the program is composed.

Also introduced were the basic forms used to build both recursive and iterative
forms in Lisp. The COND macro provides a powerful and flexible tool for controlling
recursion. The DO loop provides the basic macro for controlling iteration. In gen-

eral, recursion provides a succinct and natural way to express many Lisp functions. In general, however, it is not as computationally efficient as iteration. Several advanced concepts were mentioned that might enhance the efficiency of programming; these included destructive programming and tail recursion with continuations.

The behavior of functions and the concepts of scope and extent were introduced to provide more insight into the overall structure of the language. Fully understanding the behavior of the lexical environment takes much experience and study. Lack of understanding in this area is one of the common shortcomings of professional programmers. Common Lisp is a block-structured, lexically scoped language.

The use of local declarations using LET, LET*, FLET, and LABELS was also introduced. LABELS provides a means of encapsulating a recursive process in a covering function. It has the disadvantage that TRACE cannot be used to view the behavior of a local recursion.

In a sense, Common Lisp is three programming languages in one. One language is contained in the formatting facilities provided with Common Lisp. Formatting was introduced in Chapter 1 and will be illustrated throughout the book. A second language consists of the lambda list keywords used to build flexible argument lists for functions and macros. A third language consists of the primitives that have been introduced for composing functions and macros. This chapter introduced a number of new primitives, along with the use of lambda list keywords.

4.10 PROBLEMS

4.1 Write a function, called MY-CADAR, that is your own version of CADAR.

4.2 Write your own version of the function LAST that returns the last element of a list rather than the last element of the list as a list. For example, (A B C) would return C.

4.3 Write a function that takes any number of arguments and returns them as a list.

4.4 Using the relationship $LOG_yX=LOG_bX/LOG_bY$, write a function that returns the log of X to the base 2.

4.5 Write a function that asks the user what his or her name is, reads the name, and returns it as a string.

4.6 Write a function that converts measurements to centimeters. The input consists of a number and a designation of "cm" for centimeters, "in" for inches, or "ft" for feet. The function should always return the measurement in centimeters.

4.7 What would the call (MAPLIST #'(LAMBDA (LIS) T) '(A B C)) return?

4.8 Suppose the following function is defined: (DEFUN TEST (X) (REVERSE X)). When used in the call `(APPLY #'TEST '(A B C))`, it produced an error indicating that TEST was called with too many values. Modify the expression so that it works.

4.9 Write a recursive function that does integer multiplication on the two integers X and Y using addition only.

4.10 Write a recursive function that goes deeply into a list looking for instances of the object OBJ. Any instance of OBJ is removed from the list. The modified list is returned. This is to be done without the use of the REMOVE or DELETE series of functions.

4.11 A very abstract function is shown below. Show how a number of applications that CDR down a list could be expressed in this abstract function.

```
(DEFUN MAPS (COMBINER FUNC LIS &OPTIONAL GLUE)
    (COND ((NULL LIS) GLUE)
          (T
           (FUNCALL COMBINER
               (FUNCALL FUNC LIS)
               (MAPS COMBINER FUNC (CDR LIS) GLUE)))))
```

4.12 Write your own version of primitive APPEND called MY-APPEND. It should behave in the same way as the APPEND primitive does in terms of input and output. Show how you tested MY-APPEND for correctness. Write it so that it creates no new CONSes.

4.13 Write a function called SECOND-FROM-LAST that takes a list as an argument and returns the second-from-the-last element of the list. If the input is other than a list, the function should request a list input from the user and execute again. If the list has fewer than two elements, it should return NIL.

4.14 The fibonacci sequence has the following characteristics:
   a. FIB(0)=0
   b. FIB(1)=1
   c. FIB(N)=FIB(N-1)+FIB(N-2), where n is an integer $>=2$

   Given this information, write a function to calculate fibonacci numbers. Show a decomposition tree for the call (FIB 4).

4.15 Write an iterative version of the function MY-LENGTH that returns the length of a list. Remember length refers to the number of top level elements on the list. Write it so that it behaves in the same way the primitive length behaves. Could your version detect circular lists?

4.16 Write a boolean function, called VERIFY, that tests whether MY-LENGTH and LENGTH perform in the same fashion. Each time the two functions perform in the same fashion, true should be returned. We assume no side effects occur as a consequence of these functions.

4.17 Write a iterative form of the function MEMBER, called MY-MEMBER, that uses the test object, OBJ, to test for any member of LIS that is EQUAL to OBJ. If one is found, the list with OBJ as its CAR is returned. If OBJ is not EQUAL to any member of LIS, NIL is returned.

4.18 Write a version of MY-LENGTH that uses APPLY and MAPCAR.

4.19 What is wrong with this function?

```
(DEFUN FOOEY (A B)
    (LET ((A 10)
          (B A)
          (C 30))
        (PRINT (LIST A B C))
    )
    (LIST A B C))
```

4.20 Assume you do not have the basic stack operations, PUSH and POP, available. Write a version of a function, called ADD-TO-STACK, that operates in the same fashion as PUSH, and a function, called REMOVE-FROM-STACK, that operates like POP. Comment on the difficulty you had in writing correct and general functions for this purpose.

4.21 Write a function, called ARITHMETIC, that takes an operation $(+,/,-,*)$ and a variable number of arguments. The operation is then applied to the arguments.

4.22 What does this return and why?

```
(DEFUN FOO1 (X Y)
   (FOO2 X) (FOO3) (VALUES X Y))

(DEFUN FOO2 (X)
   (SETF X 1000))

(DEFUN FOO3 () (PRINT X))
(FOO1 3 9) =>
```

4.23 What does this return and why?

```
(DEFUN FOO1 (X Y)
   (FOO2) (FOO3) (VALUES X Y))

(DEFUN FOO2 () (SETF X 100))

(DEFUN FOO3 () (PRINT X))

(FOO1 3 9) =>
```

4.24 Using the DO macro, write a function to initialize lists.

4.25 Given the following sequence of computations, explain the values returned by each.
a. (SETF A 2 B 3 C 4 D 5) => 5
b. (SETF LIS '(A B C D) => (A B C D)
c. (DOLIST (I LIS CHOSEN)(IF (EQ I 'C)(SETF CHOSEN I))) => C
d. (DOLIST (I LIS CHOSEN)(IF (EQ I 'F)(SETF CHOSEN I))) => C
e. (DOLIST (I LIS C)(IF (EQ I 'F)(SETF C I))) => 4
f. (DOLIST (I LIS VAR) (EQ I 'F)(SETF VAR I)))
   => error: the variable VAR is unbound

4.26 Write your own version of the function DESCRIBE. When given a symbol name, the function should print the contents of the value cell, the definition cell, the property list cell, and the package cell of symbol name.

4.27 Write a self-replicating function—one that returns an exact copy of itself.

5

Macros

5.1 WHAT IS A MACRO?

A *macro,* or *macro function,* defines a template that must be expanded into an executable form before it can be evaluated. It is a function from form to form in which substitution and expansion occur. Once expanded, the resulting Lisp object is evaluated or compiled. Macros are powerful because a single template can be filled in so that the macro expresses a variety of executable forms. Figure 5.1 pictures the basic operation of a macro call.

Figure 5.2 shows some of the primary reasons for using macros. One important reason is to define abstractions that hide detail or complexity and simplify the development of higher level abstractions. Macros allow a single structure to express variable executable forms when expanded. The macro provides a means of simplifying syntax so that the idea being expressed in Lisp can be seen clearly and in an uncluttered way. Variability and clutter are handled by the macro.

Macros can also be used to define forms that do not require quoted arguments, to create side effects, and to improve the efficiency of the compiled code. It is often convenient to use macros to manage evaluation. This is essential for interface development requiring a straightforward facility for the user that does not involve quoted arguments. The macros PUSH and POP illustrate the use of macro forms to create global side effects. Both macros expand into top level forms that create side effects that persist after the call. This is essential for the proper behavior of stack operations. The macros, in this case, provide syntactic sugar. Certainly PUSH is more descriptive of intent than (SETF STK (CONS ITEM STK)). Finally, macros are expanded at compile time. This means that macro forms can be used to

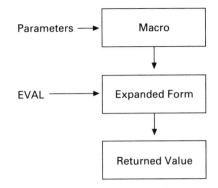

Figure 5.1   Macro Call Behavior.

reduce the number of function calls in a program. Function call (FUNCALLS) are expensive and so considerable savings in time can accrue.

5.2 MACROEXPAND AND MACROEXPAND-1

The functions MACROEXPAND and MACROEXPAND-1 are used to expand macro forms. MACROEXPAND-1 expands the macro one time and returns the expansion. It actually returns two values. If the FIRST of the *form* given to MACROEXPAND-1 is not a macro, the *form* and NIL are returned. If the FIRST of the *form* names a macro, then the macro is expanded, and the expansion and T are returned. MACROEXPAND uses MACROEXPAND-1 repeatedly until the predicate returned by MACROEXPAND-1 is NIL. This means that the CAR or FIRST of the expanded form is not a macro. The function MACRO-FUNCTION can be used to determine whether its argument names a global macro definition. If it does, the macro definition is returned.

MACROEXPAND *form* &OPTIONAL *env*
MACROEXPAND-1 *form* &OPTIONAL *env*
MACRO-FUNCTION *symbol*

1. Abstractions that hide details and variability.
2. Simplify syntax.
3. Create global side effects.
4. Control the need to quote arguments.
5. Efficient compilation.

Figure 5.2   Some Important Reasons for Defining Macros.

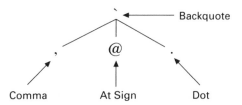

Figure 5.3 Backquote Tools for Macro Building.

5.3 BACKQUOTE

The key to building macros is to create a template that, when combined with substituted arguments, creates the form you want expressed. The backquote (') macro, along with the substitution characters shown in Figure 5.3, the comma (,), the at sign (@) and the dot (.) are provided in CL for this purpose. The backquote facility makes it easier to build a template and to visualize what the resulting expanded form with substitutions filled in will look like.

If an object is backquoted, it is simply returned. In the example, a backquoted name or list would simply be returned. In these cases, backquote behaves like a regular quote.

```
`NAME
=> NAME


`(THIS IS A BACKQUOTED LIST)
=> (THIS IS A BACKQUOTED LIST)
```

If commas are placed in front of objects on a list, the list is returned with substitutions for those objects. In the first example, the values 0 and the list (SUE PAT BILL) are bound to X and Y using LET. They are then substituted into the backquoted list. The second example shows substitution for the backquoted symbol, PATTY. In the third example, an internally generated symbol is bound to the symbol X. This is then substituted in the backquoted LET. This is a way to generate unique symbols for internal use.

```
(LET ((X 0)
      (Y '(SUE PAT BILL)))
  `(MAKE ,X THE VALUE FOR ,Y))
=> (MAKE 0 THE VALUE FOR (SUE PAT BILL))

(LET ((X 'PATTY))
  `,X)
=> PATTY

(LET ((X (GENSYM)))
  `(LET ((,X 100))
        ,X))
=> (LET ((#G100 100)) #G100)
```

The @ sign is used to splice one list into another list. The first example shows the effect of using the comma to make a substitution. The second example shows the behavior of the @ splice macro. The list (AND A LIST OF JUNK) has been spliced into the list (GOOD STUFF). The last example shows a case where the CDR primitive has been applied to the lists (A B C D) and (X Y Z) before splicing occurs.

```
(LET ((X '(AND A LIST OF JUNK)))
   '(GOOD STUFF ,X))
=> (GOOD STUFF (AND A LIST OF JUNK))

(LET ((X '(AND A LIST OF JUNK)))
   '(GOOD STUFF ,@X))
=> (GOOD STUFF AND A LIST OF JUNK)

(LET ((X '(A B C D))
      (Y '(X Y Z)))
   '(LIST ,@(CDR X) ,@(CDR Y)))
=>(LIST B C D Y Z)
```

An alternative to the @ splice is to use dot notation. Suppose X has the value '(M N O P). The result of using dot notation is shown in the following example. It should be clear that splicing with the dot is the destructive counterpart of @.

```
'(A B ,@X C D) => (A B M N O P C D)
X => (M N O P)

'(A B ,.X C D) => (A B M N O P C D)
X => (M N O P C D)
```

5.4 DEFMACRO

The DEFMACRO facility is provided for the development of user defined global macro definitions. The basic use of DEFMACRO in combination with the backquote facility is shown in the example that defines a GRIND and a GRINDE macro for expanding and then pretty printing MACRO forms. In GRIND, the backquoted argument is also quoted in the form to be expanded. This stops the form from being evaluated when the expanded form is evaluated. In the GRINDE version, the form would be evaluated after being expanded. Not controlling evaluation properly is a common source of errors when building macros.

```
(DEFMACRO GRIND (FORM)
   '(PPRINT (MACROEXPAND ',FORM)))

(DEFMACRO GRINDE (FORM)
   '(PPRINT (MACROEXPAND ,FORM)))
```

GRIND and GRINDE work for both user defined and systems defined macro expansions. They therefore provide exploratory tools for studying macro expansions. Seeing how the language designers have done it can be very educational. The elongated arrow (==>) following a form, indicates the macro expansion of FORM.

FORM ==> MACRO EXPANSION OF FORM

DEFMACRO *name lambda list {declarations | doc-string}* {form}**

Examples of Macro Expansions

SETF is a very powerful macro. A variable assignment using SETF expands in the following way. Remember PROGN simply ensures that the forms are evaluated in sequential order. What would the value of Z be?

```
(SETF X 100 Y 200 Z X) ==> (PROGN (SETQ X 100)
                                  (SETQ Y 200)
                                  (SETQ Z X))
```

Normally, if the first argument to SETF is a symbol, then the macro expands to SETQ.

PSETF *{place newvalue}**

If the parallel version of SETF (called PSETF) is expanded, the resulting form must treat each binding separately. If the previous SETF were now PSETF, the assignments of X and Y and Z would have to have been managed as parallel bindings. That means that the second X is not the same as the first. The expansion using Sun Common Lisp™ version 2.1 would be:

```
((LAMBDA (#:G6)
        ((LAMBDA (#:G7)
                ((LAMBDA (#:G8)
                        (SETQ X #:G6)
                        (SETQ Y #:G7)
```

```
                                        (SETQ Z #:G8)
                                        'NIL)
                        X))
              200))
    100)
```

On the VAX system running VaxLisp™ 2.2 program, the same expansion yields.

```
(LET* ((#:G2732 X)
       (#:G2731 200)
       (#:G2730 100))
   (SETQ Z #:G2732)
   (SETQ Y #:G2731)
   (SETQ X #:G2730)
  NIL)
```

The macros INCF and PUSH both use the SETQ form.

```
(GRIND (PUSH ITEM STACK))
==> (SETQ STACK (CONS ITEM STACK))

(GRIND (INCF X))
==> (SETQ X (1+ X))
```

Finally, a DO or DOTIMES form usually expands into an ugly TAGBODY form for implementing iteration. Using VaxLisp™ 2.2, a DO would expand into the following:

```
(GRIND (DO ((X 0 (1+ X)))
          ((= X 20) NIL)
          (PRINT X)
          (DO-OTHER-STUFF)))
==> (BLOCK NIL
      (LET ((X 0))
        (TAGBODY
          (GO #:G2736)
        #:G2735
          (PRINT X)
          (DO-OTHER-STUFF)
          (PSETQ X (1+ X))
        #:G2736
          (IF (NOT (= X 20)) (GO #:G2735))
          (RETURN-FROM NIL (PROGN NIL)))))
```

The preceding form uses a LET to establish the initial value for X. The TAGBODY defines the basic iterative loop. The (GO #:G2736) sends control to the symbol #:G2736. This ensures that the termination test precedes any other computations. If the termination test is not satisfied then we go to #:G2735, PRINT X, DO-OTHER-STUFF, and increment X. The termination condition is again tested. This loop continues until the test is satisfied. Finally, NIL is returned.

TAGBODY {*tag* | *statement*}*

Using Sun Common Lisp™, a DOTIMES expansion would look like the following:

```
(GRIND (DOTIMES (X 100) (DANCE)))

==> (BLOCK NIL
        (LET ((#:G11 100)
              (X 0))
            (DECLARE (FIXNUM X #:G11))
            (TAGBODY
              #:G12 (IF (>= X #:G11)
                          (RETURN NIL))
              (DANCE)
              (PSETQ X (1+ X))
              (GO #:G12)))))
```

This again uses a TAGBODY form. The input value for the number of iterations is reassigned to a unique GENSYM. DECLARE is used to ensure more efficient code when later compiled. In this loop, the test is first followed by the body.

Keyword Arguments

Lambda list keywords such as &BODY, &OPTIONAL, and &KEY can be used with macros. The &BODY form is preferred in place of &REST in macro definitions. In some programs you might see the argument lists that use dot notation (DEFMACRO FOO (X . Y) . . .). This has the same basic effect as (DEFMACRO FOO (X &BODY Y). Additional keywords are described in the CL specification.

An example of the use of keyword arguments in macros would be a simplified version of pretty print that will pretty print any number of interpreted functions. The arguments do not have to be quoted.

```
(DEFMACRO PP (&BODY FUNS)
  '(DOLIST (FN ',FUNS (VALUES))
     (PRINC (FORMAT () "~2%---BEGIN ~S ---" FN))
     (PPRINT (SYMBOL-FUNCTION FN))
     (PRINC (FORMAT () "~2%---END ~S ---" FN)))))
```

Building Macros with DEFMACRO

IFN.   DEFMACRO can be used to simplify syntax, to create abstractions that manage underlying variability, and to modify the normal evaluation process. Here is a simple user defined macro IFN shown with its expanded form. The purpose of IFN is to simplify syntax.

```
(DEFMACRO IFN (X Y &OPTIONAL Z)
  '(IF (NOT ,X) ,Y ,Z))

(IFN (SYMBOLP SYM) (LIST SYM) SYM)
==> (IF (NOT (SYMBOLP SYM))
        (LIST SYM)
        SYM)
```

IF+.   It might be useful to make the syntax of the IF more explicit for readability. It will be called IF+ to distinguish it from IF. Suppose we wanted it to read as follows:

IF+ <test> THEN <action1> ELSE <action2>

One macro definition for this would be:

```
(DEFMACRO IF+ (TEST THEN ACTION1 &OPTIONAL ELSE ACTION2)
  (DECLARE (IGNORE THEN ELSE))
  '(IF ,TEST ,ACTION1 ,ACTION2))
```

Using the new syntax and LET to create a temporary binding for illustration, several examples of the use of IF+ are shown below:

```
(LET ((X 100))
  (IF+ (= X 100) THEN (INCF X) ELSE (DECF X))) => 101

(LET ((X 100))
  (IF+ (= X 101) THEN (INCF X) ELSE (DECF X))) => 99

(LET ((X 100))
  (IF+ (= X 99) THEN (INCF X))) => NIL
```

The (DECLARE (IGNORE THEN ELSE)) expression in IF+, tells the compiler to ignore the names THEN and ELSE. They are never bound to values or referenced in the program. They only provide a syntactic convenience for using IF+.

LOOP.   The LOOP macro is clumsy because an explicit RETURN or THROW is required to terminate execution. We can add some syntactic sugar by defining a new macro, called UNTIL, that can be used with LOOP. The syntax would be:

(LOOP {forms}* (UNTIL <test>))

This is only one choice. The decision in this case is to use LOOP as is and provide UNTIL and an alternative to RETURN.

```
(DEFMACRO UNTIL (TEST)
    `(IF ,TEST (RETURN NIL)))
```

Now a call to LOOP would look like this:

```
(LOOP
    (DO-SOMETHING-TO LIS)
    (DO-SOMETHING-ELSE LIS)
    (UNTIL (EMPTY LIS)))
```

QUEUE.   Standard data structures that are used in a generic fashion in different parts of a program should be made macros. Here is a package for doing QUEUE operations. The queue operations do not require quoted arguments. The package controls the lexical environment so as to produce the needed side effects from the creation, insertion, and deletion operations.

```
(DEFMACRO CREATEQ (QUEUE)
    `(SETF ,QUEUE ()))

(DEFMACRO INSERTQ (ITEM QUEUE)
    `(SETF ,QUEUE (APPEND ,QUEUE (LIST ',ITEM))))

(DEFUN EMPTYQ (QUEUE)
    (NULL QUEUE))

(DEFMACRO DELETEQ (QUEUE)
    `(IF
        (NOT (EMPTY ,QUEUE))
        (POP ,QUEUE)
        (ERROR "ERROR: The queue is empty.")))
```

Note that, if the IFN macro is used in DELETEQ it reads better. The function ERROR signals a noncontinuable error.

ERROR *format-string* &REST *args*

```
(DEFMACRO DELETEQ (QUEUE)
   `(IFN
      (EMPTYQ ,QUEUE)
      (POP ,QUEUE)
      (ERROR "ERROR: The queue is empty.")))
```

Errors with User Defined Macros

One can fall into a number of traps when building macros. The next example could produce a infinite execution loop.

```
(DEFMACRO SETD (VAR VALUE)
   `(SETD ,VAR ,VALUE))
```

Sometimes you get evaluation when you don't want it.

```
(DEFMACRO MY-SET (VAR VALUE)
   `(SET ,VAR ,VALUE))
```

Suppose that X has no value. Then an error will occur when X becomes the first argument to MY-SET.

```
(MY-SET X 100)
<error>
```

Either of the following would correct the error.

```
(DEFMACRO MY-SET (VAR VALUE)
   `(SETQ ,VAR ,VALUE))
```

```
(DEFMACRO MY-SET (VAR VALUE)
   `(SET ',VAR ,VALUE))
```

A subtle problem has to do with the uniqueness of names used for local variable in macros. The macro PERCENT takes a numeric value and creates a table of percent correct. It works fine unless the argument to the macro is X. When X is the argument, local X and the substituted X cause an error. This is called the FUNARG problem.

```
(DEFMACRO PERCENT (SIZE)
  '(DO ((X 1 (1+ X)))
       ((> X ,SIZE) NIL)
     (PRINT
       (FORMAT () "~D correct is ~F percent"
         X (* 100 (/ X ,SIZE)))))))
```

The standard fix for such a potential problem is to create a unique internal symbol to preclude any possible name conflict.

```
(DEFMACRO PERCENT (SIZE)
  (LET ((X (GENSYM)))
    '(DO ((,X 1 (1+ ,X)))
         ((> ,X ,SIZE) NIL)
       (PRINT (FORMAT () "~D correct is ~F percent"
                 ,X (* 100 (/ ,X ,SIZE))))))))
```

This would expand using Golden Common Lisp 3.1 to the form:

```
(BLOCK NIL
  (LET ((#:G1001 1))
    (TAGBODY
      #G:1002
      (WHEN (> #:G1001 10) (RETURN-FROM () (PROGN NIL)))
      (PRINT (FORMAT () "~D correct is ~F percent"
                #:G1001 (* 100 (/ #:G1001 10))))
      (PSETQ #:G1001 (1+ #:G1001))
      (GO #:G1002))))
```

The Destructuring Capability of DEFMACRO

Suppose you wanted a simple FOR macro for iterating from index1 to index2 and performing a sequence of operations. You might develop a macro that looks something like this:

```
(DEFMACRO FOR (VAR INDEX1 INDEX2 &BODY FORMS)
  '(DO ((,VAR ,INDEX1 (1+ ,VAR)))
       ((> ,VAR ,INDEX2) NIL)
     ,@FORMS))
```

The call (FOR X 1 5 (PRINT X)) would print the values and then return NIL.

1

2

3

```
                                   4
                                   5
                               =>NIL
```

Or we could nest FORs so that (FOR X 1 3 (FOR Y 1 3 (PRINT (LIST X Y))))
would print.

```
                              (1 1)
                              (1 2)
                              (1 3)
                              (2 1)
                              (2 2)
                              (2 3)
                              (3 1)
                              (3 2)
                              (3 3)
                           =>NIL
```

The CL macro facility includes the capability to destructure lists. So in the
FOR example, we could choose to change the look of the function by adding an
extra set of parens around the first three arguments.

```
(DEFMACRO FOR ((VAR INDEX1 INDEX2) &BODY FORMS)
    '(DO ((,VAR ,INDEX1 (1+ ,VAR)))
        ((> ,VAR ,INDEX2) NIL)
      ,@FORMS))
```

Now the call to the FOR would be:

```
(FOR (X 1 5) (PRINT X))
1
2
3
4
5
=>NIL
```

5.5 READ MACROS

CL allows the user to build read macro characters that invoke functions when the
character is read. The first example is a dollar sign reader. Whenever a $ is encoun-
tered in any expression read, a function is called that reads the next expression and
creates the expression (*VAR* expression) in place of $expression.

The arguments to the READ function need some explanation to make this

behavior understandable. Notice that the read expression is (READ STREAM T
NIL T). Referring to the definition of READ in Chapter 1, STREAM refers to the
source of input. Normally this is the stream that is the value of *STANDARD-
INPUT*. The next argument that has the value T is *eof-error-p*. When *eof-error-p* is
true, an error is signaled when end of file (EOF) is reached. If the value of *eof-
error-p* was NIL and the next argument *eof-value* had a value, the value of *eof-value*
would be returned when EOF was reached. The final argument, *recursive-p*, is set
to T because calls to READ from read macros are not necessarily top level calls.
The system needs to know this to preserve the correct READ semantics when
recursive calls to a macro character occur. The interested reader is referred to
Steele for more discussion of this problem.

```
(DEFUN DOLLAR-SIGN-READER (STREAM CHAR)
   (DECLARE (IGNORE CHAR))
   (LIST '*VAR* (READ STREAM T NIL T)))

(SET-MACRO-CHARACTER #\$ #'DOLLAR-SIGN-READER)
=> T

'(If $X is greater than 2 then $X is set to 0)
=>(IF (*VAR* X) IS GREATER THAN 2 THEN (*VAR* X) IS SET TO 0)
```

The required arguments for SET-MACRO-CHARACTER are char and function. *Char* refers to the character that is to be read as a macro character—dollar
sign in the above example. *Function* is called when the char is encountered. The
optional argument, *non-terminating-p*, is used to make the process non-terminating
when the macro character is embedded in a expression. In the first expression, *non-
terminating-p* defaults to nil. So even the $ embedded in the OK$AY was read as a
macro character. In the second case, *non-terminating-p* was set to true. As a result,
the embedded instance of $ was not read as a macro character. Finally, *readtable*
allows the user to use any readtable with this function. Normally the default
readtable is used.

```
   '(THIS IS A $TEST OK$AY) =>
   (THIS IS A (*VAR* TEST) OK (*VAR* AY))

   (SET-MACRO-CHARACTER #\$ #'DOLLAR-SIGN-READER T) => T

   '(THIS IS A $TEST OK$AY) =>
   (THIS IS A (*VAR* TEST) OK$AY)
```

The function used by the SET-MACRO-CHARACTER function argument
must have two arguments: stream and char. *Stream* refers to the source of the
input. This is the value of the global variable *STANDARD-INPUT*, which is
usually the terminal. The *char* is the macro char and can be discarded

(DECLARE (IGNORE CHAR)). The read macro function is called whenever the macro character is encountered.

> **SET-MACRO-CHARACTER** *char function* &OPTIONAL *non-terminating-p*
>   *readtable*
> **SET-DISPATCH-MACRO-CHARACTER** *disp-char sub-char function* &
>   OPTIONAL *readtable*
> **MAKE-DISPATCH-MACRO-CHARACTER** *char* &OPTIONAL
>   *non-terminating-p readtable*

Several other examples of the use of read macros are (1) a *bang reader*, which causes the ! character to activate a pretty printer on the name that follows the !, and (2) a *macro grinder*, which uses #\% to activate a function to expand and then pretty print a macro. The grinder uses the function SET-DISPATCH-MACRO-CHARACTER, which allows for the development of a greater number of read macros by using more than one character. The first character has to be a dispatching character for the readtable. MAKE-DISPATCH-MACRO-CHARACTER can be used to define dispatching characters for a user defined readtable. The character # is a dispatching character in the default readtable and was used here:

```
(SET-MACRO-CHARACTER #\! #'(LAMBDA (STREAM CHAR)
                          "BANG READER"
                          (DECLARE (IGNORE CHAR))
                          (PPRINT (SYMBOL-FUNCTION
                                    (READ T NIL T)))
                          (TERPRI)))


(SET-DISPATCH-MACRO-CHARACTER #\# #\%
   #'(LAMBDA (STREAM SUBCHAR CHAR)
        (DECLARE (IGNORE SUBCHAR CHAR))
        (PPRINT (MACROEXPAND (READ STREAM T NIL T)))
        (TERPRI)))

#%(SETF X 100) ==>(SETQ X 100)
```

5.6 SUMMARY

The purpose of this chapter was to describe the basic macro definition facilities of CL. Macros are useful when we want to violate the normal course of evaluation or want to hide detail or complexity. Macros can be more efficient than functions since they are expanded only once—either by the interpreter or when compiled. Macro definitions should precede their use (calls) in the program. Whenever a macro is modified, the program segments that use the macro should be recompiled.

5.7 PROBLEMS

5.1 Write your own POP macro and compare it with the definition provided in your CL implementation.

5.2 Rewrite the LOOP macro with the following syntax:

LOOP {*form*}* **UNTIL** *test.*

5.3 Do these versions of DOTIMES and DOLIST work? How could you improve each definition?

```
(DEFMACRO DOTIMES+ ((NAME TIMES) . BODY)
   `(DO ((,NAME 0 (1+ ,NAME)))
        ((= ,NAME ,TIMES) NIL)
      ,@BODY))

(DEFMACRO DOLIST+ ((NAME LIS) &BODY BODY)
   `(DO ((,NAME ,LIS (CDR ,NAME)))
        ((NULL ,NAME) NIL)
      ,@BODY))
```

5.4 Do the macro definitions in Problem 5.3 take advantage of the destructuring capability of DEFMACRO? If so, show where.

5.5 Would this function work? What side effects, if any, would it produce?

```
(DEFUN SPLICE (X Y)
   (ASSERT (AND (CONSP X)(CONSP Y)) "Error")
   `(,.X ,.Y))
```

5.6 Rewrite PP the pretty printer macro using MAPCAR in place of DOLIST in the macro body.

5.7 Write a macro, called DYN, that defines local dynamic bindings. This can be simple or complex.

5.8 Write a macro called PROG3, which returns the third form evaluated and NIL if there are less than three forms.

5.9 Write a FOR macro that manages the mapping functions for you. This macro should allow you to CDR down lists performing computations on each CAR for any number of lists.

6

Advanced Data
Structures

6.1 INTRODUCTION

The purpose of this chapter is to introduce advanced data structures that are useful in developing applications. The chapter describes the most used features of DEFSTRUCTs, vectors and arrays, hash tables, closures, and streams.

6.2 DEFSTRUCT

The DEFSTRUCT macro provides a powerful tool for expressing data structures. It is used to define new data types. It supports traditional record structures and also supports frame-based and object-based programming.

DEFSTRUCT *name-and-options* [*doc-string*] {*slot-description*}+

DEFSTRUCT creates a object of type *name* with a structure defined by *slots*. A simple example is a structure called AUTO. First DEFSTRUCT is used to define the new structure AUTO with attributes, or slots: brand, model, and color. Instances of AUTO can now be created from this template. Instances can be created in any number of ways. The first example simply assigns an instance to the symbol

DAUGHTERS-CAR using SETF. The MAKE function is provided for creating
instances of any type defined using DEFSTRUCT. The second example builds a
macro called BUILD-CAR for creating instances. In the following cases, the instances MY-CAR, SONS-CAR, and WIFES-CAR were created. The macro was
used to simplify syntax. It should be noted that the syntax of what is printed when
an instance is created depends upon the print function associated with the newly
created structure. The newly created object or instance is actually returned regardless of what is printed. The distinction between what is printed and what is returned
can be subtle. The default syntax for printing is #S(defstruct-name :slot1 value1
:slot2 value2. . . .).

```
(DEFSTRUCT AUTO BRAND MODEL COLOR)
=> AUTO

(SETF DAUGHTERS-CAR
    (MAKE-AUTO :BRAND 'PORSCHE :MODEL 944
                :COLOR 'SCREAMING-YELLOW))
=>#S(AUTO :BRAND PORSCHE :MODEL 944 :COLOR SCREAMING-YELLOW)

(DEFMACRO BUILD-CAR (NAME BRAND MODEL COLOR)
   '(SETF ,NAME (MAKE-AUTO :BRAND ',BRAND
                        :MODEL ',MODEL :COLOR ',COLOR)))
=> BUILD-CAR

(BUILD-CAR MY-CAR HONDA COOP BLACK)
=> #S(AUTO :BRAND HONDA :MODEL COUP :COLOR BLACK)

(BUILD-CAR SONS-CAR HONDA ACCORD BLUE)
=> #S(AUTO :BRAND HONDA :MODEL ACCORD :COLOR BLUE)

(BUILD-CAR WIFES-CAR NISSAN MAXIMA BLUE)
=> #S(AUTO :BRAND NISSAN :MODEL MAXIMA :COLOR BLUE)
```

DEFSTRUCT is a very efficient way to build data structures because several
functions including the constructor, accessor, and print functions for the new type
are provided automatically. The function (AUTO-P sym) can be used to see if sym
is a structure of type AUTO. The syntax (STRUCTURENAME-SLOT instance)
accesses the value of the slot for any instance. The DESCRIBE function prints a
complete description of any instance and shows the slot values. Using the above
example, a comparison of wives' and sons' car color would look like the following:

```
(IF (EQ (AUTO-COLOR WIFES-CAR) (AUTO-COLOR SONS-CAR))
    (PRINT (FORMAT () "NO MORE ~S CARS"
            (AUTO-COLOR SONS-CAR))))
"NO MORE BLUE CARS"
=> "NO MORE BLUE CARS"
```

Default values can be specified when the structure is defined. As shown in the next example, if defaults are provided these are inherited by any instance that is defined. MY-CAR has automatically inherited the color red. However, the model slot was changed to a new value when the instance was created. This overrides the default value. SETF is used to change a value once the instance has been created. Any slot in an instance defines a place for SETF. The use of SETF to change values is also shown in the examples that follow:

```
(DEFSTRUCT AUTO
   (BRAND  'HONDA)
   (MODEL  'ACCORD)
   (COLOR   'RED))
=>AUTO

(SETF MY-CAR (MAKE-AUTO :MODEL 'COUP))
=> #S(AUTO :BRAND HONDA :MODEL COUP :COLOR RED)

(AUTO-COLOR MY-CAR) => RED
(AUTO-MODEL MY-CAR) => COUP

(SETF (AUTO-COLOR MY-CAR) 'GREEN)
=>GREEN
(SETF (AUTO-MODEL MY-CAR) 'SEDAN)
=>SEDAN
(AUTO-COLOR MY-CAR)
=>GREEN
(AUTO-MODEL MY-CAR)
=>SEDAN
```

CONC-NAME can be used to change the prefix used for retrieving slot values. Normally, the prefix would be the defstruct name—AUTO in the current example. AUTO-BRAND, AUTO-MODEL, and AUTO-COLOR would be used with an instance as an argument for retrieving slot values. The next example shows three different choices for prefixing. In the first, the prefix CAR is defined. Notice that no hypen is used with it when retrieving slot values. In the second example, a hyphenated prefix is used. In the third example CONC-NAME has been set to NIL, meaning that no prefix is required.

```
(DEFSTRUCT (AUTO (:CONC-NAME CAR)) BRAND MODEL COLOR)
=>AUTO

(BUILD-CAR TEST-CAR FORD MUSTANG GREEN)
=>#S(AUTO :BRAND FORD :MODEL MUSTANG :COLOR GREEN)

(CARMODEL TEST-CAR)
=> MUSTANG
```

```
(DEFSTRUCT (AUTO (:CONC-NAME CAR-)) BRAND MODEL COLOR)
=>AUTO

(BUILD-CAR TEST-CAR FORD MUSTANG GREEN)
=>#S(AUTO :BRAND FORD :MODEL MUSTANG :COLOR GREEN)

(CAR-MODEL TEST-CAR)
=> MUSTANG

(DEFSTRUCT (AUTO (:CONC-NAME NIL)) BRAND MODEL COLOR)
=>AUTO

(BUILD-CAR TEST-CAR FORD MUSTANG GREEN)
=>#S(AUTO :BRAND FORD :MODEL MUSTANG :COLOR GREEN)

(MODEL TEST-CAR)
=> MUSTANG
```

If the :TYPE option (Steele, et al., 1984) is not used then the print function can be modified to make it easier to read or to simplify the normal default of printing a description of the entire structure as shown in the previous examples. Two examples illustrate approaches to writing a new print function. The approach that develops the lambda definition within the body of the DEFSTRUCT encapsulates the definition better. Notice the use of a GENSYM to ensure a unique default name for each structure.

```
(DEFSTRUCT (AUTO (:PRINT-FUNCTION FOO))
   (NAME (GENSYM))
   BRAND
   MODEL
   COLOR)
 => AUTO

(DEFUN FOO (AUTO STREAM DEPTH)
   (DECLARE (IGNORE DEPTH))
   (FORMAT STREAM "<AUTO: ~S>" (AUTO-NAME AUTO)))
 => FOO

(SETF TEST
   (MAKE-AUTO :NAME 'MY-CAR
              :BRAND 'CHEVY
              :MODEL 'MALIBU
              :COLOR 'BLUE))

 =><AUTO: MY-CAR>
```

Note that the new print function FOO takes three arguments. This is required when rewriting a print function for a structure. The first argument is the structure type—in this case, AUTO. The second argument is STREAM, the stream to print to. The third argument is DEPTH, which determines how many levels deep an object will print. This is normally controlled by the system variable *PRINT-LEVEL*. You have probably noticed that, if a list is deeply nested at a certain level of nesting, dots (. . .) appear in printed representations. This is controlled by *PRINT-LEVEL*. We will normally ignore depth in modifying print functions.

```
(DEFSTRUCT (BIKE (:PRINT-FUNCTION
                     (LAMBDA (BIKE STREAM DEPTH)
                       (FORMAT STREAM "<~S>"
                         (BIKE-BRAND BIKE)))))
     BRAND MODEL COLOR COST)
=>BIKE


(SETF MY-BIKE (MAKE-BIKE :BRAND 'SCHWINN))
=> <SCHWINN>
```

The next example shows that a DEFSTRUCT can be used in a DEFSTRUCT. It also shows that a variety of forms can be placed in slots as values. Slot will be elaborated to include three separate facets or subslots: value, default, and when-asked. The VALUE facet of the slot BRAKES asks the user for the kind of brakes the bicycle has. The reply becomes the value of the VALUE facet of brakes. The WHEN-ASKED facet of brakes evaluates to a definition that can be applied any time. An example of this is shown for the bicycle DEFSTRUCT.

```
(DEFSTRUCT (SLOT (:CONC-NAME NIL))
   VALUE
   DEFAULT
   WHEN-ASKED)
=>SLOT


(DEFSTRUCT (BICYCLE (:CONC-NAME NIL))
   NAME
   (BRAKES
      (MAKE-SLOT
        :VALUE
           (PROGN
             (PRINT "WHAT KIND OF BRAKES DO YOU HAVE?")
                (READ))
        :DEFAULT 'HUB
        :WHEN-ASKED
           #'(LAMBDA (INS)
                 (IF (EQ (DEFAULT (BRAKES INS)) 'HUB)
                    (PRINT "GET A NEW BIKE!")(VALUES)))))
```

```
    (DERAUILER 'NONE))
=>BICYCLE


(SETF MY-BIKE (MAKE-BICYCLE :NAME 'BIKE-1))
"WHAT KIND OF BRAKES DO YOU HAVE?" LOUSY
=>#S(BICYCLE
        :NAME BIKE-1
        :BRAKES
           #S(SLOT
                  :VALUE LOUSY
                  :DEFAULT HUB
                  :WHEN-ASKED
                     #'(LAMBDA (INS)
                            (IF (EQ (DEFAULT (BRAKES INS)) 'HUB)
                                (PRINT "GET A NEW BIKE!")
                                (VALUES))))
                 :DERAUILER NONE)


(FUNCALL (WHEN-ASKED (BRAKES MY-BIKE)) MY-BIKE)
"GET A NEW BIKE"
=>"GET A NEW BIKE"
```

6.3 VECTORS AND ARRAYS

The example shows four ways to create a simple vector:

1. Use the syntax #(elements) directly.
2. Use the MAKE-SEQUENCE primitive, which also suggests that vectors, lists, and strings are all sequences in CL.
3. Use the primitive VECTOR followed by the elements the vector is to contain.
4. The general primitive MAKE-ARRAY can be used for constructing arrays of any number of dimensions.

```
    (SETF VEC1 #( 1 2 3 4 5 6))
    => #(1 2 3 4 5 6)

    (SETF VEC2 (MAKE-SEQUENCE 'VECTOR 10))
    => #(NIL NIL NIL NIL NIL NIL NIL NIL NIL NIL)

    (SETF VEC3 (VECTOR 'AUTO 'HONDA 'ACCORD 'RED))
    => #(AUTO HONDA ACCORD RED)

    (SETF VEC4 (MAKE-ARRAY '(10)))
    => #(0 0 0 0 0 0 0 0 0 0)  ;implementation dep
```

MAKE-SEQUENCE *type size* &KEY :initial-element
MAKE-ARRAY *dimensions* &KEY   :element-type
                                    :initial-element
                                    :initial-contents
                                    :adjustable
                                    :fill-pointer
                                    :displaced-to
                                    :displaced-index-offset
VECTOR &REST *objects*

MAKE-ARRAY provides a number of keyword arguments. The more useful of these are:

1. The keyword *element-type* allows you to specify the type of elements the array is allowed to contain.
2. The argument *initial-element* is used to initialize the array to some value.
3. The argument *initial-content* is used to specify the contents of the array.
4. The *adjustable argument* requires that the array be dimensionally adjustable during execution time.
5. *Fill-pointer* is used with one dimensional arrays. It allows you to specify an integer between 0 and array length. This value is incremented and decremented automatically when used with VECTOR-PUSH, VECTOR-PUSH-EXTEND and VECTOR-POP.

Examples of the use of these keywords and forms are shown below. In the example, the fill-pointer is set to 3 rather than 10 to illustrate that the primitive LENGTH is sensitive to the fill-pointer value. For a vector without a fill-pointer, length is the same as vector size. As shown, fill-pointer also defines a location for SETF.

VECTOR-PUSH *new-element vector*
VECTOR-PUSH-EXTEND *new-element vector* &OPTIONAL *extension*
VECTOR-POP *vector*

```
(SETF V1 (MAKE-ARRAY '(10)
          :INITIAL-CONTENTS '(A B C D E F G H I J)
          :FILL-POINTER 3
          :ADJUSTABLE T))
 => #(A B C)

(SETF V2 (MAKE-ARRAY '(10)))
=>#(0 0 0 0 0 0 0 0 0 0)

(LENGTH V1) => 3
(LENGTH V2) => 10
(VECTOR-PUSH-EXTEND 'K V1 10) => 3
(LENGTH V1) => 4
(FILL-POINTER V1) => 4
(SETF (FILL-POINTER V1) 10) => 10
V1 => #(A B C K E F G H I J)
(FILL-POINTER V1) => 10
```

AREF is the general accessor function for elements of an array. It is also used in conjunction with SETF to assign or change the values of array elements. The accessor function SVREF is specific to **simple** vectors.

AREF *array* &REST *subscripts*
SVREF *simple-vector index*

An example is a tic-tac-toe board represented as a 3×3 matrix. The indices range from 0 to 2 for each of the two dimensions.

```
(SETF M (MAKE-ARRAY '(3 3) :INITIAL-ELEMENT '-))
=>#2A((- - -) (- - -) (- - -))
(SETF (AREF M 0 0) 'O) => O
(SETF (AREF M 1 1) 'X) => X
(SETF (AREF M 2 2) 'O) => O

M
=> #2A((O - -) (- X -) (- - O))
```

CHAR *string index*
SCHAR *simple-string index*
STRING *x*

Strings are also sequences in Common Lisp. The functions CHAR for strings and SCHAR for simple strings can be used to access a single character in a string. A simple string has no fill-pointer and is not adjustable. MAKE-STRING returns a simple string. This definition of simple applies to vectors as well.

Suppose symbols are being extracted from a list. The program is testing each symbol to see if the first character is a "?." If so, the symbol is being used as a variable. The example shows several ways to extract and test the first symbol. The function STRING returns the print-name (a string) when a symbol is the argument.

```
(EQ (SCHAR (STRING SYMBOL) 0) #\?)
(EQ (AREF (STRING SYMBOL) 0) #\?)
```

SETF can also be used to modify a string since AREF defines a place.

```
(SETF S (STRING '?VAR))
=> "?VAR"
(SETF (AREF S 2) #\*)
=> #\*
S
=>"?V*R"
```

Bit Vectors

Bit vectors can be created by setting the keyword element-type to bit when using MAKE-ARRAY. The accessor functions are BIT and SBIT. The accessor function SBIT is used to access a bit location in simple bit vectors. BIT is the general accessor function. The next example creates two bit vectors with assignments of bits 0 and 2 in B1 and 1 and 3 in B2. Several of the variety of bit functions are then illustrated. Note that bit arrays in CL can have any number of dimensions. Bit functions usually require that the bit array arguments have the same rank and dimensions.

BIT *bit-array* &REST *subscripts*
SBIT *simple-bit-array* &REST *subscripts*

```
(SETF  B1 (MAKE-ARRAY 5 :ELEMENT-TYPE 'BIT)
       B2 (MAKE-ARRAY '(5) :ELEMENT-TYPE 'BIT))
```

```
=>#*00000
B1 => #*00000
B2 => #*00000
(SETF (BIT B1 0) 1 (BIT B1 2) 1) => 1
(SETF (SBIT B2 1) 1 (SBIT B2 3) 1) => 1
B1 => #*10100
B2 => #*01010
(BIT-AND B1 B2) => #*00000
(BIT-IOR B1 B2) => #*11110
(BIT-XOR B1 B2) => #*11110
(BIT-EQV B1 B2) => #*00001
(BIT-NOT B1)    => #*01011
(BIT-XOR B1 (BIT-NOT B1)) => #*11111
```

BIT-AND *bit-array1 bit-array2* &OPTIONAL *result-bit-array*
BIT-IOR *bit-array1 bit-array2* &OPTIONAL *result-bit-array*
BIT-XOR *bit-array1 bit-array2* &OPTIONAL *result-bit-array*
BIT-EQV *bit-array1 bit-array2* &OPTIONAL *result-bit-array*
BIT-NOT *bit-array bit-array2* &OPTIONAL *result-bit-array*

6.4 HASH TABLES

MAKE-HASH-TABLE &KEY :TEST :SIZE :REHASH-SIZE
  :REHASH-THRESHOLD
HASH-TABLE-P *object*
GETHASH *key hash-table* &OPTIONAL *default*
REMHASH *key hash-table*
MAPHASH *function hash-table*
CLRHASH *hash-table*
SXHASH *object*

A *hash table* provides a means of mapping a set of objects into a set of hash codes that preserve the retrievability of the original objects. The idea is to decrease the average search time through a linear list from O(n/2) to O(n/size), where only one level of indirection is needed to access the proper bucket, and size refers to the number of buckets or storage locations contained in the hash table. Symbol tables are an example of a data structure that is often implemented as a hash table.

```
(SETF TABLE (MAKE-HASH-TABLE))
=> <HASHTABLE POINTER>

(HASH-TABLE-P TABLE)
=> T

(SETF (GETHASH 'VAR1 TABLE) 'FLYING-WOLINDA)
=>FLYING-WOLINDA
T
(SETF (GETHASH 'VAR2 TABLE) '(A LIST OF VALUABLE JUNK))
=>(A LIST OF VALUABLE JUNK)
T
(SETF (GETHASH 'VAR3 TABLE) 'FOO-BIRD)
=>FOO-BIRD
T
(GETHASH 'VAR3 TABLE)
=>FOO-BIRD
T
  (MAPHASH #'(LAMBDA (KEY VAL)
                (IF (EQ VAL 'FOO-BIRD)
                    (SETF (GETHASH KEY TABLE)
                          'BIRD-OF-PARADISE)))
     TABLE)
 =>NIL

  (MAPHASH #'(LAMBDA (KEY VAL)
               (PRINT (LIST KEY VAL))) TABLE)
  (VAR1 FLYING-WOLINDA)
  (VAR2 (A LIST OF VALUABLE JUNK))
  (VAR3 BIRD-OF-PARADISE)
 =>NIL

(MULTIPLE-VALUE-BIND (X Y)
   (GETHASH 'VAR3 TABLE) (VALUES X Y))
=>BIRD-OF-PARADISE
   T
```

MULTIPLE-VALUE-BIND ({*var*}*) *values-form {declaration}* {form}*

In the example, the hash table TABLE is created. Three entries are put in the table: VAR1, VAR2, and VAR3. GETHASH is used to access each entry. The value is returned and also a predicate indicating T if a value was found and NIL if not. The default argument to GETHASH can be used to change what is returned if no entry for a key is found. MAPHASH is used to walk through all table entries changing foo-bird to bird-of-paradise if encountered. The arguments to MAPHASH are *key* and *val* (any two names). This is required for MAPHASH. KEY refers to the KEY upon which the original hash was based, and VAL is the value associated with the KEY. Next all entries are printed using MAPHASH. Finally, GETHASH is combined with MULTIPLE-VALUE-BIND and both the value returned and the predicate returned are bound to variables X and Y. The values of both X and Y are returned by VALUES. MULTIPLE-VALUE-BIND is the preferred way to return multiple values since the macro creates less garbage than LIST.

```
(REMHASH 'VAR3 TABLE)
=> T
(REMHASH 'NON-EXISTENT-VAR TABLE)
=> NIL
```

REMHASH is used to remove a table entry. It returns true if the entry was removed or nil if it was not found. CLRHASH removes all entries from the hash table. SXHASH returns a hash code. An interesting relationship is the following: if (EQUAL OBJ1 OBJ2) is true then (= (SXHASH OBJ1)(SXHASH OBJ2)) is true. It implies that list structures can be hash objects.

6.5 LEXICAL CLOSURES

A lexical closure includes both a definition and the binding environment at the time the definition was created. Closures can be explicitly created in several ways. A simple example is the function ONE-NAME. The symbol NAMES is given the value (PAT MIKE TOM EDDIE CARL). Since the LET is outside the DEFUN, a closure is created. The binding for NAMES is only accessible by the function ONE-NAME. As shown, a call to ONE-NAME returns one value from NAMES.

```
(LET ((NAMES '(PAT MIKE TOM EDDIE CARL)))
    (DEFUN ONE-NAME ()
        (POP NAMES)))
=> ONE-NAME

(ONE-NAME) => PAT
(ONE-NAME) => MIKE
NAMES => "ERROR"
```

When a defined function returns a definition as its value, it is returned as a closure. The function called CANDY returns two closures when called. The binding for X is shared by both closures. However, the bindings for the Ys that are local to each definition are not shared. That is shown in the example by the results of funcalls on each of the closures.

```
(DEFUN CANDY ()
    (LET ((X 10))
        (LIST
            (LET ((Y 0))
                #'(LAMBDA ()
                        (LIST :LEFT (DECF X) :EATEN (INCF Y))))
            (LET ((Y 0))
                #'(LAMBDA ()
                        (LIST :LEFT (DECF X) :EATEN (INCF Y)))))))

=> CANDY

(SETF MUNCH-TEST (CANDY))
=>(<LEXICAL-CLOSURE><LEXICAL-CLOSURE>)

(FUNCALL (FIRST MUNCH-TEST))
=>(:LEFT 9 :EATEN 1)
(FUNCALL (FIRST MUNCH-TEST))
=>(:LEFT 8 :EATEN 2)
(FUNCALL (SECOND MUNCH-TEST))
=>(:LEFT 7 :EATEN 1)
(FUNCALL (SECOND MUNCH-TEST))
=>(:LEFT 6 :EATEN 2)
(FUNCALL (SECOND MUNCH-TEST))
=>(:LEFT 5 :EATEN 3)
(FUNCALL (FIRST MUNCH-TEST))
=>(:LEFT 4 :EATEN 3)
```

Closures can provide a means of encapsulating a data object making it available to a function but not to a user. An example of the use of a closure for this purpose is shown below. The idea is to create factorials for N equal to any value between 0 and 59 while never recalculating any factorial more than once.

```
(LET ((HISTORY (MAKE-ARRAY 60 :INITIAL-ELEMENT NIL)))
   (DEFUN FACT (N)
      (ASSERT (AND (INTEGERP N) (>= N 0) (<= N 60))
      (COND ((AREF HISTORY N))
            (T (SETF (AREF HISTORY N)
                  (LABELS ((REC-FAC (N)
                              (IF (= N 0) 1
                                  (* N (REC-FAC (1- N))))))
                     (REC-FAC N))))))))
```

This is a history-sensitive version of factorial. A private array is maintained in a closure. The function FACT contains an error checker in ASSERT and has its own local recursive function REC-FAC. Since all locations in HISTORY were initialized to NIL, the argument to COND (AREF HISTORY N) will return itself if not nil. Otherwise, it evaluates to NIL and a new factorial is calculated using REC-FAC. Since the function returns the value of the last evaluated form. SETF enters the value into the HISTORY array and then returns the value.

6.6 STREAMS

Streams provide data structures for managing reading and writing. They define sources and sinks for input and output. The system variables *TERMINAL-IO*, *STANDARD-INPUT* and *STANDARD-OUTPUT* are among a number of system variables that have streams as values and that are used to control input and output.

MAKE-STRING-INPUT-STREAM *string* &OPTIONAL *start end*
MAKE-STRING-OUTPUT-STREAM

Input Streams

An example of a stream is shown using MAKE-STRING-INPUT-STREAM to create and initialize the stream S1.

```
(LET ((S1 (MAKE-STRING-INPUT-STREAM
             "THIS IS A STREAM TEST.")))
    (PRINT (READ S1))
    (PRINT (READ S1))
    S1)

THIS
IS
=><INPUT STREAM>        ;implementation dep
```

There is a problem in using a string in this manner. The next example illustrates what happens if you try to read a value from an empty stream. An end of file error occurs.

```
(SETF TEST (MAKE-STRING-INPUT-STREAM "THIS IS A TEST"))
=><INPUT STREAM>

(READ TEST)
=> THIS
(READ TEST)
=> IS
(READ TEST)
=> A
(READ TEST)
=>TEST
(READ TEST)
=><END OF FILE ERROR>
```

End of File

The end of file (EOF) problem is controlled by taking better advantage of the capabilities of the READ function. The READ function allows you to specify a number of options. This includes which stream to read from, whether or not to signal an end of file error, and what value to return if EOF occurs. To control end of file, we will turn off the option that signals an end of file error and provide a value to be returned when EOF occurs. This provides a means of taking explicit control of the end of file condition.

```
(LET ((S1 (MAKE-STRING-INPUT-STREAM
             "THIS IS A TEST OF EOF TESTING"))
      (*EOF* (GENSYM)))
    (FLET ((EOF? (OBJ)
             (EQ *EOF* OBJ)))
      (DO ((OBJ (READ S1 NIL *EOF*) (READ S1 NIL *EOF*)))
          ((EOF? OBJ) (VALUES))
        (PRINT OBJ))))
```

```
THIS
IS
A
TEST
OF
EOF
TESTING
=>
```

Broadcast Streams

MAKE-BROADCAST-STREAM &REST *streams*
MAKE-CONCATENATED-STREAM &REST *streams*
MAKE-TWO-WAY-STREAM *input-stream output-stream*
GET-OUTPUT-STREAM-STRING *string-output-stream*

Broadcast streams can be used to take input from an input stream and broadcast it to multiple streams. In the example, one input and three output streams are generated. The broadcast stream CHANNEL includes all three output streams: OUT1, OUT2, and OUT3. When a message is printed to CHANNEL, it is received by OUT1, OUT2, and OUT3 using GET-OUTPUT-STREAM-STRING as the string accessor function.

```
(LET* ((OUT1 (MAKE-STRING-OUTPUT-STREAM))
       (OUT2 (MAKE-STRING-OUTPUT-STREAM))
       (OUT3 (MAKE-STRING-OUTPUT-STREAM))
       (CHANNEL (MAKE-BROADCAST-STREAM OUT1 OUT2 OUT3)))
  (PRINT "MESSAGE FROM PROCESS ONE" CHANNEL)
  (PRINC (GET-OUTPUT-STREAM-STRING OUT1))
  (PRINC (GET-OUTPUT-STREAM-STRING OUT2))
  (PRINC (GET-OUTPUT-STREAM-STRING OUT3)))
"MESSAGE FROM PROCESS ONE"
"MESSAGE FROM PROCESS ONE"
"MESSAGE FROM PROCESS ONE"
=>"\"MESSAGE FROM PROCESS ONE"\"      ;value returned
```

Bidirectional Streams

Two way streams are created using MAKE-TWO-WAY-STREAM. Separate input and output streams are the arguments to this function. In the example, the input stream IN and the output stream OUT become the arguments for the two way stream BI. The expression (PRINT (READ BI) BI) illustrates that it can then be used to both read from and print to.

```
(SETF IN (MAKE-STRING-INPUT-STREAM "JOLLY GREEN GIANTS"))
=><INPUT Stream>

(SETF OUT (MAKE-STRING-OUTPUT-STREAM))
=><OUTPUT Stream>

(SETF BI (MAKE-TWO-WAY-STREAM IN OUT))
=><TwoWay stream>

(PRINT (READ BI) BI)
=>JOLLY

(GET-OUTPUT-STREAM-STRING OUT)
=>"
   JOLLY "
```

Concatenating Streams

Streams can be glued together using the function MAKE-CONCATENATED-STREAM. This is useful when input is to be taken in order from more than one stream. The first of the concatenated streams is used for input until it is empty. Input is then taken from the next stream in the concatenation, and so on.

```
(LET* ((IN1 (MAKE-STRING-INPUT-STREAM " THE ITSY BITSY"))
       (IN2 (MAKE-STRING-INPUT-STREAM " SPIDER RAN UP THE"))
       (IN3 (MAKE-STRING-INPUT-STREAM " COFFEE CUP"))
       (CAT (MAKE-CONCATENATED-STREAM IN1 IN2 IN3)))
  (LET ((*EOF* (GENSYM)))
    (FLET ((EOF? (OBJ)
             (EQ OBJ *EOF*)))
      (DO ((OBJ (READ CAT NIL *EOF* NIL)
                (READ CAT NIL *EOF* NIL)))
          ((EOF? OBJ) (PRINC " SQUASH") (VALUES))
        (PRINC (FORMAT () " ~A " OBJ))))))

THE ITSY BITSY SPIDER RAN UP THE COFFEE CUP SQUASH
=>
```

6.7 USING STREAMS TO MANAGE FILE INPUT AND OUTPUT

The user defined function READ-FROM-STREAM takes a stream as an argument and reads objects from the stream until it is empty. An explicit EVAL would be placed in the LOOP if READ-FROM-STREAM was used to process a program file. Normally LOAD would be used for that purpose. The function for testing the EOF value is encapsulated in a FLET. A simple LOOP controls iteration until the EOF test is true. READ-LOOP is a more readable version of READ-FROM-STREAM.

```
(DEFUN READ-FROM-STREAM (STR)
   (LET ((*END-OF-STREAM* (GENSYM)))
      (FLET ((EOF-P (OBJ)
                (EQ OBJ *END-OF-STREAM*)))
         (LOOP
            (LET ((ITEM (READ STR () *END-OF-STREAM* ())))
               (IF (EOF-P ITEM) (RETURN ()))
                  (PRINT ITEM))))))

(DEFUN READ-LOOP (STREAM &OPTIONAL (EOF (GENSYM)))
   (FLET ((EOF-P (OBJ) (EQ OBJ EOF)))
      (LOOP
         (LET ((EXP (READ STREAM () EOF ())))
            (IF (EOF-P EXP) (RETURN T))
            (PRINT EXP)))))
```

CLOSE *stream* &KEY :ABORT
DIRECTORY *pathname* &KEY
OPEN *filename* &KEY :DIRECTION :ELEMENT-TYPE :IF-EXISTS :IF-DOES-
   NOT-EXIST
PROBE-FILE *file*
UNWIND-PROTECT *protected-form* {*cleanup-form*}*
WITH-OPEN-FILE (*stream filename* {*options*}*) {*declarations*}* {*form*}*
FILE-NAMESTRING *pathname*

The next function is for reading from files. The OPEN primitive creates a stream with :DIRECTION determining whether the stream is for input or output. Again the EOF is tested using a local function. Notice that an UNWIND-PROTECT with an explicit CLOSE is used with the OPEN primitive. The UNWIND-PROTECT with the CLOSE ensures that all files are closed properly if an error produces a nonstandard termination of the function READ-FROM-FILE1.

```
(DEFUN READ-FROM-FILE1 (FILE)
   (LET ((STR (OPEN FILE :DIRECTION :INPUT))
         (EOF (GENSYM)))
      (FLET ((EOF-P (OBJ) (EQ OBJ EOF)))
         (UNWIND-PROTECT
            (LOOP
               (LET ((ITEM (READ STR () EOF ())))
                  (IF (EOF-P ITEM ) (RETURN 'DONE))
                  ))
            (CLOSE STR :ABORT :ERROR-CONDITION)))))
```

READ-FROM-FILE1 is messy. The macro WITH-OPEN-FILE takes care of protecting and closing files automatically. It is therefore preferred to OPEN.

```
(DEFUN READ-FROM-FILE2 (FILE)
   (IF (PROBE-FILE FILE)
       (WITH-OPEN-FILE
          (STR FILE :DIRECTION :INPUT)
          (READ-LOOP STR))))
```

The function READ-FROM-FILE2 uses PROBE-FILE to make sure the file exists. If it exists, the stream STR is created within WITH-OPEN-FILE, and the previous function READ-LOOP is used to read expressions from the stream STR.

The function PRINT-TO-FILE takes an expression and file. If the file exists, the expression EXP is appended to the end of the file. If the file does not exist, it is created.

```
(DEFUN PRINT-TO-FILE (EXP FILE)
   (WITH-OPEN-FILE
      (STR FILE :DIRECTION :OUTPUT :IF-EXISTS :APPEND
               :IF-DOES-NOT-EXIST :CREATE)
      (PRINT EXP STR)))
```

A final example shows a function that prints the file names for whatever directory path is provided. The file namestring is printed. A useful exercise would be to modify this function so that it prints the names of five files per line rather than one.

```
(DEFUN SHOW-DIRECTORY (&OPTIONAL (PATH "*.*"))
   (DOLIST (ITEM (DIRECTORY PATH))
      (LET ((FILE (FILE-NAMESTRING ITEM)))
         (IF (NOT (EQUAL FILE ""))
             (PRINC (FORMAT () "~%~5T~A " FILE))))))
```

6.8 SUMMARY

This chapter introduced a number of data structures that become more useful as one's Lisp programming ability matures. Most of the concepts presented can only be understood fully after experimentation by the programmer. The most commonly used options were discussed. It is important to experiment with some of the more esoteric options that were not discussed to build an awareness of their usefulness for future reference.

DEFSTRUCT and the Lisp facilities for creating and manipulating hash tables are particularly important. DEFSTRUCT will become the primary means of encapsulating, abstracting, and separating data structures from programs. Hash tables will be a workhorse for storing and sequentially accessing databases.

6.9 PROBLEMS

6.1 Write your own version of a STACK data structure using a DEFSTRUCT, called STACK. Write EMPTYS to test for an empty stack, PUSHS for pushing new values onto the stack, and POPS for coping objects from the stack. STACK should only accept FIXNUMs as data elements. House the entire data structure both representation and operations in the DEFSTRUCT.

6.2 Use DEFSTRUCT to design a data structure called AND-GATE and OR-GATE so that any combination of instances of these could be connected to form a simulated circuit.

6.3 Write additional code that sets values at the input terminals of the circuits created in Problem 6.2 and propagates values through the circuit.

6.4 Build a macro for putting values into locations in arrays with any number of dimensions.

6.5 Using a vector implement the list operations:

CREATE-LIST *length* =>

HEAD *lis* => returns the first element on the list or NIL

TAIL *lis* => all but the first element of list or NIL

V-NTH *n lis* => returns the nth car

6.6 Write a history-sensitive version of factorial using a hash table rather than an array. What are the advantages or disadvantages of doing this? Modify it so that it takes advantage of the factorials that have already been calculated.

6.7 Using bit vectors and DEFSTRUCT build a representation of an AND and OR gate.

6.8 You are given the following closure:

```
(DEFMACRO FOOD-GAME  (CACHE)
   `(LET ((LARDER ' (BEANS COFFEE BACON)))
       (PROGN
         (SETF EAT  #' (LAMBDA ()
                         (COND ((LARDER (POP LARDER)))
                               (T (FUNCALL RESUPPLY)
                                  (POP LARDER)))))
         (SETF RESUPPLY #' (LAMBDA ()
                             (SETF LARDER (APPEND ,CACHE LARDER)))))))
```

When EAT is FUNCALLed after (FOOD-GAME '(APPLE CHERRIES)) is
executed, the following is returned:

```
(FUNCALL EAT)  => BEANS
(FUNCALL EAT)  => COFFEE
(FUNCALL EAT)  => BACON
(FUNCALL EAT)  => APPLE
(FUNCALL EAT)  => CHERRIES
(FUNCALL EAT)  => APPLE
(FUNCALL EAT)  => CHERRIES
```

Explain why this is happening? Change it so that the larder is only restocked
once.

7

Program Development

7.1 WHERE IS THE PROGRAM?

When students are first learning to write functions, they often ask, "But where is the program? Where are the BEGIN and END statements?" The answer is that Common Lisp is an environment you compute in. A Common Lisp program is a set of Lisp expressions that use the Lisp environment to solve a problem. Your program modifies or extends the basic environment to serve a particular purpose. When students ask, "Where is the program?" they are really searching for some sort of *glue* that ties all the pieces together and provides coherence to the developed application. This could be a top level description of the program or an overarching abstraction residing in the Lisp environment that provides a focused view of the application. In this chapter, the concept of program in Lisp will be discussed, and an example developed fully, to illustrate both the concept of program and some good principles of abstraction and program development.

As mentioned earlier, assume in learning Lisp that you are exploring the nature of knowledge from an imperative point of view. You are interested in using a procedural approach to understanding. You want to create abstractions that can be programmed into the computer and directly subjected to experiments. The key concepts in doing this without getting overwhelmed by detail are abstraction, levels of description, and modularization. The very concepts that make for a concise, readable, organized, and integrated knowledge system are the basis for well designed programs.

The concepts of levels of description and abstraction evolve from the same processes of analysis and synthesis. Abstraction implies removing details that encumber an idea so that its essential nature is exposed. The general way to remove detail is to decompose a problem, driving detail down to what are called "primitive levels." Levels of description can be defined by using decomposition or by working from the bottom up. The idea with levels of description is that problems are expressible at more than one level and each level has its own language suited for procedural description (Rich, 1981). The process of building programs involves layering the abstractions developed and expressed at each level. An example would be a program to visually control a robotic arm. At the lowest level of description, there would be data structures and operations for controlling the micromovement of the arm and the micromovements of the eye. At another level, there would be data structures and operations for controlling higher level motor sequences, such as grasping and reaching with the arm and tracking with the eye. Finally, at a higher level data structures and operations for controlling and executing visually directed there might be grasping.

The program developed in this chapter defines a symbol table and an interface for using it. The purpose is to provide the user with an educational tool to explore or view the behavior of the symbol table. The program is to be constructed so that the underlying implementation of the data structure can be changed without changing the abstract program that uses the data structure. The idea is that these procedures represent abstractions that you will see again in different guises. Part of the power of the Lisp language is that it was designed to facilitate the layering of abstractions, the development of generic components, and the generation of functional specifications that translate easily into executable code.

7.2 THE PROBLEM

The example project is to implement a symbol table in such a manner that either a vector or a hash table can be used as the underlying data structure. It should not matter to the abstract program which representational system is used. A symbol table defines a namespace for symbols. The table contains an indexing system and a number of indexed buckets into which symbols can be placed along with their values. For a vector, a bucket is a list of pairs indexed by a simple vector index. The indexed bucket could be organized in a number of ways. An association list will be used in this example, because it supports needed operations in a clear, direct way. Figure 7.1 illustrates the organization of a symbol table as a vector containing association lists. Note that each bucket is a list of lists, with each sublist being a dotted pair consisting of symbol and value (SYMBOL . VALUE).

The following procedures are the minimum needed to implement the symbol table;

1. *Addition*: This procedure takes a symbol, value, and a symbol table. If the symbol does not exist in the table, add the symbol and value to the table. If the symbol does exist, then update the value. Assume that no symbol can

have more than one value at a time in a symbol table. That is, symbols are EQ in the same table. Nothing needs to be returned.

2. Retrieval: This procedure takes a symbol and a symbol table, and retrieves the value of the symbol. If the symbol has no current value, the value <UNBOUND> is returned. A symbol has no value if it is not in the symbol table.

3. *Deletion:* This procedure takes a symbol and a symbol table as arguments. It deletes the symbol. An indication of whether or not the symbol was deleted should be returned or printed as a side effect.

7.3 THE GLUE

Knowing what the representation will be and what operations are required does not give us enough information to proceed. It is also important to know how the data structure will be used. Knowing how the data structure will be used, effects implementation decisions and interface design decisions. In this example, the goal is to understand the nature of small program development in Lisp. Therefore, an interface is required that allows the user to interactively add, delete, and retrieve symbols from the symbol table as well as to print the contents of the entire symbol table whenever desired. There are two major conceptual pieces: the data structure and the abstract program that uses the data structure. There is no one way to begin coding these two concepts. However, in general, writing the top level function that describes the overall operation of the program and provides a perspective on how it interfaces with the user is a typical starting place.

The Top Level Glue

The function SYMBOL-TABLE defines a version of the top level program described earlier. A symbol table is created by making an instance of the data structure. A loop is then initiated that presents the user with a menu of choices from which to choose a symbol table operation. The PRINT-RETURN and READ-

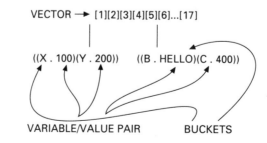

Figure 7.1   Organization of the Symbol Table Using a Vector Representation.

CHAR, which reads a single character, pauses the LOOP until any keyboard character is input. The menu in then redisplayed and so on until the user chooses to stop the process. The catcher (CATCH) is used to re-execute the menu if a bad value is entered. When this top level function is initially written, the procedure calls in the body of the top level function serve as a rough functional specification of what is needed underneath the top level. The expressions that represent procedure calls that have not been implemented yet are written as simple function *stubs* that have the correct input syntax but that only echo the input parameter values. This provides a means of monitoring data flows until the actual function body can be created and tested. This allows code to be tested while development proceeds. Each procedure can be tested and developed within the evolving top level description. This allows for more realistic testing *in context* and maintenance of *locality of reference* while each procedure is being developed into working code and then tested. The top level function describes the basic intent of the program and is the *glue* that defines the functionality and limitations of the program.

CATCH *tag {form}**
THROW *tag result*
READ-CHAR &OPTIONAL *input-stream eof-error-p eof-value recursive-p*
CASE *keyform {({({key}*)|key} {form}*)}**

```
(DEFUN SYMBOL-TABLE ()
"SYMBOL-TABLE() generates an interactive symbol-table
manipulation program"
    (LET ((TABLE (MAKE-SYMBOLTABLE)))
        (LOOP
            (CATCH 'AGAIN
                (MENU)
                (LET ((CHOICE (READ)))
                    (IF (NOT (NUMBERP CHOICE)) (THROW 'AGAIN ()))
                    (CASE CHOICE
                        ((1)(ADD-FUNCTION (PROMPT 'SYM)
                                (PROMPT 'VAL) TABLE))
                        ((2)(DELETE-FUNCTION (PROMPT 'ITEM) TABLE))
                        ((3)(RETRIEVE-FUNCTION (PROMPT 'ITEM) TABLE))
                        ((4)(SHOW-TABLE TABLE))
                        ((5)(RETURN-FROM SYMBOL-TABLE 'DONE))
                        (OTHERWISE ()))))
                (PRINT-RETURN)
                (READ-CHAR)
    )))))
```

A problem with this version of the function SYMBOL-TABLE is that the code mixes levels of abstraction. The section;

```
(CATCH 'AGAIN
    (MENU)
    (LET ((CHOICE (READ)))
        (IF (NOT (NUMBERP CHOICE)) (THROW 'AGAIN ())))
```

is low level code and should not be present in the top level function. It does not contribute to the abstract quality and readability of the function. Conceptually, the code all relates to the behavior of MENU and should be part of the MENU abstraction. MENU could be written;

```
(DEFUN MENU ()
"MENU() returns a number between 1 and 5 indicating
the choice from the menu."
    (PRINC
        (FORMAT ()
            "~|~14% WELCOME TO SYMBOL TABLE ~%
            ~20T 1. ADD A SYMBOL ~%
            ~20T 2. DELETE A SYMBOL ~%
            ~20T 3. RETRIEVE A VALUE ~%
            ~20T 4. PRINT THE TABLE ~%
            ~20T 5. STOP ~3% ~2T AND WHAT IS YOUR CHOICE>>>> "))
    (LET ((CHOICE (READ)))
        (IF (AND (NUMBERP CHOICE) (MEMBER CHOICE '(1 2 3 4 5)))
            CHOICE
            (MENU)))))
```

The code beginning with the LET captures a value and if the value is a number returns it. Now the function SYMBOL-TABLE is more uniform.

```
(DEFUN SYMBOL-TABLE ()
"SYMBOL-TABLE() generates an interactive symbol-table
manipulation program"
    (LET ((TABLE (MAKE-SYMBOLTABLE)))
        (LOOP
            (CASE (MENU)
                ((1) (ADD-FUNCTION (PROMPT 'SYM)
                        (PROMPT 'VAL) TABLE))
                ((2) (DELETE-FUNCTION (PROMPT 'ITEM) TABLE))
                ((3) (RETRIEVE-FUNCTION (PROMPT 'ITEM) TABLE))
                ((4) (SHOW-TABLE TABLE))
                ((5) (RETURN-FROM SYMBOL-TABLE 'DONE))
                (OTHERWISE ()))
            (PRINT-RETURN)
            (READ-CHAR))))
```

SYMBOL-TABLE can still be improved, however. The expressions (PRINT-RETURN) and (READ-CHAR) do not contribute to the function nor do they convey what they are intended to do. The idea is to pause the LOOP, keeping the result just printed on the screen visible until the user hits any key. The key press indicates that the user is ready to reactivate the menu. These two expressions will be replaced by the new expression (PAUSE-UNTIL-KEYPRESSED), which conveys much more clearly what is intended and buries the implementation details in a low level function.

Note that the CASE statement ends with OTHERWISE. This protects the case statements from numbers greater than 5. However, this is not really the purpose of the case statement in this function. It manages the choice points for the user. The MENU abstraction should take care of *guarding* the value given to the case statement. The guard in MENU could read;

```
(IF (AND (INTEGERP CHOICE)
         (MEMBER CHOICE '(1 2 3 4 5)))
    CHOICE
    (MENU))
```

This ensures that CHOICE is an INTEGER between 1 and 5.

The final version of the function SYMBOL-TABLE now has been layered with implementation details driven down into lower level abstractions. It is easy to read and describes what it does in a uniform way.

```
(DEFUN SYMBOL-TABLE ()
"SYMBOL-TABLE () generates an interactive symbol-table
manipulation program"
   (LET ((TABLE (MAKE-SYMBOLTABLE)))
      (LOOP
         (CASE (MENU)
            ((1)(ADD-FUNCTION (PROMPT 'SYM)
                   (PROMPT 'VAL) TABLE))
            ((2)(DELETE-FUNCTION (PROMPT 'ITEM) TABLE))
            ((3)(RETRIEVE-FUNCTION (PROMPT 'ITEM) TABLE))
            ((4)(SHOW-TABLE TABLE))
            ((5)(RETURN-FROM SYMBOL-TABLE 'DONE)))
         (PAUSE-UNTIL-KEYPRESSED)))))

(DEFUN PAUSE-UNTIL-KEYPRESSED ()
"PAUSE-UNTIL-KEYPRESSED () pauses computation until
any key on the keyboard is pressed."
   (PRINC
      (FORMAT () "~%HIT ANY KEY TO CONTINUE ~%"))
   (READ-CHAR))
```

```
(DEFUN PROMPT (NAME)
 "PROMPT (NAME) takes a name and substitutes the name
 into the formatted expression. This prompts
 the user for input which is read. The expression read
 is returned by the function."
   (PRINC (FORMAT () "~%INPUT THE ~S " NAME))
   (READ))
```

7.4 THE DATA STRUCTURE

The next step is designing the data structure or structures. The idea is to encapsulate the data structure so that it is self-contained, sharing with the abstract program only a minimum either of symbols that name procedures or of data structure slots that contain procedures. The abstract program does not care about the implementation details encapsulated in the data structure. It only cares about the procedure names it needs.

DEFSTRUCT, used in this example, is the preferred way to build encapsulated data structures. The DEFSTRUCT called SYMBOLTABLE contains both a representation of the actual table, and the procedures or functions defined on the table. In keeping with the additional requirements defined in the interface, the function ACCESS-ALL was added to the data structure even though it is not part of the essential definition of SYMBOLTABLE.

```
(DEFCONSTANT *SYMBOL-TABLE-SIZE* 18
"This value minus 1 is the symbol table size.")

(DEFSTRUCT (SYMBOLTABLE (:CONC-NAME NIL))

;---------------INTERNAL SLOTS-------------

  (-SIZE- *SYMBOL-TABLE-SIZE*)

  (-INDEX- #'(LAMBDA (ITEM TABLE)
              (MOD (SXHASH ITEM) (-SIZE- TABLE))))

  (-BUCKET- #'(LAMBDA (ITEM TABLE)
               (AREF (REPRESENTATION TABLE)
                 (FUNCALL (-INDEX- TABLE) ITEM TABLE))))

  (-PAIR- #'(LAMBDA (ITEM TABLE)
             (ASSOC ITEM (FUNCALL (-BUCKET- TABLE)
                              ITEM TABLE))))

;-----------EXTERNAL INTERFACE SLOTS--------
```

```
(REPRESENTATION (MAKE-SEQUENCE 'VECTOR
                  *SYMBOL-TABLE-SIZE*))


(RETRIEVE
   #'(LAMBDA (ITEM TABLE)
       (LET ((PAIR (FUNCALL (-PAIR- TABLE) ITEM TABLE)))
          (IF PAIR
              (VALUES (REST PAIR) T)
              (VALUES '<UNBOUND> NIL)))))


(ADD
   #'(LAMBDA (ITEM VALUE TABLE)
       (LET ((PAIR (FUNCALL (-PAIR- TABLE) ITEM TABLE))
             (BUCKET (FUNCALL (-BUCKET- TABLE) ITEM TABLE)))
          (IF PAIR (RPLACD PAIR VALUE)
              (SETF (AREF (REPRESENTATION TABLE)
                          (FUNCALL (-INDEX- TABLE) ITEM TABLE))
                    (ACONS ITEM VALUE BUCKET))))))


(DEL
   #'(LAMBDA (ITEM TABLE)
       (LET ((BUCKET (FUNCALL (-BUCKET- TABLE) ITEM TABLE)))
          (IF (MEMBER ITEM BUCKET :KEY 'FIRST)
              (FUNCALL (ADD TABLE) ITEM '<UNBOUND> TABLE)))))


(ACCESS-ALL
   #'(LAMBDA (TABLE)
       (LET ((REP (REPRESENTATION TABLE)))
          (DOTIMES (I (LENGTH REP) (VALUES))
             (LET ((BUCKET (AREF REP I)))
                (IF BUCKET
                    (MAPCAR #'(LAMBDA (ITEM)
                                (PRINC
                                   (FORMAT ()
                                      "~% KEY= ~A AND VAL= ~A"
                                      (FIRST ITEM)
                                      (REST ITEM))))
                            BUCKET)))))))
```

One global definition was used in this program. DEFCONSTANT was used to define symbol table size. DEFCONSTANT protects the variable *SYMBOL-TABLE-SIZE* from being modified during execution of the program. Once a constant is defined and given a value, it cannot be changed during execution of the program. Global definitions of this sort should be the first thing in your program.

Following the DEFCONSTANT, the new type or structure called SYM-
BOLTABLE is defined. The internal slots refer to lambda expressions that are only
needed by internal forms. They define low level accessor functions. There is no
need to define them outside the body of DEFSTRUCT. The first external interface
slot in the DEFSTRUCT, called REPRESENTATION, creates a symbol table
representation using an underlying data structure. In this case, it is a vector or one-
dimensional array of length *SYMBOL-TABLE-SIZE*. This function would *naturally* come first in the DEFSTRUCT since it defines the implementation strategy
required by the rest of the symbol table procedures. Following this are slot names
and lambda forms that define the procedures providing the functionality for the
symbol table. ADD, DEL, RETRIEVE, and SHOW-ALL are the slot names and
provide the necessary interface to the abstract program.

The function SXHASH was used to generate a hash code for this representation, and the MOD function was used to keep it within vector bounds. The value 18
was chosen to provide hash numbers up to 17 (a prime) since (MOD 18 18) is zero.
Normally, a large prime would be best for sizing a symbol table.

The Abstract Program

The abstract program that uses the symbol table to solve a problem would be
designed and implemented next. The key is to write the code for these functions in a
manner that uses only the interface and *never* accesses the underlying representation. The code for each function is transparent. It is only interested in the operations defined on the data structure such as (REPRESENTATION TABLE), (ADD
TABLE) or (DEL TABLE).

```
(DEFUN ADD-FUNCTION (SYM VAL TABLE)
"ADD-FUNCTION(SYM VAL TABLE)->
Adds a symbol/value to the symbol table by side-effect."
   (FUNCALL (ADD TABLE) SYM VAL TABLE))


(DEFUN DELETE-FUNCTION (ITEM TABLE)
"DELETE-FUNCTION(ITEM TABLE)->
Deletes an item if found by side-effect and reports result."
  (IF (FUNCALL (DEL TABLE) ITEM TABLE)
      (PRINC (FORMAT () "~%THE ITEM ~S WAS DELETED" ITEM))
      (PRINC (FORMAT () "~%THE ITEM ~S DOES NOT HAVE A VALUE"
             ITEM))))

  (DEFUN RETRIEVE-FUNCTION (ITEM TABLE)
  "RETRIEVE-FUNCTION(ITEM TABLE)->
  Prints the result of retrieving an item from the table."
     (MULTIPLE-VALUE-BIND (VALUE FLAG)
        (FUNCALL (RETRIEVE TABLE) ITEM TABLE)
        (IF FLAG
```

```
(PRINC (FORMAT () "~%THE VALUE OF ~S IS ~S"
               ITEM VALUE))
(PRINC (FORMAT ()
               "~%THE VALUE OF ~S WAS NOT FOUND"
               ITEM)))))
```

```
(DEFUN SHOW-TABLE (TABLE)
 "SHOW-TABLE (TABLE)->
 Prints all table entries."
    (FUNCALL (ACCESS-ALL TABLE) TABLE))
```

The ADD-FUNCTION takes a symbol, value, and table, and adds the symbol/value pair to the table. The DELETE-FUNCTION takes an item and table, and deletes the symbol from the table. If the symbol is not found, then this fact is printed.

The RETRIEVE-FUNCTION is more complex. If the symbol is found then the symbol value is returned. This could be an actual value or '<UNBOUND> if the symbol once had a value and subsequently was deleted. If the symbol is not found, then NOT FOUND is returned. One interpretation of this operation would require that <UNINTERNED> be returned if the symbol was not in the table and <UNBOUND> be returned if the symbol was in the table but had no current value. Since the READ function in CL interns names when they are read in, this would be transparent to us (we are ignoring GENSYM). Therefore, DEL never removes a symbol. It changes the value to <UNBOUND>. If an attempt is made to either retrieve or delete a nonexistent symbol, the symbol is interned in the table and <UNBOUND> returned. The final versions of DEL and RETRIEVE that implement this are shown next:

```
(DEL #'(LAMBDA (ITEM TABLE)
         (FUNCALL (ADD TABLE) ITEM '<UNBOUND> TABLE)))
```

```
(RETRIEVE
  #'(LAMBDA (ITEM TABLE)
       (LET ((PAIR (FUNCALL (-PAIR- TABLE) ITEM TABLE)))
          (COND (PAIR (REST PAIR))
                (T (FUNCALL (ADD TABLE) ITEM '<UNBOUND> TABLE)
                   '<UNBOUND>)))))
```

The only changes necessary to the abstract program are shown next (both DELETE-FUNCTION and RETRIEVE-FUNCTION have been simplified):

```
(DEFUN DELETE-FUNCTION (ITEM TABLE)
   (FUNCALL (DEL TABLE) ITEM TABLE)
   (PRINC (FORMAT () "~%THE VALUE OF ~S IS UNBOUND" ITEM)))
```

```
(DEFUN RETRIEVE-FUNCTION (ITEM TABLE)
   (PRINC (FORMAT () "~%THE VALUE OF ~S IS ~S" ITEM
                (FUNCALL (RETRIEVE TABLE) ITEM TABLE)))))
```

The Basic Structure

Figure 7.2 summarizes that basic schema used to organize this program. The figure shows the contextual organization of the program and does not imply the order of development, which is:

- GLOBAL DEFINITIONS.
- DATA STRUCTURES and MACROS (remember MACROS are different in the sense that they *must be defined* before they can be referenced).
- The interface or top level glue, which provides the top level view of the functionality of the program.
- The abstract program, which defines the various operations performed on the data structures.
- The utilities, which provide low level support to the program. The utilities represent (in the main) reusable software components that abstract away clutter and detail.

Hash Table Representation

To change the presentation used in the previous program, it is only necessary to change the DEFSTRUCT. The interface and abstract program need no modification since they are ignorant of the implementation details. The DEFSTRUCT shown on page 143 and 144 implements SYMBOLTABLE using hash table functions provided by Common Lisp. This will work with the program with no changes to the rest of the code. In general, it is a safe assumption that primitive functions are to be preferred to user defined functions since the primitive functions are likely to be more efficient. It is clear that the hash table representation takes better advantage of the Lisp environment than did the vector representation. Figure 7.3 shows a dribble file of an interactive session using this program.

```
GLOBAL DECLARATIONS
DEFSTRUCTS & MACRO DEFINITIONS
TOP LEVEL INTERFACE
ABSTRACT PROGRAM
UTILITIES AND SUPPORT FUNCTIONS
```

Figure 7.2 General Schema for Small Program Development.

```
WELCOME TO SYMBOL TABLE
    1. ADD A SYMBOL
    2. DELETE A SYMBOL
    3. RETRIEVE A VALUE
    4. PRINT THE TABLE
    5. STOP
AND WHAT IS YOUR CHOICE>>>>1
  INPUT A SYM x
  INPUT A VAL 100
.............................
AND WHAT IS YOUR CHOICE>>>>1
  INPUT A SYM y
  INPUT A VAL 200
.............................
AND WHAT IS YOUR CHOICE>>>>1
  INPUT A SYM lis
  INPUT A VAL (this is a list of symbols)
.............................
AND WHAT IS YOUR CHOICE>>>>4
  KEY = Y AND VAL = 200
  KEY = LIS AND VAL = (THIS IS A LIST OF SYMBOLS)
  KEY = X AND VAL = 100
.............................
AND WHAT IS YOUR CHOICE>>>>3
  INPUT A ITEM x
  THE VALUE OF X IS 100
.............................
AND WHAT IS YOUR CHOICE>>>>1
  INPUT A SYM x
  INPUT A VAL 5555
.............................
AND WHAT IS YOUR CHOICE>>>>3
  INPUT A ITEM x
  THE VALUE OF X WAS 5555
```

Figure 7.3   Sample Run of (SYMBOL-TABLE)*.

*The dotted line indicates where the menu was repeated.

```
(DEFSTRUCT (SYMBOLTABLE (:CONC-NAME NIL))
"Implements a symbol-table data structure using a hash table."

  (REPRESENTATION (MAKE-HASH-TABLE))

  (RETRIEVE
    #'(LAMBDA (ITEM TABLE)
        (COND ((GETHASH ITEM (REPRESENTATION TABLE)))
              (T (FUNCALL (ADD TABLE) ITEM '<UNBOUND> TABLE)
                 '<UNBOUND>)))))
```

```
(ADD #' (LAMBDA (ITEM VALUE TABLE)
         (SETF (GETHASH ITEM (REPRESENTATION TABLE))
               VALUE)))

(DEL #' (LAMBDA (ITEM TABLE)
         (FUNCALL (ADD TABLE) ITEM '<UNBOUND> TABLE)))

(ACCESS-ALL
   #' (LAMBDA (TABLE)
        (MAPHASH
          #' (LAMBDA (KEY VAL)
               (PRINC
                 (FORMAT ()
                   "~% KEY= ~A AND VAL= ~A" KEY VAL)))
          (REPRESENTATION TABLE)))))
```

7.5 DEFSYS

For programs that are large enough to require multiple files, a component management system is desirable. Such a facility is available on Lisp machines and is described in the *Lisp Machine Manual* (Moon, 1981). A simple version of DEFSYS
would organize the files containing system components so that the developer could
more easily load and compile the system being developed. Instead of many load or
compile commands, the developer would use something like (SYS-DO :LOAD
<sys-instance>). This would load all the files mentioned in the system definition.

A simple version of such a system is described by the DEFSTRUCT named
SYS in the next example. NAME refers to the print name of the system being
defined. The value of PATH would be a default pathname describing the path to the
files that the system uses. This would act as a default when creating and loading files
and is merged with file information when individual files are loaded. The value of
PACKAGE would be the name of the package to be used as the home package for
the system. This would be the argument to the function IN-PACKAGE. FILES
would contain an ordered list of files stored as strings. Any non-standard file path
information would be contained in the file string. An example would be the unix file
"/bin/harrison/lisp/unify/foo". The functions LOAD, COMPILE, ADD, and DE-
LETE are utilities that support typical systems activity. LOAD creates a implementation independent pathname using MERGE-PATHNAMES. TYPE extensions
such as *lsp or lisp* for source code and *fas, 1bin or f2s* for compiled files are
implementation dependent. The global variables *SOURCE-TYPE* and *COM-
PILE-TYPE* are used to store the standard extensions for your implementation.
The values of these variables are used with MERGE-PATHNAMES to provide
pathname arguments to PROBE-FILE. If no extension is provided in the file list, a
standard TYPE extension is assumed. If there is a choice between source and

compiled files, by default, the newest is chosen. Newest meaning the file with the newest FILE-WRITE-DATE. The function uses PROBE-FILE to make sure that a source or compiled version of the file exists. If found, the file is loaded. All files specified in the FILES slot are loaded in order. If a file has a non-standard type extension, it must be a part of the file string in FILES. In our earlier example; "/bin/harrison/lisp/foo.bar". COMPILE works in the same way. The function COM-PILE-FILE is used to compile each file. It checks to see if the source file exists. If it does then it is compiled. The functions ADD and DELETE can be used to add or delete files from the FILES slot.

COMPILE-FILE *input-pathname* &KEY :output-file
FILE-WRITE-DATE *file*
MAKE-PATHNAME &KEY :host :device :directory :name :type :version
    :defaults
MERGE-PATHNAMES *pathname* &OPTIONAL *defaults default-version*

```
(DEFVAR *SOURCE-TYPE* ".lisp")
(DEFVAR *COMPILE-TYPE* ".lbin")

(DEFSTRUCT SYS
"Defines a system for managing large programming projects."
   NAME
   PATH
   PACKAGE
   FILES
   (LOAD #'(LAMBDA (SYS)
             (MAPCAR
               #'(LAMBDA (FIL)
                   (LET ((PATH
                           (MERGE-PATHNAMES
                             FIL
                             (SYS-PATH SYS))))
                     (IF (OR
                           (PROBE-FILE
                             (MERGE-PATHNAMES
                               *SOURCE-TYPE* PATH))
                           (PROBE-FILE
                             (MERGE-PATHNAMES
                               *COMPILE-TYPE* PATH)))
```

```
                                  ;fault is to load newest
                             (LOAD PATH)
                             (PRINC
                                (FORMAT ()
                                   "~% The file ~S was not found."
                                   FIL)))))
                    (SYS-FILES SYS))))
(COMPILE #'(LAMBDA (SYS)
              (MAPCAR
                 #'(LAMBDA (FIL)
                      (LET ((PATH
                               (MERGE-PATHNAMES
                                  (MERGE-PATHNAMES
                                     *SOURCE-TYPE*
                                     FIL)
                                  (SYS-PATH SYS))))
                        (IF (PROBE-FILE PATH)
                            (COMPILE-FILE PATH)
                            (PRINC
                               (FORMAT ()
                                  "~% The source file ~S was not found."
                                  PATH)))))
                    (SYS-FILES SYS))))
(ADD #'(LAMBDA (SYS &REST FILES)
          (SETF (SYS-FILES SYS)
             (APPEND FILES (SYS-FILES SYS)))))

(DELETE #'(LAMBDA (SYS &REST FILES)
             (LET ((FILE-LIST (SYS-FILES SYS)))
                (MAPCAR #'(LAMBDA (FILE)
                             (SETF (SYS-FILES SYS)
                                (REMOVE FILE FILE-LIST
                                   :TEST #'EQUAL)))
                   FILES)
                (SYS-FILES SYS)))))
```

The macro DEFSYS is used to define a system.

```
(DEFMACRO DEFSYS (&KEY
                    NAME
                    (PATH *DEFAULT-PATHNAME-DEFAULTS*)
                    (PACKAGE NAME)    (FILES ()))
  "DEFSYS (&KEY NAME PATH PACKAGE FILES)->SYS INSTANCE"
This macro creates an instance of SYS and SETFs it to NAME.
```

```
PATH defines a default for loading files. PACKAGE is
given NAME as its argument. FILES is an unquoted list of
files in the order they should be loaded."
  '(PROGN
      (SETF ,NAME
          (MAKE-SYS :NAME ',NAME
                    :PATH ',PATH
                    :PACKAGE  (MAKE-PACKAGE  ',PACKAGE)
                    :FILES ',FILES)))))
```

The function SYS-DO manages the utilities when the system is loaded.

```
(DEFUN SYS-DO (KEY SYS &OPTIONAL FILES)
"SYS-DO (KEY SYS &OPTIONAL FILES)-->
 Key determines what action will be computed. SYS is an
 instance of the structure type SYS. Any number of
 files made be mentioned for ADD and DELETE. All actions
 involve side-effects."
  (CASE KEY
      ((:LOAD)(FUNCALL (SYS-LOAD SYS) SYS))
      ((:COMPILE) (FUNCALL (SYS-COMPILE SYS) SYS))
      ((:ADD) (FUNCALL (SYS-ADD SYS) SYS FILES))
      ((:DELETE) (FUNCALL (SYS-DELETE SYS) SYS FILES))
      (OTHERWISE ()))))
```

The system definition would be kept in a separate file and loaded after the
general system management and definition file. An example would be the definition
for SYMBOL-TABLE. It should be noted that implementations of Common Lisp
may handle filename extensions differently. This would require a change to the
TYPE keyword of MAKE-PATHNAME.

```
(DEFSYS :NAME SYMBOL-TABLE
        :FILES ( "FOR" "IFN" "LOOP-UNTIL" "SYM-P SYM-D"))
```

IN-PACKAGE *package-name* &KEY :nicknames :use
USE-PACKAGE *packages-to-use* &OPTIONAL *package*
IMPORT *symbols* &OPTIONAL *package*
MAKE-PACKAGE *package-name* &KEY :nicknames :use

To house the instantiated system in a package use the IN-PACKAGE command either at the beginning of the file containing the system definition:

```
(MAKE-PACKAGE 'NAME :USE '(LISP ...other packages))
(IMPORT '(DEFSYSTEM SYS-FILES SYS-NAME SYS-PATH....) 'NAME)
(IN-PACKAGE 'NAME)
(DEFSYS :NAME SYMBOL-TABLE :PACKAGE 'NAME :FILES
   ("FOR" "IFN" "LOOP-UNTIL" "SYMH-P" "SYMH-D")))
```

Or before files are loaded:

```
(IN-PACKAGE 'NAME :USE '(LISP ...other packages))
(LOAD "DEFSYS.LSP")
(DEFSYS :NAME SYMBOL-TABLE :PACKAGE 'NAME :FILES
   ("FOR" "IFN" "LOOP-UNTIL" "SYM-P" "SYM-D")))
```

EVAL-WHEN ({*situation*}*) {*form*}*

It may sometimes be desirable to keep components in separate files during development and then merge them when the system is compiled. The function EVAL-WHEN can be used to merge files in certain situations. Suppose the file FOO uses a utility kept in a file called UTIL.LSP. It might be desirable to load it separately when using interpreted code because it is subject to modification. However, since the utility services only FOO and is isolated from the rest of the program, when the system is compiled, it might be desirable to compile the utility with FOO. If the command (EVAL-WHEN (COMPILE) (LOAD "UTIL.LSP")) is placed in the file FOO, when FOO is compiled, UTIL.LSP will first be loaded and then compilation will occur. Using this command, with SYS modified to include a *files to be compiled* slot, would provide a means of adding this capability to the system management program.

7.6 GENERAL RULES FOR PROGRAM DEVELOPMENT

To pull things together, the following list summarizes some rules for program development (discussed in this and previous chapters) that provide general guidelines for program development. The list is not complete at this point: more items will be added to this list in subsequent chapters.

1. A general model for development consists of levels of abstraction, modularization of data structures, the abstract program, and some sort of *top level interface/control glue* that acts as a program description.

2. Bury implementation details in low level functions. Layer functions to provide a clear and uniform abstraction.

3. Minimize *CONSing* by using DEFSTRUCTS and arrays instead of lists to house data structures and by returning multiple values instead of lists. When doing list modifications, use destructive list functions and modifications when possible (carefully).

4. Take advantage of built-in primitives. In general, it is fair to assume that user defined versions of primitive Lisp functions will not be as efficient as the primitives provided with the language.

5. Use built-in assertion checking and type declarations to guard functions.

6. Use type declarations to provide information for the compiler to build more efficiency into your code. In conjunction with this, use FIXNUM arithmetic as much as possible.

7. BIND using LET rather than bind using SETF whenever possible. This is a matter of minimizing undesirable and unnecessary side effects. SETF can create side effects that mask unbound variables and create subtle bugs during program development. This is one of the habits that differentiates novice from experienced programmers.

8. Use macros to bury detail and to avoid FUNCALLS. Remember that many macros are expanded at compile time. Function calls are expensive. When defining macros, protect symbols from the *FUNARG* problem by using internally generated, unique symbol names.

9. Use iteration rather than recursion. Iteration is, in general, more efficient both in time and space requirements.

10. Re-initialize the Lisp environment before testing a program. Side effects from interactive sessions can create or mask bugs that are not actually part of the program being tested.

11. Minimize the use of dynamic or special variables. Try to limit these to global proclamations using DEFVAR, DEFCONSTANT, and so on.

12. Learn to take advantage of your Lisp compiler. The flexibility of Lisp carries a price. The programmer must take a more explicit role in directing the behavior of the compiler.

13. Using LET to create closures can encapsulate an environment for a function. However, the code may not compile as a consequence.

7.7 SUMMARY

This chapter described concepts important to the development of programs in the small and in the large. The concepts of layered abstractions, modularization, and top level glue or control provided a general approach to development of a program or module. The management of implementation details provided a key focus in determining the proper level of abstraction for a functional concept. There are irreducible complex problems, but in general most complex problems will yield to decomposition and layered recomposition.

The symbol table example showed clearly some basic organizational components of a program or program module. These were global declarations, DEF-STRUCTS and macro definitions, top level interface, the abstract program, and the supporting utilities. No order of development is always correct. The order is often dictated by the nature of the problem and by the complexity of the components. However, in general, a global sketch of each component, made before the development of any one component, can contribute to the overall design integrity of the finished program.

The use of a *system definition tool* can manage a system that is too big to house in one file. Various utilities for loading, compiling, printing, and so on can be managed by the systems tool. The package structure of Common Lisp can also be used to isolate the namespace of a system during development.

Finally, the chapter summarized some rules of programming that have emerged from the current and previous chapters. These center around taking advantage of the Lisp environment and compiler to build efficient code. It should be noted, however, that efficiency at the expense of good program design practice is questionable, especially in view of the fact that Lisp programs often have long evolutionary periods requiring many adjustments to the original code.

7.8 PROBLEMS

7.1   Modify the SYMBOL TABLE program so that it uses list structures to represent the symbol table.

7.2   Change the SYMBOL TABLE program so that a new parameter, called PACKAGE, is added. Now ADD requires an ITEM VALUE and PACKAGE where PACKAGE refers to a particular symbol table. Likewise with DEL and RETRIEVE. Use a DEFVAR called *CURRENT-PACKAGE* to house the name of the default package. If no package is specified in an operation, use the default package.

7.3   Modify SYMBOLTABLE so that the variable *SYMBOL-TABLE-SIZE* is contained in a slot in the structure.

7.4   Modify SYMBOLTABLE so that each symbol can have *both* a value and a definition.

7.5   Many of the functions in this chapter are not *guarded*. Using declarations or ASSERT, guard each function as necessary.

7.6   What is the relationship between the concept of a symbol table and the concept of a package in Common Lisp?

7.7   Add the slot PATCHES to DEFSYS. Modify DEFSYS and any supporting definitions that are necessary for using the PATCHES facility. PATCHES should contain the names of files containing patches or fixes to the current system that are under evaluation and that have not been incorporated into the permanent file structure yet.

7.8   Build a new function into DEFSYS called RECOMPILE that compiles any files that have been modified since the last compilation.

8

State Space Search

8.1 INTRODUCTION TO STATE SPACE SEARCH

States, Operators, and Goals

Search is a very basic problem solving mechanism that is applicable in most areas of artificial intelligence. Playing games, solving problems, understanding language, learning and making plans are examples of activities that involve search. The problem is that search can be efficient, inefficient, or impossible depending upon the nature of the activity and the expertise of the system doing the search.

A basic first generation model for thinking about the problem of efficient search in artificial intelligence is the production system model (Nilsson, 1980). It describes the search problem in terms of a state space model with an initial problem state, a goal state, and a set of operators used to generate or produce new states. An example would be a checkers game, in which the starting board configuration is the initial state. Having none of the opponent's checkers on the board defines the goal state. The operators are the legal checkers moves. It is assumed that the operators can potentially produce every possible state in the domain of interest and can produce no states that are not part of the domain of interest. That is, the operators as a set are inclusive of the domain. The idea is to apply operators to states producing new states until the desired goal state is produced.

If this is done by simply applying operators and then looking for a match between the current state and the goal state, the search being conducted is called an *uninformed search of the state space*. An uninformed search of such a space could be very time-consuming and even impossible. Imagine, for example, that you are

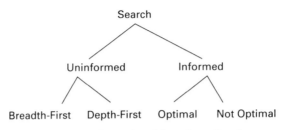

Figure 8.1 Categories of State Space Search.

sitting in front of a chess board. Your opponent has just made a move. You are deciding what to do next based on thinking about all possible outcomes for all possible games that could be played from this point. The board represents the current state of the problem. The possible chess moves represent the operators or production rules. Possible stalemates or checks of the opponent's king represent goal states. The state space is beyond your comprehension in size. It is estimated that the chess tree has 10^{120} nodes. Your only hope is to use your experience of past games to devise a plan and then revise it based on the opponent's behavior by looking ahead only several steps.

Figure 8.1 shows various categories of informed and uninformed state space search. We will first write a program that will accomplish either a breadth-first or depth-first uninformed search. Then we will explore ways to reduce the size of the search space by bringing knowledge about the problem to bear on deciding what to do next. Informed search is intended to accomplish the same thing as an uninformed, exhaustive search would accomplish while exploring a smaller portion of the state space of the problem.

There are several classes of search problems. This chapter concentrates on the class of problems called *path finding* problems (Korf, 1987). These are problems that have a definable solution path. This solution path is usually the shortest (in some sense) path from some start state to some goal state. The water jug problem and the traveling salesperson problems are examples.

The other two classes are two player games, such as chess and checkers, and constraint satisfaction problems that require a reaching a goal state without violating certain constraints (Korf, 1987). The eight queens problem is a classic example. The idea is to place eight queens on a 8 by 8 chess board so that no queen can endanger (capture) any other queen. The placement of the queens is controlled by this constraint.

It might be noted at the outset that the problem of search is a very important and central problem in understanding the concept of an expert. How an expert solves a problem differs from how a novice solves a problem. Experts have developed many rules of thumb, hunches, and so on that enable them to solve problems in their area of expertise in an efficient and correct manner. The overhead associated with problem solving is less than for the novice who must search the set of possibilities more fully in the absence of those rules of thumb. The term *heuristic* is used to note rules of thumb, recipes, intuitions, hunches, and so forth used by an expert to improve efficiency in problem solving. So informed search will be called "heuristic search" to emphasize that heuristic information is used in developing efficient search strategies, which better contain the potential combinatorial explosion of states in uninformed search.

Representing States

The search space is represented as a directed graph in which the nodes are states and the edges implicitly represent operators. Several examples of the basic terminology used are shown in Figure 8.2. In the figure, the results of applying the successor operation on N_0 are the successors N_1 and N_2. The successors may be generated or may be represented explicitly as in the top left part of the figure. The basic terminology used in describing graphs and solutions is demonstrated in the figure.

The problem of path finding is based on the assumption that, because of the

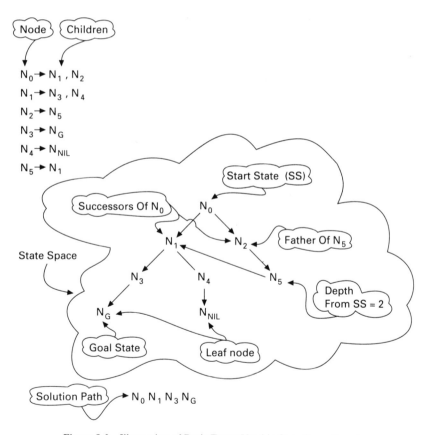

Figure 8.2   Illustration of Basic Terms Used in State Space Search.

size of the search space, it is not reasonable to represent the entire space in memory at one time. A representation for problem states must be decided upon, and a function or a set of functions constructed that will generate all successors of the state. A generating function takes a state and a set of operators, and produces the set of all subsequent states. It is assumed that the set of operators are *complete*, that is, they generate *all* possible children (potentially).

8.2 UNINFORMED STATE SPACE SEARCH

Figure 8.3 shows a simple graph representing a search space. The nodes labeled G represent the goal state so A-B-D-G and A-C-G are paths to the goal from the initial state A. The initial node A is at level 0. The nodes labeled B and C are at level 1. The nodes D, E, and the G to the far right are at level 2. The nodes F and the other G are at level 3. Nodes B and C, called the *children* or *successors* of A, were generated from applying the appropriate operators to A and so on.

Depth-First Search

A depth-first search proceeds by searching states at successive levels first. An example from Figure 8.3 is a search represented by the sequence A-B-D-F. After F, there are no more children; so another path must be explored—the path A-B-D-G, for example. The general idea is to explore the search space deeply a path at a time until a solution is found or all paths have been explored.

Algorithms for depth-first search are presented in many references such as Winston (1984) or Nilsson (1980). A basic algorithm is:

1. *Initialize the problem.*
    a. Define a start state S and a goal state G. Create an UNEXPLORED list and an EXPLORED list. Put the start state on the UNEXPLORED list. Set the EXPLORED list equal to NIL.
2. *Search* (UNEXPLORED EXPLORED G).
    a. IF EMPTY (UNEXPLORED) THEN GOTO 3.
    b. Set CS = First state on the unexplored list.
    c. Take CS off the UNEXPLORED list.
    d. IF CS = G THEN GOTO 3.
    e. Generate the children of CS and establish a pointer back to the predecessor (CS).
    f. IF they are not on the EXPLORED list, then ADD them to FRONT of the UNEXPLORED LIST.
    g. ADD CS to the EXPLORED list.
    h. SEARCH (UNEXPLORED EXPLORED G).
3. *Report results.*
    IF CS = G, then use pointers to RETURN PATH ELSE RETURN NIL.

Node   Children

A → B, C
B → D, E
C → GOAL
D → F, GOAL
E → NIL
F → NIL

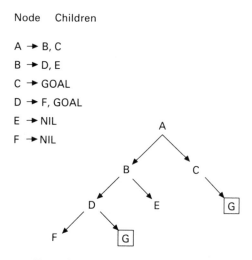

Figure 8.3 An Abstract Search Problem.

The algorithm checks to see if the current state is equal to the goal state. If it is, then you are done. Otherwise, you generate the portion of the search space that is immediately reachable from the state just tested. Two lists are used to control the search of these states. An UNEXPLORED list is used to store the states that generated but not looked at yet. By putting successors on the front of this list, a depth-first search is programmed. The EXPLORED list is used to control redundancy in the search space. It is used to store states that have been looked at (tested). It ensures that no state is seen more than once.

Problems with Depth-First Search

There are several problems with depth-first search. First, suppose that the tree shown was very deep. How far should the search of a single path continue before another alternate is tried? Some sort of depth cutoff may be appropriate, so a control algorithm would state:

IF s has no successors or the depth of s is >= d
THEN discontinue the search of this path.

Another problem occurs if you are looking for the optimal solution. Suppose that optimal in this example means shortest path from the start state to a goal state. If search proceeded in a depth-first fashion and stopped after a solution was found, then there is no guarantee that the path A-C-G would be returned rather than the path A-B-D-G. There is no guarantee that the solution found is the best solution as "best" is defined.

Breadth-First Search

To modify the depth-first search algorithm so as to conduct a breadth-first search, modify the control portion of the algorithm. Within the search loop at 2.f., the newly generated successors are placed on the *back* of the *unexplored* list rather than on the front. This change forces the exploration of all states on a level before proceeding to the next level. The breadth-first search strategy offers the advantage that, if there is a shortest path solution, it will be found.

   Both depth- and breadth-first search strategies are brute force. They are uninformed. If a quick solution is all that is required, if states have lots of children, if there are a number of paths to the goal, and if less than an optimal solution is satisfactory, then a depth-first search is the choice. If you want to ensure a shortest path solution if a solution exists, then a breadth-first search is preferable.

8.3 IMPLEMENTING DEPTH- AND BREADTH-FIRST SEARCH

We will try to develop a general engine for executing depth- or breadth-first searches of a variety of data representations. The goal is to make the search implementation as independent of the data abstraction as possible. In fact, depth- and breadth-first search are kinds of search and so the top level abstraction is SEARCH. We want to embed depth-first search and breadth-first search in SEARCH.

   The first step is to define the basic data structures needed for a path search. This would include a structure for the data representation (NODE) and a structure for the representation of the control strategy (CONTROL). These data structures should be abstract and constructed so that they are easily modifiable. DEF-STRUCT will be used to define these data structures.

   Each NODE in the search space must carry as a minimum a description of the current state and information that allows us to trace the path back to the starting state if a solution is found. The DEFSTRUCT called NODE describes this minimum. It also carries with it information concerning the name of the function that computes successors to any state, as well as the name of the appropriate function for testing equality among members of the state space.

```
(DEFSTRUCT (NODE (:CONC-NAME NIL)) STATE (FATHER ())
    (SUCCESSOR-FN 'SUCCESSORS) (EQUALITY-TEST 'EQUAL))
```

Since STATE, FATHER, SUCCESSOR-FN, and EQUALITY-TEST will not interfere with the names used in the CONTROL structure, CONC-NAME is set to nil. This means that each of the preceding can be referred to without the NODE preface. SUCCESSOR-FN and EQUALITY-TEST have default values. Carrying the successor function and equality test names with each node costs extra memory.

However, it allows us the potential to actually search a space with heterogeneous structures in it.

The basic control strategy in path search is to visit states only once but to control the search such that potentially all states can be visited. The search process stops when a solution is found or all states have been visited. This requires some means of backtracking when a dead end is found so that alternatives can be explored. Think of a maze problem as an example. You try a particular path. If it dead-ends, you must remember the path so you can back up until you find an alternative; then search continues. Ideally, you would also keep information concerning the paths you have already tested so that you do not waste valuable time retracing paths that are sure to fail.

The structure CONTROL defines two slots for this purpose, UNEXPLORED and EXPLORED. The UNEXPLORED list is a list of NODEs that have been generated by the SUCCESSOR-FN but that have not been explored yet. The UNEXPLORED list provides a backtracking mechanism for us, because it enables us to ensure that no state is left unexplored. The EXPLORED list is a list of the states that have been explored. This list is used to ensure that no state is visited more than once. A description of the goal state will also be carried in the control structure. It will be used when comparisons are needed between the current state representation and the goal representation.

```
(DEFSTRUCT (CONTROL (:CONC-NAME NIL))
    UNEXPLORED (EXPLORED ()) GOAL)
```

Given the basic data structures, the top level search function can be defined. Since the function SEARCH is a Common Lisp primitive, it would not be appropriate to use SEARCH as the name of the program. Instead we will call it SER.

```
(DEFUN SER (START GOAL)
    (LET ((BACK
            (MAKE-CONTROL
              :UNEXPLORED
                (LIST (MAKE-NODE :STATE START))
              :GOAL GOAL)))
        (SER-REC BACK)))
```

The function SER takes two arguments: START and GOAL. It returns the results of the search. This function will take any representation as an argument. It uses the data structures to *abstract out* problem details. All the accessor functions and print functions are automatically provided by DEFSTRUCT.

The function SER-REC is the workhorse of the program. It actually executes the search. Because we have chosen our data structures well, SER-REC is easy to write and easy to read. If all possibilities in the search space have been exhausted, the unexplored list will be empty and the search will fail. If a match is found using SOLVED, the search is done and the solution path is printed. Otherwise, the controls are updated and the search is continued.

```
(DEFUN SER-REC (BACK)
   (COND ((NULL (UNEXPLORED BACK)) (FAIL BACK))
         ((SOLVED BACK) (PRINT-RESULTING-PATH BACK))
         (T (SER-REC (UPDATE BACK))))))
```

Notice that SER-REC was written as a recursive process. It happens that search problems of this type can be expressed in a natural way using a recursive model. The same thing could be accomplished using an iterative approach. It would not be the natural way to express this kind of problem, however. Since SER-REC is only used by SER, it could also be written as a local function.

```
(DEFUN SER (START GOAL)
   (LABELS ((SER-REC (BACK)
               (COND ((NULL (UNEXPLORED BACK)) (FAIL BACK))
                     ((SOLVED BACK)
                         (PRINT-RESULTING-PATH BACK))
                     (T (SER-REC (UPDATE BACK)))))))
      (SER-REC
         (MAKE-CONTROL
            :UNEXPLORED (LIST (MAKE-NODE :STATE START))
            :GOAL GOAL))))
```

This version of SER encapsulates the recursion that defines the basic top level program description. It also ensures that SER-REC gets a control structure as a starting argument.

All of the supporting functions could be defined locally for the SER program. However, in this version the decision is to keep all supporting function visible.

```
(DEFUN FAIL (BACK)
   (LET ((LIS (EXPLORED BACK)))
      (PRINT
         (FORMAT () "~%Search failed ~D nodes were visited."
            (LENGTH LIS)))
      (IF (Y-OR-N-P
            "Do you want to see a list of visited nodes?")
         (DOLIST (VISITED LIST (VALUES))
            (PRINC (FORMAT () "~%<node: ~S>" VISITED))))))

(DEFUN SOLVED (BACK)
   (LET ((CURRENT-NODE (FIRST (UNEXPLORED BACK))))
      (FUNCALL (EQUALITY-TEST CURRENT-NODE)
         (STATE CURRENT-NODE) (GOAL BACK))))

(DEFUN PRINT-RESULTING-PATH (BACK)
   (LABELS ((PATH (STATE FATHER)
               (COND ((NULL FATHER) (LIST STATE))
```

```
(T (CONS STATE
          (PATH (STATE FATHER)
                (FATHER FATHER))))))))
(LET ((CURRENT-NODE (POP (UNEXPLORED BACK))))
    (NREVERSE (PATH (STATE CURRENT-NODE)
                    (FATHER CURRENT-NODE))))))
```

The function FAIL prints out housekeeping details if desired. The function SOLVED matches the current state against the goal state using the node's equality test value. If SOLVED is true, then PRINT-RESULTING-PATH uses the FATHER information and the local recursive function PATH to reconstruct the successful search path.

The heart of the control process is the function UPDATE. This function updates the UNEXPLORED and EXPLORED lists using the function name in SUCCESSOR-FN. How the successor function operates is a detail for the application to worry about. The result of application of the successor function is a nonredundant list of successor states. The SET-DIFFERENCE function ensures that only states not on the EXPLORED list will be considered for addition to the UNEXPLORED list. If the state has not been visited, it is retained on a list to be added to the UNEXPLORED list. This is the second argument to the MAPCAR function.

```
(DEFUN UPDATE (BACK)
   (LET* ((CURNODE (POP (UNEXPLORED BACK)))
          (CURSTATE (STATE CURNODE)))
      (PUSH CURSTATE (EXPLORED BACK))
      (MAPCAR
         #'(LAMBDA (ST)
              (ADDNEW (MAKE-NODE :STATE ST :FATHER CURNODE)
                      (UNEXPLORED BACK)))
         (SET-DIFFERENCE
             (FUNCALL (SUCCESSOR-FN CURNODE) CURNODE)
             (EXPLORED BACK) :TEST (EQUALITY-TEST CURNODE)))
      BACK))
```

FIND *item sequence* &KEY :from-end :test :test-not :start :end :key
UNLESS *test* {*form*}*

The manner in which the new states are added to the UNEXPLORED list is the essence of the control strategy. If the new nodes are PUSHed onto the front of the UNEXPLORED list, a depth-first search is being employed. If the new states are added onto the back of the UNEXPLORED list, a breadth-first search is being employed. The user defined macro ADDNEW implements queue behavior and ensures that only states not already on the UNEXPLORED list are added to the back of the UNEXPLORED list. The macro ADDNEW can be modified to behave in a stack-like manner for a depth-first search. The macro ADDNEW now adds new unique states to the beginning of the UNEXPLORED list.

```
;;; QUEUE LIKE VERSION

(DEFMACRO ADDNEW (ITEM Q)
"Adds to back of queue"
    `(UNLESS
        (FIND (STATE ,ITEM) ,Q :TEST (EQUALITY-TEST ,ITEM)
                                :KEY #'STATE)
        (SETF ,Q (APPEND ,Q (LIST ,ITEM))))))


;;; STACK LIKE VERSION

(DEFMACRO ADDNEW (ITEM S)
"Adds to front of stack"
    `(PUSHNEW ,ITEM ,S :TEST (EQUALITY-TEST ,ITEM)
                        :KEY #'STATE))
```

8.4 STATE SPACE SEARCH EXAMPLE

Representation of the Water Jug Problem

The water jug problem will be used to illustrate how path finding is done. This classic problem has been around a long time. In this version of it, assume there are two jugs. One holds 5 gallons of water and one holds 8 gallons of water. There is an infinite supply of water, and the goal is to end up with x gallons of water in the smaller jug and y gallons in the larger jug. The amount x is in the closed interval [0,5], and the amount y is in the closed interval [0,8] . Only one operation at a time can be used. It must be one of the following;

1. Pour water from the smaller jug into the larger (none can spill and none can be thrown away).
2. Pour water from the larger into the smaller (none can spill and none can be thrown away).
3. Fill up either jug.
4. Empty out either jug (throw the water away).

The first step is to decide upon a representation for the problem state. Start with two empty jugs—a 5 gallon jug called SMALL and an 8 gallon jug called LARGE. End up with x gallons in the small jug and y gallons in the large jug. In the process of solving this problem, it will be necessary to generate the successors of any state and to have a test of equality. To generate successors, it will be necessary to define the more primitive operations for accessing and modifying either the small or large jug value. Figure 8.4 shows both the organization and the interface descriptions required to plug the water jug representation into the search program.

The issue in deciding how to represent the problem state is to consider what operations must be performed on the state during the execution of a state space search. As done in earlier chapters, the basic strategy will be to define a representation using a data type or macro facility provided by Lisp, and then build a data abstraction that contains the functions necessary to manipulate the state as needed to execute the problem. A vector or structure offers the advantage that any element can be accessed or modified in constant time. A list requires CONSing, which is expensive. However, since Common Lisp provides primitives to access both of these elements (x and y), lists are conceptually simple, and the list in this application has only two members, a list will be used as the underlying representation for state.

The list representation is (SMALL LARGE). The FIRST element of the list is the number of gallons in the small jug, and the SECOND element of the list is the number of gallons in the large jug. A start state could be (0 0) and the goal state could be (X Y), where X is in [0,5] and Y is in [0,8].

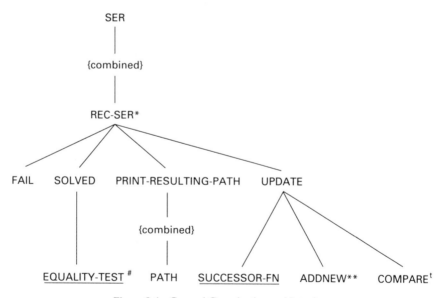

Figure 8.4   General Organization and Interface.

* Indicates a recursive function.
** This is the control and will change with strategy.
#Underlined functions are the interface with the application.
† SET-DIFFERENCE used in application for compare.
DEFSTRUCTs were used to house application components.

```
DEFSTRUCT NODE state father successor-fn equality-test
DEFSTRUCT CONTROL unexplored explored goal
ADDNEW (node queue) --> queue

SER (start goal) --> solution path | NIL
    REC-SER (control) -->
        if null (unexpl) then fail else
        if solved then show path else
        else update controls
        REC-SER (controls)
FAIL (control) --> NIL | a list of states visited
SOLVED (control) --> boolean
PRINT-RESULTING-PATH (control) --> solution path list
    PATH (state father) --> solution path list
UPDATE (control) --> control
SUCCESSOR-FN (node) --> list of successors
EQUALITY-TEST (state1 state2) --> boolean
SET-DIFFERENCE (lis1 lis2) --> lis1 − (lis1 intersection lis2)

All other functions are primitives or are representation specific
and of no interest to search. Underlined functions interface the
representation with the abstract search program. Equality-test is
used by SOLVED and UPDATE. It is used to test the equality of
members of the application representation. It is housed in
DEFSTRUCT NODE. Some of the arguments named were
changed in text.
```

Figure 8.4 (cont)   Operational Specification for Search.

```
(DEFUN F-TO-S (F S MAX)
    (COND ((OR (= F 0) (>= S MAX)) (LIST F S))
          (T (F-TO-S (1- F) (1+ S) MAX))))
```

The natural way to think about this problem is to think about pouring the contents of one jug (F) into the other jug (S) until either the first one is empty or the second one is full. The function F-TO-S expresses this idea. If the first jug is empty, there is nothing to pour and F-TO-S returns whatever state was input. The same is true if the second jug is full. The ((OR (= F 0) (>= S MAX)) (LIST F S)) takes care of these two cases. If F has water in it and S is not full, then water is poured (one unit at a time) from F to S. This continues until, by condition one, either F is empty or S is full. This function is employed by the function SUCCES-SORS to generate the successors to any legitimate problem state.

```
(DEFUN SUCCESSORS (NODE)
    (LET ((SJ (FIRST (STATE NODE)))
          (LJ (SECOND (STATE NODE))))
        (REMOVE-DUPLICATES
            (LIST `(0 ,LJ) `(,SJ 0) `(5 ,LJ) `(,SJ 8)
                (F-TO-S SJ LJ 8)
                    (REVERSE (F-TO-S LJ SJ 5)))
                        :TEST (EQUALITY-TEST NODE)))))
```

The business of filling and emptying either of the two jugs is handled directly using the backquote macro. The F-TO-S function is only needed to simulate the pouring of water from one jug into the other. The primitive REMOVE-DUPLICATES is used to remove duplicate states that might occur. An alternative would have been to have a more involved set of rules that would create no duplicates. That would seem cumbersome for this problem. The example shows such a set.

REMOVE–DUPLICATES *sequence* &KEY :from-end :test :test-not :start :end :key

---

```
(IF (AND (> SJ 0) (< SJ 5)) (LIST (F-TO-S 5 LJ LJ)
    (F-TO-S 0 LJ LJ) (F-TO-S SJ LJ 8)))
(IF (AND (> LJ 0) (< LJ 8)) (LIST (F-TO-S SJ 8 8)
    (F-TO-S SJ 0 0) (REVERSE (F-TO-S LJ SJ 5))))
(IF (= SJ 0) (LIST (F-TO-S 5 LJ LJ)))
(IF (= LJ 0) (LIST (F-TO-S SJ 8 8)))
(COND ((AND (= SJ 5) (= LJ 8)) (LIST (F-TO-S 0 LJ LJ)
                                     (F-TO-S SJ 0 0)))
      (T (COND ((= SJ 5)) (LIST (F-TO-S 0 LJ LJ)
                               (F-TO-S SJ LJ 8)))
           ((= LJ 8) (LIST (F-TO-S SJ 0 0)
                          (REVERSE (F-TO-S LJ SJ 5))))
           (T NIL)))))))
```

These two functions implement all that is necessary for using the search program to solve the water jug problem. We have successfully separated the implementation details of the water jug application from the more abstract search program. The interface between the application and the search program is contained in the CONTROL data structure as SUCCESSOR-FN and EQUALITY-TEST.

The Water Jug Solution

The first test problem has a start state (0 0), indicating both jugs are empty and a solution state (2 0) indicating 2 gallons in the small jug and nothing in the large jug. A depth-first search visited 7 nodes and produced the following solution.

(0 0) the start state
(5 0) fill small jug
(0 5) pour small into large
(5 5) fill small
(2 8) pour small into large until large is full
(2 0) empty large

A breadth-first search visited 12 nodes and produced the same solution path as the depth-first search. In this case, the depth-first approach was faster (visited fewer nodes) and produced the same solution as the breadth-first approach. However, the second example suggests caution in overgeneralizing this case. Here the start state is again (0 0) and the goal state is (3 0). The breadth-first solution to this problem visited 9 nodes. Since this is a breadth-first solution, it is a shortest path solution. You cannot solve the problem in fewer steps.

(0 0) the start state
(0 8) fill large
(5 3) pour large into small
(0 3) empty small
(3 0) pour large into small

The depth-first solution to this problem visited 23 nodes, 22 of which are in the solution path. Clearly this is not the way to solve this problem.

(0 0) start
(5 0) fill small
(0 5) pour small into large
(5 5) fill small
(2 8) pour small into large
(2 0) empty large
(0 2) pour small into large
(5 2) fill small
(0 7) pour small into large
(5 7) fill small
(4 8) pour small into large
(4 0) empty large
(0 4) pour small into large
(5 4) fill small
(1 8) pour small into large
(1 0) empty large
(0 1) pour small into large
(5 1) fill small
(0 6) pour small into large
(5 6) fill small
(3 8) pour small into large
(3 0) empty large

A third illustration is the problem with start state (0 2) and goal state (2 0). A breadth-first search visits 2 nodes and finds the solution ((0 2) (2 0)). That is, empty the large jug into the small jug. A depth-first solution visited 26 nodes before it discovered the same solution.

The depth-first strategy may give you a shortest path solution opening fewer nodes than a breadth-first approach. However, a breadth-first strategy will always give you a shortest path solution if a solution exists. It cannot guarantee it will give you the shortest path solution while opening the visiting the fewest nodes, however.

The program was given the problem with start state (0 0) and goal state (3 1). It could not solve this problem and visited 26 nodes with each strategy. This defines the size of the search space.

The Representation for the Eight Tiles Problem

The representation and operations written for the water jug problem were designed to make the representation as independent of the program using the representation as possible. The separation of the representation and the formula or program promotes clear thinking about the two pieces. It also promotes the proper development of abstractions. We will now develop a representation for a second search problem that can be run using the same search program. This problem is called the eight tiles problem.

The eight tiles game uses a small board with eight inlaid square sliding pieces with the values 1 through 8 marked on top of them. One vacant square area allows for limited movement of the individual tiles. Figure 8.5 shows a picture of the board

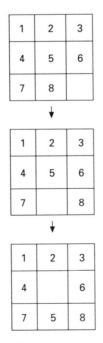

Figure 8.5 The Tile Game with Sample Moves.

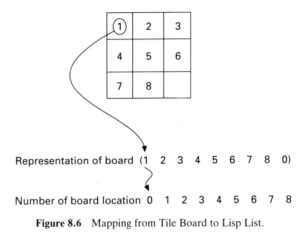

Figure 8.6 shows the numbering system used to identify each location on the board.

Representation of board (1 2 3 4 5 6 7 8 0)

Number of board location 0 1 2 3 4 5 6 7 8

Figure 8.6 Mapping from Tile Board to Lisp List.

and several sample moves. The idea is to move the tiles about until you achieve whatever goal state is specified. A typical goal state is also shown in the figure.

Figure 8.6 shows the numbering system used to identify each location on the board. There are nine locations, eight of which will have numbers on them and one that will be the empty square. The nine locations will be numbered 0 through 8. The values of any location can range from 0 to 8 where 0 indicates the empty square. The state representation will be a simple list with 9 elements. Each element represents a location on the board. The mapping of list positions to board positions is shown in Figure 8.6.

The starting and goal representations are given. For example, the start state could be (2 8 3 1 6 4 7 0 5) and the goal state could be (1 2 3 8 0 4 7 6 5). To use SER, all that is needed is to define SUCCESSOR-FN and EQUALITY-TEST. Since the default for EQUALITY-TEST is EQUAL, it does not need to be redefined. Successor function is defined as SUCCESSORS. It takes a node, accesses the state, defines the location of the blank tile, and applies a generating rule in the form of a list of numbers. The location of the blank tile determines which generating rule should be applied. If, for example, the blank tile is in the first position (0), then it can be moved to either position 1 or to position 3. This is described by the rule (0 1 3), which can be read "if 0 then 1 or 3". The function MAKE-MOVES uses this information and a copy of the current state to generate new moves.

```
(DEFUN SUCCESSORS (NODE)
   (LET* ((ST (STATE NODE))
          (BLANK (- 9 (LENGTH (MEMBER 0 ST)))))
      (MAKE-MOVES ST BLANK
         (CASE BLANK
            ((0) '(1 3))
            ((1) '(0 2 4))
            ((2) '(1 5))
```

```
((3) '(0 4 6))
((4) '(1 3 5 7))
((5) '(2 4 8))
((6) '(3 7))
((7) '(4 6 8))
((8) '(5 7)))))))

(DEFUN MAKE-MOVES (ST BLANK MOVES)
  (MAPCAR #'(LAMBDA (POS)
              (LET ((CHILD (COPY-LIST ST)))
                (SETF (NTH BLANK CHILD) (NTH POS CHILD))
                (SETF (NTH POS CHILD) 0) CHILD))
        MOVES))
```

Solution to the Eight Tiles Problem

The search space for the eight tiles problem is much larger than the search space for the jug problem. Depending on what kind of machine you have and how much memory you have available, you can run out of space in a hurry.

The first problem has the start state (2 8 3 1 6 4 7 0 5) and goal state (1 2 3 8 0 4 7 6 5). A depth-first strategy found a solution after visiting only 6 nodes.

```
2 8 3    2 8 3    2 0 3    0 2 3    1 2 3    1 2 3
1 6 4-->1 0 4-->1 8 4-->1 8 4-->0 8 4-->8 0 4
7 0 5    7 6 5    7 6 5    7 6 5    7 6 5    7 6 5
```

The breadth-first was the same but visited 61 nodes.

The second problem was another story. The start state was (2 8 3 1 6 4 7 0 5) and the goal state was (2 8 3 1 6 4 7 5 0). A breadth-first search visited 2 nodes before finding the solution.

```
2 8 3    2 8 3
1 6 4-->1 6 4
7 0 5    7 5 0
```

The depth-first search opened a very large number of nodes before finding the same solution. The problem was trivial but, because the depth-first strategy didn't happen to make the move shown in the solution above first, it traveled deep into the state space before visiting (2 8 3 1 6 4 7 5 0).

One thing this problem suggests is the need for a *depth bound* when using depth-first search. Without some control on depth, the search could get out of hand very quickly. Look back at the code and think about where you would put this control and how you would express it in the problem. One approach would be to set the depth bound equal to the estimated path length of a solution.

8.5 HEURISTIC SEARCH

Suppose that a hypothetical path problem is such that every state produced four new states to explore with no duplication for the top few levels. The start state would produce four new states to explore. Each of these four states would in turn produce four new children. The number of state nodes that have to be contended with is growing from 1 to 4 to 16 to 64 and so on. At the top level, called *level zero,* there was only one node, the start node. At the next level there were 4, at the next 16, then 64, and so on. This could also be written 4^0, 4^1, 4^2, 4^3, and so on. If this is plotted as in Figure 8.7, it is clear that the number of states to contend with grows exponentially as a search progresses. For this reason, it is very costly in both time and memory to use uniformed search as a problem solving technique. The kind of search we are really interested in is informed search. The idea is to achieve the same results one would get from an uninformed search while looking at only a small portion of the potential search space. The purpose of informed search is to contain (to a degree) this exponential explosion of possibilities.

Looking back at the general search program, two things can be done to add heuristic power to the program. First, the representation needs to be modified (extended) to accommodate the new information that will be required to compute a heuristic value. Second, a function must be added that selects, according to the value of the heuristic, the best state to explore from the UNEXPLORED list.

Figure 8.8 shows a start state, some state deeper in the search space, and a

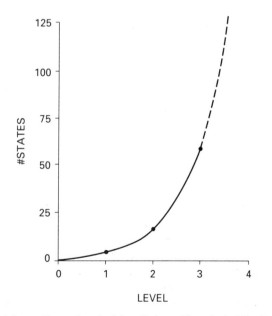

Figure 8.7 Number of States Versus Level of Search for a Hypothetical Problem with Each State Producing Four Successors.

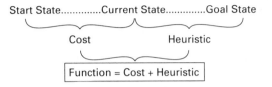

Figure 8.8 The Cost and Heuristic Components of Search.

goal state. Suppose you are standing at a current state somewhere between the start state and the goal state. If you turn and look back at the start state, you can assess the cost of getting from the start state to the current state. The measure could be the distance traveled in miles, the cost for visiting each state in dollars, or simply the depth of the current state. If you now turn and face the goal state, you can assess (maybe) how close you are to the goal. This second component is the heuristic component. The heuristic function used for the informed search will include both of these components.

$$\text{Heuristic function} = \text{Cost from start to current state}$$
$$+ \text{Estimated distance from the goal}$$

Both the cost and the heuristic components of the heuristic function are properties of the representation. For any representation, the creator function must include provision for these two components.

The search program must include a provision for either reordering the UNEX-PLORED list or for choosing the best state to visit based on the value of the heuristic function. By convention, the state with the smallest heuristic function value is considered the best choice. It will also be necessary to extend the function that creates the general structure housing all the information pertinent to each state.

Modifying the Search Program

The NODE DEFSTRUCT that houses the state and other information must be extended to include both depth and heuristic information. Since we want to be able to experiment with various combinations of these components, the array will be extended to include COST, HEURISTIC, and HEURISTIC FUNCTION (HF) data. The new NODE DEFSTRUCT is:

```
(DEFSTRUCT (NODE (:CONC-NAME NIL))
   STATE
   (FATHER ())
   (SUCCESSOR-FN    'SUCCESSORS)
   (EQUALITY-TEST 'EQUAL)
   (COST 0)
   HEURISTIC
   HF)
```

Assume that COST is a function of information contained in the previous state. It has a default value of 0. The HEURISTIC computation is a function of the current state and the goal state. The values of COST and HEURISTIC are representation-specific. They must be defined for each problem representation. HF is simply the sum of the cost and the heuristic HF = COST + HEURISTIC. It could be calculated when needed or put into the HF slot.

Modifications are also required for SER and UPDATE. In SER, we need only modify MAKE-NODE so that it now includes initialization of HEURISTIC and HF. The LET now becomes a LET* since the value of H is needed in MAKE-NODE. COST is automatically initialized to 0.

```
(DEFUN SER (START GOAL)
    (LABELS
        ((SER-REC (BACK)
            (COND ((NULL (UNEXPLORED BACK)) (FAIL BACK))
                  ((SOLVED BACK) (PRINT-RESULTING-PATH BACK))
                  (T (SER-REC (UPDATE BACK)))))))
    (LET ((H (H-FN START GOAL)))
       (SER-REC
          (MAKE-CONTROL
             :UNEXPLORED
               (LIST (MAKE-NODE
                        :STATE START
                        :HEURISTIC H
                        :HF H))
             :GOAL GOAL))))))
```

The function UPDATE also requires modification since the control strategy requires that the state with the smallest value of HF be chosen as the next to explore. This requires some additional time for comparisons among members of the unexplored list. The basic idea is to always choose the state with the smallest value of HF. If two or more states have the smallest value, the choice is arbitrary. The primitive function SORT will be used to accomplish this. All that is required is that the modified UNEXPLORED list be sorted by HF values.

Modification is also required to compute the cost, heuristic value, and HF value for each new node that is added to the UNEXPLORED list. A LET has been added so that the value of H need only be calculated once. It is used as the value of the heuristic and is also used to calculate HF.

The change to UPDATE is minimal.

```
(DEFUN UPDATE (BACK)
    (LET* ((CURNODE (POP (UNEXPLORED BACK)))
           (CURSTATE (STATE CURNODE))
           (GOA (GOAL BACK))
           (COS (DEPTH CURNODE)))
          (PUSH CURSTATE (EXPLORED BACK))
          (MAPCAR
```

```
                        #' (LAMBDA (ST)
                            (LET ((H (H-FN ST GOA)))
                                (ADDNEW (MAKE-NODE
                                            :STATE ST
                                            :FATHER CURNODE
                                            :COST COS
                                            :HEURISTIC H
                                            :HF (+ COS H))
                                    (UNEXPLORED BACK))))
                    (SET-DIFFERENCE
                        (FUNCALL
                            (SUCCESSOR-FN CURNODE) CURNODE)
                        (EXPLORED BACK)
                        :TEST (EQUALITY-TEST CURNODE)))
                (SETF (UNEXPLORED BACK)
                    (SORT (UNEXPLORED BACK) #'< :KEY #'HF))
            BACK))
```

Application to the Eight Tiles Problem

Depth will be used as a unit cost factor for this problem. The depth of the start node is assumed to be zero. Therefore, the cost function would be:

```
            (DEFUN DEPTH (FATHER)
                (1+ (COST FATHER)))
```

As a measure of closeness to the goal (the heuristic), use the number of tiles (excluding the blank) that are not in their proper positions in the goal state. In the next example, suppose that the current state was as pictured to the left and the goal state as pictured to the right. The heuristic would be 2 since 4 and 5 are not in their proper position relative to the goal state. In the example to the right, HEURISTIC would equal 5.

```
            1 2 3   1 2 3           2 8 3   1 2 3
            8 4 5-->8 0 4           1 6 4-->8 0 4
            7 6 0   7 6 5           7 5 0   7 6 5
```

In this case, the function H-FN is quite simple. It simply makes a sequential comparison of the two representations counting differences and excluding the blank position in the current representation.

```
        (DEFUN H-FN (ST1 ST2)
            (LET ((CNT 0))
                (MAPCAR #' (LAMBDA (E1 E2)
                                (IF (AND (/= E1 0) (/= E1 E2))
                                    (INCF CNT)))
                    ST1 ST2)
                CNT))
```

Heuristic Search of the Eight Tiles Problem

Given the start state (2 8 3 1 6 4 7 0 5) and the goal state (1 2 3 8 0 4 7 6 5), the heuristic search visited 7 nodes to generate a solution. Below each step in the solution is the computed value of the heuristic function (HF), the cost (C), in this case simply the depth of the node, and the computed heuristic (H). Notice that H approaches zero while depth increases as search gets closer to the goal. The starred node (*) was not on the solution path.

```
                          *
      2 8 3    2 8 3    2 8 3    2 0 3    0 2 3    1 2 3    1 2 3
      1 6 4-->1 0 4-->0 1 4-->1 8 4-->1 8 4-->0 8 4-->8 0 4
      7 0 5    7 6 5    7 6 5    7 6 5    7 6 5    7 6 5    7 6 5

HF    (4)      (4)      (5)      (5)      (5)      (5)      (5)
C     (0)      (1)      (2)      (2)      (3)      (4)      (5)
H     (4)      (3)      (3)      (3)      (2)      (1)      (0)
```

If the start state was (2 8 3 1 6 4 7 0 5) and the goal state was (2 8 3 1 6 4 7 5 0), heuristic search does better than either breadth- or depth-first search. It visited 2 nodes in getting this solution.

A more difficult problem adapted from Nilsson (1980) begins with start state (2 1 6 4 0 8 7 5 3) and goal state (2 8 1 4 6 0 7 5 3). The solution path is:

```
      2 1 6    2 1 6    2 1 0    2 0 1    2 8 1    2 8 1
      4 0 8-->4 8 0-->4 8 6-->4 8 6-->4 0 6-->4 6 0
      7 5 3    7 5 3    7 5 3    7 5 3    7 5 3    7 5 3
```

Heuristic search visited 10 nodes in solving this problem. Breadth-first search visited 51 nodes in solving it, and depth-first search was terminated after 540 states were visited.

The Optimal Solution

If you had a perfect heuristic in the preceding search, you would only visit nodes on the solution path. If you had no heuristic (H=0) and cost equal to the depth of the search, you have a breadth-first search. Call the perfect heuristic H_f, and the actual heuristic H_e. If the relation $H_e <= H_f$, is true for estimates of H_f at all states visited, you are guaranteed to get a shortest path solution. If H_e is greater than zero, you will realize the optimal solution while visiting fewer nodes than with a breadth-first search. As H_e approaches H_f, the solution opens fewer and fewer nodes. If H_e is greater than H_f, optimality is lost.

8.6 SUMMARY

In this chapter the problem of state space search was explored. Path finding problems were used to illustrate how search was accomplished and how heuristics could improve efficiency in terms of both time and memory requirements.

8.7 PROBLEMS

8.1 Modify the SER program so that it keeps track of the number of nodes visited and reports the number with the solution.

8.2 Rewrite the SER program so that the states for all nodes visited are reported, as well as the solution path.

8.3 Add a depth bound capability to the present SER code to further control depth-first search.

8.4 Another kind of uninformed search is called *depth-first with progressive deepening*. An exhaustive search at depth 1 is executed. If no solution is found, all the nodes are thrown out and a depth-first search is executed at depth bound 2. If no solution is found, the nodes are thrown out and a depth-first search is conducted with depth bound 3 and so on. Rewrite or expand the program so that it can also execute a depth-first search with progressive or iterative deepening.

8.5 MAKE-NODE had to be modified in both SER and UPDATE when heuristic search was introduced. Write MAKE-NODE so that this duplication of effort would no longer be required.

8.6 Rewrite the SER program so that either breadth-first, depth-first, or heuristic search could be executed without changing the program code. In other words, generalize the program to handle all three choices.

8.7 The start state and the goal state for a problem might be such that no solution exists. What problem with simple uninformed search does this possibility suggest?

8.8 Modify the jug problem so that a wild card can be used in either the first or second position of the goal state indicating that it does not matter what is in the small or large jug. For example, if the current state was (3 4) this would match (3 *), where * indicates any value will match.

8.9 Would it have been better to use an array for the eight tiles representation rather than a list? What would be gained or lost?

8.10 What would be gained in efficiency and what would be lost in readability if we rewrote SER-REC using iterative forms?

8.11 When using the heuristic version of SER, would it be better to simply choose the item with the smallest value of HF each time rather than sort the whole unexplored list? Why or why not?

8.12 Show how the concept of backtracking was included in the control strategies used in the SER program.

8.13 What would be the impact on the eight tiles search if COPY-LIST were not used? When would it be appropriate to use COPY-TREE?

9

Unification and Pattern-Directed Inference

9.1 INTRODUCTION

One of the fundamental assumptions made about human behavior is that thinking involves complex pattern matching. If we know that when A occurs, B is likely to follow, the occurrence of A allows us to *infer* B. If the sky is cloudy and gray, we can infer that there is a likelihood of rain. The patterns, clouds and gray taken together, match an internal inference structure that has been associated with rain in the past. Thus rain is inferred in the present situation. This can be abstracted for any combination of occurrences and following inferences without regard to whether they exist in the real world or not.

The problem can be given some formal treatment by generating rules of inference. In fact, the preceding example involving A and B has as its basis a rule of logical inference called *Modus Ponens*. Stated formally, it says that if A implies B and A has been asserted, we can conclude B. From a pattern matching point of view, the rule says that given A=>B and A, the pattern A and the left hand side of the inference A=>B match, if a match occurs then do whatever is on the right-hand side of A=>B. The implicit action here is to assert B. This can be quickly generalized by using variables [by convention starting with a question mark (?)] in place of A and B. Now the implicative reads ?X => ?Y, so that for any variable ?X if ?X=>?Y and ?X have been asserted, then ?Y can be asserted.

A central problem in building a machine that can do this sort of thing is determining what we mean by a pattern match. The concept of equal or equality must be defined in some sense. Identical and fraternal twins look alike on the

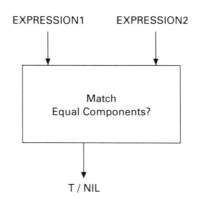

Figure 9.1   The Concept of a Simple Match.

surface, and they are equal in that sense. However, if our criterion for equality is equivalent genetic structures, then identical twins are still equal but fraternal twins are not.

EQ and EQUAL provide us a means for expressing the equality of pattern matches using Lisp. EQ means equivalent or the same pointer. EQUAL means the same structure. This, however, stills leaves room for interpretation as with the twins example. Are they EQ or EQUAL? The first problem tackled in this chapter is the problem of matching and equality. From that start, a unification algorithm is developed, and then, a simple deductive engine is prototyped for reasoning about a limited world. Feldman and Rich (1988) provide algorithms and background concepts upon which the material in this chapter is based.

9.2 PATTERN MATCHING

Figure 9.1 shows the basic concept of matching. Two expressions are compared for equality a component at a time. If the two expressions have the same structure and the same order, they match and T is returned. If they do not have the same order or if they do not have the same components then NIL is returned.

The first consideration in developing a MATCH algorithm is to determine what kinds of objects will be recognized by the MATCH function. To express the kinds of information that MATCH will be given, it need only recognize three kinds of terms; constants, variables and patterns consisting of lists containing constants and variables. Constants will include symbols and numbers, and variables will be symbols that start with a question mark (?).

Now the question becomes what defines a constant, variable or pattern for MATCH? A constant will be recognized as either a number or an atomic structure that is not a variable. In Lisp this could be:

```
(CONST? (EXP)
   (OR (NUMBERP EXP)
       (AND (ATOM EXP) (NOT (VAR? EXP))))))
```

By convention a variable is a symbol that starts with ?. In Lisp this might be;

```
(VAR? (EXP)
   (AND (SYMBOLP EXP)
        (EQ #\? (SCHAR (STRING EXP) 0))))
```

A pattern could be defined as a CONS. So the test would be:

```
(PATTERN? (EXP)
   (CONSP EXP))
```

Obviously, there are alternative ways to implement these ideas so that what is recognized is more or less constrained. The definition of a CONST is, for example, not very restrictive. The use of ATOM rather than SYMBOLP defines a rather loose constraint since (AND (ATOM ARRAY) (NOT (VAR? ARRAY))) is T. Since it is unclear how arrays would fit into the kinds of inferencing we want to do, it might be appropriate to reconsider this definition and introduce an additional constraint;

```
(CONST? (EXP)
   (OR (NUMBERP EXP)
       (AND (SYMBOLP EXP) (NOT (VAR? EXP))))))
```

With the tests defined, a shell version of MATCH can be implemented. Since these tests are only needed by MATCH, they will be implemented as local functions to encapsulate them. The argument P is a pattern. The argument TE is a term or fact being matched against the pattern. B is initialized to NIL and is used to store bindings.

```
(DEFUN MATCH (P TE B)
   (LABELS ((VAR? (EXP)
               (AND (SYMBOLP EXP)
                    (EQ #\? (SCHAR (STRING EXP) 0))))
            (CONST? (EXP)
               (OR (NUMBERP EXP)
                   (AND (SYMBOLP EXP) (NOT (VAR? EXP)))))
            (PATTERN? (EXP)
               (CONSP EXP)))
      (COND ((VAR? P) (LIST 'VAR P))
            ((PATTERN? P) (LIST 'PATTERN P))
            ((CONST? P) (LIST 'CONST P))
            (T "ERROR"))))
```

This is what was called earlier a *stubs* program that implements the *schema* for the full MATCH abstraction. It allows us to test the behavior of input parameters, as well as the ability of our conditionals to discriminate cases and to incrementally debug the function while maintaining locality of reference when errors occur. AS-SERT could have been used in place of LIST in the conditional for a stronger constraint on the data.

MATCH-UNIFY

Consider now the purpose of MATCH. It will be used to provide bindings for unifying expressions. Unification requires more than a simple MATCH program can offer. An expression is unified by substituting constants, variables and functions for variables. The name of the function is changed to MATCH-UNIFY to make the function's use apparent. All constants in the pattern P must match constants in the data element or term TE. Figure 9.2 provides an illustration of this idea. The term (TALL TREE) and the pattern (TALL ?X) unify using the substitution (?X TREE). The substituted expression, which is the value of B (?X TREE), is returned.

The general case for MATCH-UNIFY is PATTERN? since any recursive calls to the function will occur here in the process of decomposing list structures into variables or constants. Both VAR? and CONST? will be terminating cases. They will return bindings to the previous level or signal failure. If (PATTERN? P) is true then the obvious next test is to make sure that TE is also a pattern. If not, processing can stop since the expressions are not matchable. If both P and TE are patterns,

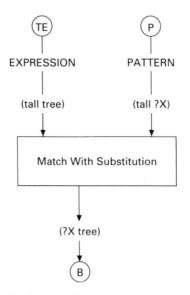

Figure 9.2 The Concept of Pattern Matching with Substitution.

then call MATCH-UNIFY on subexpressions being sure to maintain the integrity of the bindings that are being accumulated as components of the TE and P are compared. The terminating case will be when either P or TE becomes the null list. If both are null, then the match succeeded. However, if only one of the two is empty, the match failed. The conditional could be expressed in this way:

```
((OR (NULL P) (NULL TE))
  (IF (EQ P TE) B '()))     ;the '() can be implicit
```

If either P or TE is empty then if they are equal (i.e., both nil) then return bindings B else return failure '(). That is, the term TE has been successfully reduced relative to the pattern P. The basic idea is:

```
(DO ((PATS P (REST PATS))
     (ELES TE (REST ELES)))
    ((OR (NULL PATS) (NULL ELES))
     (IF (EQ PATS ELES) B))
  (SETF B (MATCH-UNIFY (FIRST PATS) (FIRST ELES) B)))
```

The DO is used to walk down the ribs of both P and TE. Each time we have successfully completed the decomposition of a CAR, B is updated using SETF on the bindings returned by MATCH-UNIFY. The next rib is then processed and this continues until at least one of P or TE is null. The combination of a DO and a recursive call is more readable and more efficient than using recursions on the FIRST and REST of P and TE.

The CONST? would seem to be immediately clear. If the pattern is a constant, and if the pattern and the term are equal, then return whatever bindings have been accumulated. If they are not equal, then return failure since MATCH has failed.

For VAR?, four cases must be considered:

- If there are no current bindings, add (LIST P TE) to the bindings list.
- If there are bindings, check to see whether the variable P already has a binding.
- If it has a binding and the value is equal to TE, then return the bindings.
- If P has a binding but the values are not equal, then return failure.

```
(LET ((BINDING (FIND P B :KEY #'FIRST)))
  (COND ((NULL BINDING) (PUSH (LIST P TE) B) B)
        ((NAME-OCCURS? P BINDING)
         (IF (VALUE-OCCURS? TE BINDING) B))
        (T (PUSH (LIST P TE) B))))
```

The preceding code expresses the variable case in a fairly succinct way. The only problem is that MATCH-UNIFY is recursive. If a failure occurs at any level, then there is no need to continue. It might therefore be appropriate to use a top level function called MATCH-UNIFY and a subordinate recursive function MATCH+. When MATCH+ detects failure, control can immediately be returned to MATCH-UNIFY. This is expressed in the final form of MATCH-UNIFY and MATCH+:

```
(DEFUN MATCH-UNIFY (P TE B)
"MATCH-UNIFY(P TE B)-->BINDINGS|NIL
NON-STANDARD EXIT ON FAILURE TO MATCH AT ATOMIC LEVEL"
    (CATCH 'FAILURE
        (MATCH+ P TE B)))


(DEFUN MATCH+ (P TE B)
"MATCH+(P TE B)-->BINDINGS|NIL
    (LABELS ((VAR? (EXP)
                (AND (SYMBOLP EXP)
                    (EQ #\? (SCHAR (STRING EXP) 0))))
             (CONST? (EXP)
                (OR (NUMBERP EXP)
                    (AND (SYMBOLP EXP) (NOT (VAR? EXP)))))
             (PATTERN? (EXP)
                (CONSP EXP))
             (NAME-OCCURS? (P BIND)
                (EQ P (FIRST BIND)))
             (VALUE-OCCURS? (TE BIND)
                (EQUAL TE (SECOND BIND))))
        (COND ((VAR? P)
               (LET ((BINDING (FIND P B :KEY #'FIRST)))
                   (COND ((NULL BINDING) (PUSH (LIST P TE) B) B)
                         ((NAME-OCCURS? P BINDING)
                             (IF (VALUE-OCCURS? TE BINDING) B))
                         (T (PUSH (LIST P TE) B)))))
              ((PATTERN? P)
               (IF (PATTERN? TE)
                   (DO ((PATS P (CDR PATS))
                        (ELES TE (CDR ELES)))
                       ((OR (NULL PATS) (NULL ELES))
                        (IF (EQ PATS ELES) B))
                       (SETF B (MATCH+ (FIRST PATS)
                                       (FIRST ELES) B)))))
              ((CONST? P)
               (IF (EQUAL P TE) B (THROW 'FAILURE ()))))))
```

9.3 TESTING THE PATTERN MATCHER

Now that MATCH-UNIFY has been implemented, the program needs to be tested. It should be able to handle both simple and nested expressions. If both P and TE are matching constants then B should be returned. On the other hand, if P and TE do not match, failure should be signaled.

- The expression (DOG ?X) should unify with (DOG BONE) returning (?X BONE).
- (?ZIZZY DOG) should unify with (?Y DOG) returning (?ZIZZY ?Y) or (?Y ?ZIZZY).
- The expression (?X FOO ?Y BAR) should unify with the expression (OYSTER FOO EATING BAR) returning ((?Y EATING)(?X OYSTER)).
- (?F ?X) should unify with (FUNC 100) returning ((?X 100)(?F FUNC)).

More difficult tests would be (?X ?Y) with (?Y ?X). This should return (?X ?Y) or (?Y ?X). The expressions (?X ?X) and (100 100) should return (?X 100). A more complex and nested test would be (STAR ?X ?X) and (STAR (JABBA ?Z)(JABBA (SOLO ?G)). This expression should return something like ((?Z (SOLO ?G))(?X (JABBA ?Z))). The expression (FOO ?X ?X) and (FOO ?Y (BAR ?Y) should return NIL. Several such test results are shown. All tests that failed are starred:

```
(MATCH-UNIFY 'ATOM 'ATOM '((TEST))) => ((TEST))
(MATCH-UNIFY 'ATOM 'ATOM '()) => ()
(MATCH-UNIFY 'ATOM 'ADAM '((TEST))) => ()
(MATCH-UNIFY '(DOG ?X) '(DOG BONE) ()) => ((?X BONE))
(MATCH-UNIFY '(DOG ?X) '(DOG BONE) '((?X BONE)))
=> ((?X BONE))
(MATCH-UNIFY '(FOO ?X ?X) '(FOO BAR BAR) ())
=> ((?X BAR))
(MATCH-UNIFY '(FOO ?X) '(FOO BAR EXTRA) ()) => ((?X BAR))*
(MATCH-UNIFY '(?X ?Y) '(?Y ?X) ()) => ((?Y ?X)(?X ?Y))*
(MATCH-UNIFY '((FOO BAR) ?Y) '((FOO ?Y) ?Y) ()) => ()*
(MATCH-UNIFY 100 '?X ()) => ()*
(MATCH-UNIFY '(STAR ?X ?X) '(STAR (JABBA ?Z)
   (JABBA (SOLO ?G))) ()) => ()*
(MATCH-UNIFY '?X '((FOO ?X) HELLO) ()) =>
   ((?X ((FOO ?X) HELLO))*
```

The first problem that arises is that the current system fails to distinguish between failure and a match without any unification as illustrated in the first three test examples. The unifier is of more utility for our use if it can return any of three values; NIL for failure, T for a literal match and BINDINGS for unifications.

Inspection of the existing code suggests that this is a fairly trivial fix. It is a matter of taking better advantage of the catcher being used for failure. A throw to the catcher for failure returns NIL. There are two remaining cases. If no bindings are returned and no failure has occurred, the two expressions are literal matches. In this case, T should be returned. If bindings are found then they should be returned.

```
(DEFUN MATCH-UNIFY (P TE B)
   (CATCH 'FAILURE
      (LET ((RES (MATCH+ P TE B)))
         (IF RES
             RES
             T)))))
```

The first starred test example is not a failure but points out the need to make sure that when both P and TE are patterns they are of equal length. Currently this is checked after P and TE are evaluated an expression at a time to collect bindings. When either P or TE has been fully evaluated if both P and TE have been fully evaluated (are NULL) then the resulting bindings are returned. The new discriminator checks length before the bindings are collected. This is much more efficient. It would look like this in MATCH+:

```
(AND (PATTERN? P)
     (PATTERN? TE)
     (= (LENGTH P) (LENGTH TE)))
```

The first failed test points out the necessity of propagating bindings as the function is executing. In this way, no duplication will occur. MATCH+ would have a new program line that would check for bindings and propagate them in both P and TE. A new function called INST will be developed that given a pattern and bindings will return instantiated patterns and terms. This basic code is shown next. INST is developed in the next section:

```
(IF B
    (SETF P (INST P B) TE (INST TE B)))
```

This code would just precede the COND that performs the expression analysis and unification. In the example (MATCH-UNIFY '(?X ?Y) '(?Y ?X) ()), the first pass through MATCH-UNIFY would produce the binding '((?X ?Y)). This would be propagated by the new code segment into '(?Y) '(?Y) '((?X ?Y)) before unification on the second pass was done. The two terms (?Y) and (?Y) would match returning '((?X ?Y)) as the unification. Instantiation is discussed in section 9.4.

The next two failed tests point out the necessity of doing the VAR? test on TE if it fails on P. First check (VAR? P). If the test fails check (VAR? TE). If this passes then call MATCH+ with TE as the first argument and P as the second.

```
((VAR? TE) (MATCH+ TE P B))
```

The last thing we can learn from the failed tests is that if P is a variable, it is necessary to test for the presence of the same variable name in both the P and TE expressions. This should return failure unlike the last test shown. The control for this might be:

```
((VAR? P)
    (LET ((BINDING (FIND P B :KEY #'FIRST)))
        (COND ((VAR-OCCURS-IN P TE)
               (THROW 'FAILURE NIL))
              ((NULL BINDINGS)
               (PUSH (LIST P TE) B) B)
              ((VALUE-OCCURS? TE BINDING) B)
              (T (THROW 'FAILURE NIL)))))
```

If P is a variable then make sure it does not occur in both P and TE. If it does not then check to see if there are current bindings. If there are none then create a new binding and put it on the binding stack. If there are already bindings for P then make sure they are still consistent. If they are return the binding as is. If they are not then return failure.

With all these corrections our robust match-unifier now looks like this:

```
(DEFUN MATCH-UNIFY (P TE B)
"MATCH-UNIFY(P TE B)-->BINDINGS|T|NIL
BINDINGS INDICATE UNIFICATION. T INDICATES MATCHING
CONSTANTS. NIL INDICATES FAILURE. NON-STANDARD
EXIT ON FAILURE TO MATCH AT ATOMIC LEVEL"
    (CATCH 'FAILURE
        (LET ((RES (MATCH+ P TE B)))
            (IF RES
                RES
                T))))


(DEFUN MATCH+ (P TE B)
"MATCH+(P TE B)-->BINDINGS|NIL
SHOULD ONLY BE USED THROUGH MATCH-UNIFY
WHICH CONTROLS CATCHER"
    (LABELS ((VAR? (EXP)
                (AND (SYMBOLP EXP)
                    (EQ #\? (SCHAR (STRING EXP) 0))))
             (CONST? (EXP)
                (OR (NUMBERP EXP)
                    (AND (SYMBOLP EXP) (NOT (VAR? EXP)))))
             (PATTERN? (EXP)
                (CONSP EXP))
```

```
                  (VALUE-OCCURS? (TE BIND)
                     (EQUAL TE (SECOND BIND)))
                  (VAR-OCCURS-IN (P TE)
                     (COND ((ATOM TE)
                            (IF (EQ P TE) (THROW 'FAILURE ())))
                           (T (VAR-OCCURS-IN P (FIRST TE))
                              (VAR-OCCURS-IN P (REST TE)))))
                  ;A version is here so that unify
                  ;is a complete implementation.
                  (INST (PAT BINDINGS)
                     (DOLIST (BINDING BINDINGS PAT)
                        (SETF PAT (SUBST (SECOND BINDING)
                                         (FIRST BINDING) PAT)))))
  ;body of MATCH+
  ;propagate-bindings first
  (IF B (SETF P (INST P B) TE (INST TE B)))
  ;now check attributes of P and TE
  (COND ((EQUAL P TE) B)
        ((VAR? P)
         (LET ((BINDING (FIND P B :KEY #'FIRST)))
            (COND ((VAR-OCCURS-IN P TE)
                   (THROW 'FAILURE ()))
                  ((NULL BINDING)
                   (PUSH (LIST P TE) B) B)
                  ((VALUE-OCCURS? TE BINDING) B)
                  (T (THROW 'FAILURE NIL)))))
        ((VAR? TE) (MATCH+ TE P B))
        ((AND (PATTERN? P)(PATTERN? TE)
              (= (LENGTH P)(LENGTH TE)))
         (DO ((PATS P (CDR PATS))
              (TES TE (CDR TES)))
             ((NULL PATS) B)
           (SETF B
             (MATCH+ (FIRST PATS)
                     (FIRST TES)
                     B))))
        ((OR (CONST? P) (CONST? TE))
         (IF (EQUAL P TE)
             B
             (THROW 'FAILURE ())))
        (T (THROW 'FAILURE ()))))))
```

Running the failed tests again, we get correct answers for each:

```
(MATCH-UNIFY '(FOO ?X) '(FOO BAR EXTRA) ()) => ()
(MATCH-UNIFY '(?X ?Y) '(?Y ?X) ()) => (((?X ?Y))
(MATCH-UNIFY '((FOO BAR) ?Y) '((FOO ?Y) ?Y) ())
=> ((?Y BAR))
(MATCH-UNIFY 100 '?X ()) => ((?X 100))
(MATCH-UNIFY '(STAR ?X ?X) '(STAR (JABBA ?Z)
    (JABBA (SOLO ?G))) ())
=> ((?Z (SOLO ?G)) (?X (JABBA ?Z)))
(MATCH-UNIFY '?X '((FOO ?X) HELLO) ()) => ()
```

The ideas for some of these tests came from Nilsson etal., (1988). This book is an excellent source for unification algorithms and for test sets for implementation testing.

9.4 INSTANTIATING RULES

In pattern directed inference, *production rules* or *weak implicative* statements are used to describe the possible inferences that can be made in an application. The rules represent the knowledge or knowledge base of the system. A database is used to store facts or assertions that represent the current state of the system when it is inferencing.

Suppose the rules are of the form IF <patterns> THEN <action> or more simply the form (PATTERNS) −> (ACTIONS), and the data base is a list of facts that are TERMs in the first order predicate calculus such as (PREDICATE IN-STANCE). To use MATCH-UNIFY to make simple pattern directed inferences, it is necessary to use both the database of facts (TERMs) and the rulebase. Suppose, for example, the database contained (DOG BILL) and the rulebase contained the rule, (DOG ?X) −> (BEGS ?X). The process of making pattern directed inferences would require first that the program try unification of left-hand side (LHS) patterns with database elements. If a unification was found, the bindings would be used to instantiate variables on the right-hand side (RHS) of the rule. The assumption is being made for now that the action on the right side consists of instantiation followed by insertion of the instantiated right-hand side form into the database. If the pattern (DOG ?X) is matched against the database item (DOG BILL), the binding (?X BILL) is returned. The variable ?X in the form (BEGS ?X) would be replaced by BILL to create the new database item (BEGS BILL). This is an example of the rule of inference that was mentioned in the introduction:

1. DOG BILL => BEGS BILL
2. DOG BILL
3. Therefore BEGS BILL

Instantiation in Lisp

The new function called INST, will take a pattern (PAT) and a set of bindings (BINDINGS) and return the instantiated pattern.

$$PAT \wedge BINDINGS-->\{INST\}-->INSTANTIATED\ PAT$$

The pattern could be either a simple pattern [such as (FOO ?X), (?X FOO), or (?X ?Y)] or a complex pattern [such as (AND (OR (NOT ?X) ?Y) ?Z)]. The function must consider all of these cases. The top level primitive function SUBSTITUTE could be used for this purpose if all of the expressions were flat, but it will not work for nested expressions. However, the function SUBST or NSUBST would work. NSUBST would minimize CONSing, but it would destructively modify the pattern. This would not only modify the right-hand side pattern before database entry, but the right-hand side of the rule would be modified in the process. Therefore, in this case, SUBST would seem to be the best choice even though it copies the entire pattern. The basic code might be as follows:

```
NSUBST new old tree &KEY :test :test-not :key
SUBST new old tree &KEY :test :test-not :key
SUBSTITUTE newitem olditem sequence &KEY :from-end :test :test-not
                                         :start :end :count :key
```

```
(DEFUN INST (PAT BINDINGS)
    (DOLIST (BINDING BINDINGS PAT)
        (SETF PAT (SUBST (SECOND BINDING)
                    (FIRST BINDING)   PAT)))))
```

Some applications might call for a PAT that is not a list. In that case, INST might work in some Lisp implementations and not in others. It depends on their definition of the *tree* argument to SUBST. It, therefore, might be advisable to add an assertion to this function that guards against faulty arguments or to include provisions for this case in the function. We will add additional code to the function since it generalizes the ability of INST to deal with PAT arguments. The current version might fail for the call (INST '?X '((?X 100))).

```
(DEFUN INST (PAT BINDINGS)
"INST(PAT BINDINGS)-->INSTANTIATED PATTERN"
    (IF (CONSP PAT)
        (DOLIST (BINDING BINDINGS PAT)
```

```
(SETF PAT (SUBST (SECOND BINDING)
                 (FIRST BINDING) PAT)))
(DOLIST (BINDING BINDINGS PAT)
  (IF (EQ PAT (FIRST BINDING))
      (RETURN-FROM INST (SECOND BINDING)))))))
```

Since the new version of INST uses a RETURN-FROM and is used by external functions as well, we will take it out of the local definitions in MATCH+ and make it a DEFUN.

The Database and the Rulebase

The form of the database (DB) and rulebase (RB) is a matter of efficiency. The first question in determining efficiency is to determine how DB and RB will be used. If a new instance is added to DB, an attempt will be made to pattern match the LHS of each rule with the item in DB. If a match is found, the RHS of the rule is instantiated and another item is added to the DB. This, in turn, starts another recursive process with the new instance being compared to the LHS of each rule. This process continues until each *new* instance has been matched against every rule's LHS. The terminating condition is that no instances are created that are not already in the DB. This means that both DB and RB are being searched in a sequential fashion. Therefore, a list structure that provides for sequential search and also allows very simple accessing functions would be a reasonable choice for housing DB and RB.

The choice is based on the simplicity of the supporting functions for list structures. Suppose, for example, that RB contains the rules (((DOG ?Y)(FLEAS ?Y))((BARKS ?X)(DOG ?X))((SMALL ?Z)(MOVE ?Z))). The term (BARKS CHARLIE) is added to DB. Matching (DOG ?Y) against (BARKS CHARLIE) produces no unification. The pattern (BARKS ?X) does unify with CHARLIE bound to ?X. The term (DOG CHARLIE) is now added to DB. At this point, (DOG CHARLIE) can be put on an agenda of potential DB items to be evaluated, and (BARKS CHARLIE) can be compared with the rest of the rules for additional agenda items. In this example, (DOG CHARLIE) turns out to be the only additional agenda item. It is now unified against all the rules looking for additional agenda items. All agenda that are not already in DB are added to DB in addition to their role in creating new inferences. This process terminates when the agenda is empty. In the example, (DOG CHARLIE) will unify against FLEAS with CHARLIE bound to ?Y. Translating this to Lisp:

```
(DEFUN ADD-TERM (TERM)
  (ASSERT (CONSP TERM))
  (UNLESS
    (MEMBER TERM DB :TEST #'EQUAL)
    (PUSH TERM DB)
    (DOLIST (RULE RB)
      (TRY (FIRST RULE) TERM (SECOND RULE))))))
```

```
(DEFUN ADD-RULE (LHS RHS)
   (ASSERT (AND (CONSP LHS) (CONSP RHS)))
   (UNLESS
       (MEMBER LHS RB :TEST 'EQUAL :KEY #'FIRST)
       (PUSH (LIST LHS RHS) RB)
       (DOLIST (TERM DB)
          (TRY LHS TERM RHS))))


(DEFUN TRY (LHS TERM RHS)
   (LET ((B (MATCH-UNIFY LHS TERM ())))
       (IF B
           (LET ((INSTANT (INST RHS B)))
               (UNLESS (MEMBER INSTANT DB :TEST #'EQUAL)
                   (APPLY-INSTANT INSTANT))))))


(DEFUN APPLY-INSTANT (INSTANT)
   (ADD-TERM INSTANT))
```

9.5 GENERALIZING THE FIRST PROTOTYPE

The problem with the previous implementation is that it restricts the left-hand side of each rule to one predicate. It would be desirable to be able to have multiple ANDed predicates on the left-hand side. The Lisp code shown next generalizes the previous code so that any number of predicates can be accommodated on the left-hand side of a rule. TERM is no longer needed as an argument to TRY since TEST works through the entire DB. DOLIST can now be removed from ADD-TERM for the same reason.

```
(DEFUN TRY (LHS RHS)
"TRY(LHS RHS)-->
BY SIDE-EFFECT CAUSES APPLICATION OF AN INSTANT"
   (LET ((BINDINGS (TEST LHS)))
       (IF BINDINGS
           (DOLIST (B BINDINGS)
               (LET ((INSTANT (INST RHS B)))
                   (UNLESS  (MEMBER INSTANT DB :TEST 'EQUAL)
                       (APPLY-INSTANT INSTANT)))))))

(DEFUN TEST (P &OPTIONAL BINDS)
"TEST(PAT)-->BINDINGS OR NIL
TEST RETURNS A LIST OF BINDINGS THAT MATCHED ALL
PREDICATES. RETURNING NIL MEANS NO LHS MATCH"
   (LABELS ((BOOLEAN (EXPS OP BINDS)
       ;This takes care of ORed expressions
```

```
(IF (EQ OP 'OR)
    (LET (EXT)
        (DOLIST (P EXPS EXT)
            (SETF EXT
                (UNION EXT (TEST P BINDS)
                    :TEST #'EQUAL))))
        ;this takes care of ANDed expressions or subs
        (LET ((EXT BINDS))
            (DOLIST (P EXPS EXT)
                (SETF EXT (TEST P EXT))
                (UNLESS EXT
                    (RETURN-FROM
                        BOOLEAN ()))))))
    (FETCH (P BINDS)
        (LET (EXT)
            (IF BINDS
                (DOLIST (ELE  DB)
                    (DOLIST (B BINDS)
                        (LET ((B (MATCH-UNIFY P ELE B)))
                            (IF B (PUSH B EXT)))))
                (DOLIST (ELE DB)
                    (LET ((B
                            (MATCH-UNIFY P ELE ())))
                        (IF B
                            (PUSH B EXT)))))
            EXT)))
(LET ((FST (FIRST P))
      (RST (REST P)))
    (COND ((ENDP P) ())
          ((MEMBER FST  '(OR AND))
           (BOOLEAN RST FST BINDS))
          (T
           (FETCH P BINDS))))))
```

The functions INST and APPLY-INSTANT are as before.

9.6 PATTERN-DIRECTED INFERENCE

What remains is to define a top level control with a user interface that glues the pieces together. When this is completed, testing and development of this simple prototype can proceed. The top level might look something like this:

```
(DEFVAR RB () "GLOBAL RULEBASE")
(DEFVAR DB () "GLOBAL DATABASE")

;;; TOPLEVEL DEFINITION

(DEFUN PDI ()
"PDI()-->
TOPLEVEL CONTROL FOR PATTERN DIRECTED INFERENCE"
   (LOOP
      (CASE (MENU)
         ((1) (ADD-TERM (PROMPT 'TERM)))
         ((2) (ADD-RULE (PROMPT 'LHS) (PROMPT 'RHS)))
         ((3) (SHOW-DB))
         ((4) (SHOW-RB))
         ((5) (CLEAR (PROMPT 'CLEAR)))
         (OTHERWISE (RETURN-FROM PDI 'DONE)))))

(DEFUN CLEAR (VALUE)
   (COND ((EQ VALUE 'ALL) (SETF DB () RB ()))
         ((EQ VALUE 'RB) (SETF RB ()))
         ((EQ VALUE 'DB) (SETF DB ()))
         (T (PRINC
               (FORMAT ()
                  "NOTHING WAS CLEARED-MUST BE
                     ALL or DB or RB")))))

(DEFUN MENU ()
   (PRINC (FORMAT () "~%~20T WELCOME TO PDI~%"))
   (PRINC
      (FORMAT () "~2%~10T CHOOSE ONE OF THE FOLLOWING:~2%"))
   (MAPCAR #'(LAMBDA (MENU-ITEM)
               (PRINC (FORMAT () "~%~10T~A" MENU-ITEM)))
      '("1. ADD A TERM"
        "2. ADD A RULE"
        "3. SHOW DATABASE"
        "4. SHOW RULEBASE"
        "5. CLEAR <USE ALL or DB or RB>"
        "6. QUIT"))
   (LET ((N (PROMPT 'CHOICE)))
      (IF (INTEGERP N) N (MENU))))

(DEFUN PROMPT (CATEGORY)
   (PRINC (FORMAT () "~4%~10T~A-->" CATEGORY))
   (READ))
```

```
(DEFUN SHOW-DB ()
  (PRINC (FORMAT () "~5%DATABASE:~%~%"))
  (DOLIST (ITEM DB)
     (PRINC (FORMAT () "~5TDATABASE ITEM: ~A~%" ITEM)))
  (PRINC (FORMAT () "~%~%HIT ANY KEY TO CONTINUE"))
  (READ-CHAR)) ;pauses until character read

(DEFUN SHOW-RB ()
  (PRINC (FORMAT () "~4%RULEBASE:~%~%"))
  (DOLIST (RULE RB)
     (PRINC (FORMAT () "~%~5TLHS: ~A RHS: ~A"
                 (FIRST RULE) (SECOND RULE))))
  (PRINC (FORMAT () "~%~%HIT ANY KEY TO CONTINUE"))
  (READ-CHAR))
```

A potential problem with PDI is that there is no control over the uniqueness of variable names. They could be the same across all rules depending on what is input. The problem with this is that referencing errors could occur for some variable/value bindings. The function GET-VARS, along with a minor change to ADD-RULE, makes sure all variable references across rules are unique. When a rule is added to the rule base, an internal symbol is generated for each separate variable. These unique internal symbols are substituted in both the LHS and RHS of the rule.

```
(DEFUN ADD-RULE (LHS RHS)
"RULES OF THE FORM '(PATTERN ?X) '(BODY)"
  (LET* ((UNIQUE-VAR-NAMES (GET-VARS LHS))
         (LHS (INST LHS UNIQUE-VAR-NAMES))
         (RHS (INST RHS UNIQUE-VAR-NAMES)))
    (UNLESS
      (COMPARE-LHS LHS)   ;discussed later
      (PUSH (LIST LHS RHS) RB)
      (TRY LHS RHS)))))

(DEFUN GET-VARS (LHS)
"GET-VARS (LHS)--> LIST OF VAR/INTERNAL SYMBOL PAIRS"
  (LET ((STK ()))
    (LABELS ((UNIQUE-VARS (LHS)
               (COND ((VAR? LHS)
                      (PUSHNEW
                        (LIST LHS (GENTEMP '?)) STK
                        :KEY #'FIRST))
                     ((ATOM LHS) LHS)
                     (T (UNIQUE-VARS (FIRST LHS))
                        (UNIQUE-VARS (REST LHS))))))
      (UNIQUE-VARS LHS))
    STK))
```

Rule Equality

Before testing can commence, an additional guard must be considered. What happens if redundant rules are entered? Both are added to the rule base so that both would fire when a left-hand side match occurred. Since this is undesirable, some sort of protection against this problem should be added to the prototype. This is not a simple problem, however. Consider the following rules:

R1: (AND (FOO ?X)(BAR ?X)) -> (FOOY ?X)
R2: (AND (FOO ?X)(BAR ?X)) -> (FOOY ?X)
R3: (AND (FOO ?X)(BAR ?X)) -> (BARY ?X)
R4: (AND (BAR ?X)(FOO ?X)) -> (FOOY ?X)
R5: (FOO ?X) -> (FOOY ?X)

R1 and R2 are equal and in the same order. R3 is equal to R1 and R2 on the left-hand side, but it differs on the right-hand side. R4 is equal to R1, R2, and R3 on the left-hand side, but the order of the predicates is different. R5 subsumes R1, R2, and R4. It always fires when they do but will also fire when only FOO is in the database. Therefore, with R5 in the rulebase, R1, R2, and R4 are not necessary.

Since potentially any level of nesting of the left-hand side of an expression is allowed, testing for such conditions is complex. As a result, rather than test all possible permutations of the ordering on the left-hand side, it would be better to choose a solution that is quick rather than complete. Two rules will be considered to have equal left-hand side components if they contain the same fringe, that is, if they have the same symbols as leaves, regardless of other structural properties. It will be assumed that one left-hand side is subsumed by the other if the fringe of one is a subset of the other. In both cases, a warning will be printed to the screen, advising the user of a possible problem and asking for a decision concerning the problem.

The function FRINGE takes any tree as an argument and returns the symbol fringe with NULL leaves and variables stripped off. A temporary stack, called TEMSTACK, is used to contain either numbers or symbols that are not variables.

```
(DEFUN FRINGE (TREE)
  (LET ((TEMSTACK ()))
    (LABELS ((REC-FRINGE (TREE)
               (COND ((NULL TREE) TEMSTACK)
                     ((NUMBERP TREE)(PUSH TREE TEMSTACK))
                     ((SYMBOLP TREE)
                      (IF (NOT (EQ #\?
                                   (SCHAR (STRING TREE) 0)))
                          (PUSH TREE TEMSTACK)))
                     (T (REC-FRINGE (FIRST TREE))
                        (REC-FRINGE (REST TREE))))))
      (REC-FRINGE TREE))))
```

The function COMPARE-LHS takes the fringes and uses SET-DIFFER-ENCE to compare the left-hand side of the new rule with the left-hand side of rules already in the rule base. SET-DIFFERENCE will take care of both equal and subsumed cases.

```
(DEFUN COMPARE-LHS (LHS)
   (LET ((FLHS (FRINGE LHS)))
      (DOLIST (RULE RB)
         (LET ((FRULE (FRINGE (FIRST RULE))))
            (UNLESS
               (AND
                  (SET-DIFFERENCE FLHS FRULE)
                  (SET-DIFFERENCE FRULE FLHS))
               (PRINC
                 (FORMAT ()
                  "~%IT WOULD APPEAR THAT THE NEW RULE~%
                  ~% ~S ~%~% IS IN CONFLICT WITH THE OLD RULE~%
                  ~%~S~%" LHS (FIRST RULE)))
               (IF (Y-OR-N-P "ENTER ANYWAY?")
                   (RETURN-FROM COMPARE-LHS ())
                   (RETURN-FROM COMPARE-LHS T))))))
      (RETURN-FROM COMPARE-LHS T)))))
```

Testing the Prototype

Figure 9.3 shows the results of a simple test run of PDI. All of the redundant menu interaction has been stripped from the run to simplify analysis. A question that occurs immediately is whether or not expressions with variables are allowed in the data base. For this prototype, variables will not be allowed. So a new test CONTAINS-VAR? must be added to ADD-TERM.

```
(DEFUN CONTAINS-VAR? (EXP)
   (DOLIST (ELE EXP ())
      (IF (EQ #\? (SCHAR (STRING ELE) 0))
          (RETURN-FROM CONTAINS-VAR? T))))
```

ADD-TERM now tests for variables in the database entry as well as redundancy before entering the item.

```
(DEFUN ADD-TERM (TERM)
   (ASSERT (CONSP TERM))
   (UNLESS
      (OR (MEMBER TERM DB :TEST #'EQUAL)
          (CONTAINS-VAR? TERM))
      (PUSH TERM DB)
      (DOLIST (RULE RB)
         (TRY (FIRST RULE) (SECOND RULE)))))
```

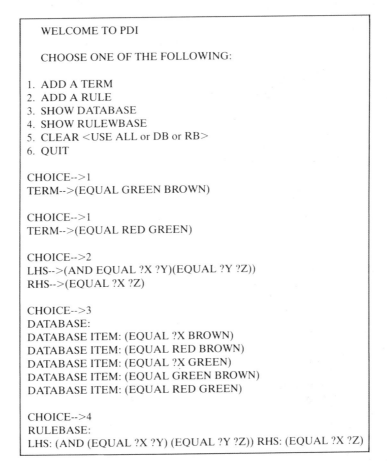

```
WELCOME TO PDI

CHOOSE ONE OF THE FOLLOWING:

1. ADD A TERM
2. ADD A RULE
3. SHOW DATABASE
4. SHOW RULEWBASE
5. CLEAR <USE ALL or DB or RB>
6. QUIT

CHOICE-->1
TERM-->(EQUAL GREEN BROWN)

CHOICE-->1
TERM-->(EQUAL RED GREEN)

CHOICE-->2
LHS-->(AND EQUAL ?X ?Y)(EQUAL ?Y ?Z))
RHS-->(EQUAL ?X ?Z)

CHOICE-->3
DATABASE:
DATABASE ITEM: (EQUAL ?X BROWN)
DATABASE ITEM: (EQUAL RED BROWN)
DATABASE ITEM: (EQUAL ?X GREEN)
DATABASE ITEM: (EQUAL GREEN BROWN)
DATABASE ITEM: (EQUAL RED GREEN)

CHOICE-->4
RULEBASE:
LHS: (AND (EQUAL ?X ?Y) (EQUAL ?Y ?Z)) RHS: (EQUAL ?X ?Z)
```

Figure 9.3 Sample Run without Variable Control.

The example in Figure 9.4 shows that the system now seems to behave correctly for simple entries. However, it cannot deal with equality. That is, suppose that (P1 FOO) and (P2 FOO) allow us to conclude (P3 FOO). Also suppose that BAR is equal to FOO, in the sense that this implies (P1 BAR) and (P2 BAR) should also be added to the data base. This prototype would be unable to conclude from the equality relation that it should assert (P1 BAR) or (P2 BAR) when given (P1 FOO) and (P2 BAR).

9.7 SUMMARY

This chapter introduced the concept of pattern-directed inference. A unification algorithm was implemented and used to build a simple prototype inference engine that uses a database and a rulebase to make inferences and add entries to its own

```
WELCOME TO PDI
CHOOSE ONE OF THE FOLLOWING:
1. ADD A TERM
2. ADD A RULE
3. SHOW DATABASE
4. SHOW RULEWBASE
5. CLEAR <USE ALL or DB or RB>
6. QUIT

CHOICE-->1
TERM-->(EQUAL RED GREEN)
CHOICE-->1
TERM-->(EQUAL GREEN BROWN)
CHOICE-->2
LHS-->(AND (EQUAL ?X ?Y)(EQUAL ?Y ?Z))
RHS-->(EQUAL ?X ?Z)
CHOICE-->3
DATABASE:
DATABASE ITEM: (EQUAL RED BROWN)
DATABASE ITEM: (EQUAL GREEN BROWN)
DATABASE ITEM: (EQUAL RED GREEN)
CHOICE-->1
TERM-->(EQUAL GREEN ORANGE)
CHOICE-->3
DATABASE:
DATABASE ITEM: (EQUAL RED ORANGE)
DATABASE ITEM: (EQUAL GREEN ORANGE)
DATABASE ITEM: (EQUAL RED BROWN)
DATABASE ITEM: (EQUAL GREEN BROWN)
DATABASE ITEM: (EQUAL RED GREEN)
CHOICE-->2
LHS-->(ORANGE ?X)
RHS-->(THEN ?X CAN BE EATEN)
CHOICE-->4
RULEBASE:
LHS: (ORANGE ?11) RHS: (THEN ?11 CAN BE EATEN)
LHS: (AND (EQUAL ?12 ?13) (EQUAL ?13 ?14)) RHS: (EQUAL ?12 ?14)
CHOICE-->1
TERM-->(ORANGE FRUIT)
CHOICE-->3
DATABASE:
DATABASE ITEM: (THEN FRUIT CAN BE EATEN)
DATABASE ITEM: (ORANGE FRUIT)
DATABASE ITEM: (EQUAL RED ORANGE)
DATABASE ITEM: (EQUAL GREEN ORANGE)
DATABASE ITEM: (EQUAL RED BROWN)
DATABASE ITEM: (EQUAL GREEN BROWN)
DATABASE ITEM: (EQUAL RED GREEN)
```

Figure 9.4   Sample Run with Variable Control and Unique Variable Names in Database.

database. Tests were added to the initial prototype to deduce redundancy in the inference process. Both rule entries and data entries are checked for duplication. The functions FRINGE and COMPARE-LHS were used to test rules for equality and subsumption. The function ADD+ allows multiple predicates on the left-hand side of the rules.

The summarized, final version of the PDI prototype is:

```
;;; GLOBALS

(DEFVAR RB () "GLOBAL RULEBASE")
(DEFVAR DB () "GLOBAL DATABASE")


;;; TOPLEVEL DEFINITION

(DEFUN PDI ()
"PDI()-->
TOPLEVEL CONTROL FOR PATTERN DIRECTED INFERENCE"
   (LOOP
      (CASE (MENU)
         ((1) (ADD-TERM (PROMPT 'TERM)))
         ((2) (ADD-RULE (PROMPT 'LHS) (PROMPT 'RHS)))
         ((3) (SHOW-DB))
         ((4) (SHOW-RB))
         ((5) (CLEAR (PROMPT 'CLEAR)))
         (OTHERWISE (RETURN-FROM PDI 'DONE))))))


(DEFUN MATCH-UNIFY (P TE B)
"MATCH-UNIFY(P TE B)-->BINDINGS|T|FAILURE
Bindings indicate unification. T indicates matching constants.
NIL indicates failure. NON-STANDARD EXIT ON FAILURE TO
MATCH AT ATOMIC LEVEL"
   (CATCH 'FAILURE
      (LET ((RES (MATCH+ P TE B)))
         (IF RES RES T))))


(DEFUN MATCH+ (P TE B)
"MATCH+(P TE B)-->BINDINGS|NIL
SHOULD ONLY BE USED TRU MATCH-UNIFY WHICH CONTROLS CATCHER"
   (LABELS ((VAR? (EXP)
               (AND (SYMBOLP EXP)
                  (EQ #\? (SCHAR (STRING EXP) 0))))
            (CONST? (EXP)
               (OR (NUMBERP EXP)
                  (AND (SYMBOLP EXP) (NOT (VAR? EXP)))))
            (PATTERN? (EXP)
```

```
                        (CONSP EXP))
                (VALUE-OCCURS? (TE BIND)
                    (EQUAL TE (SECOND BIND)))
                (VAR-OCCURS-IN (P TE)
                    (COND ((ATOM TE)
                            (IF (EQ P TE) (THROW 'FAILURE ())))
                          (T (VAR-OCCURS-IN P (FIRST TE))
                             (VAR-OCCURS-IN P (REST TE)))))))
;body of MATCH+
;propagate-bindings first
(IF B (SETF P (INST P B) TE (INST TE B)))
;now check attributes of P and TE
(COND ((EQUAL P TE) B)
       ((VAR? P)
          (LET ((BINDING (FIND P B :KEY #'FIRST)))
             (COND ((VAR-OCCURS-IN P TE) (THROW 'FAILURE ()))
                   ((NULL BINDING) (PUSH (LIST P TE) B) B)
                   ((VALUE-OCCURS? TE BINDING) B)
                   (T (THROW 'FAILURE '())))))
       ((VAR? TE) (MATCH+ TE P B))
       ((AND (PATTERN? P)
             (PATTERN? TE)
             (= (LENGTH P)(LENGTH TE)))
          (DO ((PATS P (CDR PATS))
               (TES TE (CDR TES)))
              ((NULL PATS) B)
              (SETF B (MATCH+
                        (FIRST PATS)
                        (FIRST TES)
                        B))))
       ((OR (CONST? P) (CONST? TE))
        (IF (EQUAL P TE)
            B
            (THROW 'FAILURE ())))
       (T (THROW 'FAILURE ())))))

(DEFUN TRY (LHS RHS)
"TRY(LHS TERM RHS)-->
BY SIDE-EFFECT CAUSES APPLICATION OF AN INSTANT"
   (LET ((BINDINGS (TEST LHS)))
      (IF BINDINGS
          (DOLIST (B BINDINGS)
             (LET ((INSTANT (INST RHS B)))
                (UNLESS (MEMBER INSTANT DB :TEST 'EQUAL)
                   (APPLY-INSTANT INSTANT)))))))
```

```
(DEFUN TEST (P &OPTIONAL BINDS)
"TEST(PAT)-->BINDINGS OR NIL
TEST RETURNS A LIST OF THE BINDINGS THAT MATCHED ALL PREDICATES
RETURNING NIL INDICATES NO LHS MATCH IN DB"
    (LABELS ((BOOLEAN (EXPS OP BINDS)
    ;This takes care of ORed expressions
                (IF (EQ OP 'OR)
                    (LET (EXT)
                        (DOLIST (P EXPS EXT)
                            (SETF EXT
                                (UNION EXT (TEST P BINDS) :TEST #'EQUAL))))
    ;this takes care of ANDed expressions or subs
                (LET ((EXT BINDS))
                    (DOLIST (P EXPS EXT)
                        (SETF EXT (TEST P EXT))
                            (UNLESS EXT
                                (RETURN-FROM BOOLEAN ())))))))
            (FETCH (P BINDS)
                (LET (EXT)
                    (IF BINDS
                        (DOLIST (ELE  DB)
                            (DOLIST (B BINDS)
                                (LET ((B (MATCH-UNIFY P ELE B)))
                                    (IF B (PUSH B EXT)))))
                        (DOLIST (ELE DB)
                            (LET ((B
                                    (MATCH-UNIFY P ELE ())))
                                (IF B
                                    (PUSH B EXT)))))
                    EXT)))
        (LET ((FST (FIRST P))
              (RST (REST P)))
          (COND ((ENDP P) ())
                ((MEMBER FST  '(OR AND))
                 (BOOLEAN RST FST BINDS))
                (T
                 (FETCH P BINDS))))))

(DEFUN INST (PAT BINDINGS)
"INST(PAT BINDINGS)-->INSTANTIATED PATTERN"
    (IF (CONSP PAT)
        (DOLIST (BINDING BINDINGS PAT)
            (SETF PAT (SUBST (SECOND BINDING)
                             (FIRST BINDING) PAT)))
        (DOLIST (BINDING BINDINGS PAT)
```

```
        (IF (EQ PAT (FIRST BINDING))
            (RETURN-FROM INST (SECOND BINDING))))))))

(DEFUN APPLY-INSTANT (INSTANT)
"APPLY-INSTANT(INSTANT)-->
RECURSIVELY CALLS ADD-TERM"
    (ADD-TERM INSTANT))


(DEFUN ADD-TERM (TERM)
"ADD-TERM(TERM)-->
NOTHING BUT ADDS TERM TO DATABASE
IF IT IS A NEW ITEM AND TRIGGERS TRY"
    (ASSERT (CONSP TERM))
        (UNLESS
            (OR (MEMBER TERM DB :TEST #'EQUAL)
                (CONTAINS-VAR? TERM))
            (PUSH TERM DB)
            (DOLIST (RULE RB)
                (TRY (FIRST RULE) (SECOND RULE))))))

(DEFUN CONTAINS-VAR? (EXP)
    (DOLIST (ELE EXP ())
        (IF (EQ #\? (SCHAR (STRING ELE) 0))
            (RETURN-FROM CONTAINS-VAR? T))))

(DEFUN ADD-RULE (LHS RHS)
"RULES OF THE FORM '(PATTERN ?X) '(BODY)"
    (ASSERT (AND (CONSP LHS)(CONSP RHS)))
    (LET* ((UNIQUE-VAR-NAMES (GET-VARS LHS))
           (LHS (INST LHS UNIQUE-VAR-NAMES))
           (RHS (INST RHS UNIQUE-VAR-NAMES)))
        (UNLESS
           (COMPARE-LHS LHS)
           (PUSH (LIST LHS RHS) RB)
           (TRY LHS RHS))))

(DEFUN GET-VARS (LHS)
"GET-VARS (LHS)--> LIST OF VAR/SYMBOL PAIRS"
    (LET ((STK ()))
        (LABELS
           ((UNIQUE-VARS (LHS)
                (COND ((VAR? LHS)
                       (PUSHNEW (LIST LHS (GENSYM '?)) STK
                          :KEY #'FIRST))
```

```
                          ((ATOM LHS) LHS)
                          (T (UNIQUE-VARS (FIRST LHS))
                             (UNIQUE-VARS (REST LHS)))))))
      (UNIQUE-VARS LHS))
      STK))


   ;;; UTILITIES

   ;;; VAR? was developed in MATCH+ for MATCH-UNIFY and is
   ;;; duplicated here for general use by PDI.

   (DEFUN VAR? (EXP)
      (AND (SYMBOLP EXP)
           (EQ #\? (SCHAR (STRING EXP) 0))))


   (DEFUN CLEAR (VALUE)
      (COND ((EQ VALUE 'ALL) (SETF DB () RB ()))
            ((EQ VALUE 'RB) (SETF RB ()))
            ((EQ VALUE 'DB) (SETF DB ()))
            (T (PRINC
                  (FORMAT ()
                     "MUST BE ALL or DB or RB"
      )))))


   (DEFUN MENU ()
      (PRINC (FORMAT () "~%~20T WELCOME TO PDI~%"))
      (PRINC (FORMAT () "~2%~10T CHOOSE ONE OF THE FOLLOWING:~2%"))
      (MAPCAR #'(LAMBDA (MENU-ITEM)
                  (PRINC (FORMAT () "~%~10T~A" MENU-ITEM)))
         '("1. ADD A TERM"
           "2. ADD A RULE"
           "3. SHOW DATABASE"
           "4. SHOW RULEBASE"
           "5. CLEAR <USE ALL or DB or RB>"
           "6. QUIT"))
      (LET ((N (PROMPT 'CHOICE)))
         (IF (INTEGERP N) N (MENU))))

   (DEFUN PROMPT (CATEGORY)
      (PRINC (FORMAT () "~4%~10T~A-->" CATEGORY))
      (READ))

(DEFUN SHOW-DB ()
   (PRINC (FORMAT () "~5%DATABASE:~%~%")))
```

```
    (DOLIST (ITEM DB)
       (PRINC (FORMAT () "~5TDATABASE ITEM: ~A~%" ITEM)))
    (PRINC (FORMAT () "~%~%HIT ANY KEY TO CONTINUE"))
    (READ-CHAR))

(DEFUN SHOW-RB ()
    (PRINC (FORMAT () "~4%RULEBASE:~%~%"))
    (DOLIST (RULE RB)
       (PRINC (FORMAT () "~%~5TLHS: ~A RHS: ~A"
                 (FIRST RULE) (SECOND RULE))))
    (PRINC (FORMAT () "~%~%HIT ANY KEY TO CONTINUE"))
    (READ-CHAR))

(DEFUN FRINGE (TREE)
    (LET ((TEMSTACK ()))
       (LABELS ((REC-FRINGE (TREE)
                   (COND ((NULL TREE) TEMSTACK)
                         ((NUMBERP TREE)(PUSH TREE TEMSTACK))
                         ((SYMBOLP TREE)
                          (IF (NOT (EQ #\? (SCHAR (STRING TREE) 0)))
                              (PUSH TREE TEMSTACK)))
                         (T (REC-FRINGE (FIRST TREE))
                            (REC-FRINGE (REST TREE))))))
          (REC-FRINGE TREE))))

(DEFUN COMPARE-LHS (LHS)
"COMPARE-LHS (LHS)--> T|NIL"
    (LET ((FLHS (FRINGE LHS)))
       (DOLIST (RULE RB)
          (LET ((FRULE (FRINGE (FIRST RULE))))
             (UNLESS
                (AND
                   (SET-DIFFERENCE FLHS FRULE)
                   (SET-DIFFERENCE FRULE FLHS))
                (PRINC
                   (FORMAT () "~%IT WOULD APPEAR THAT THE NEW RULE~%
                      ~% ~S ~%~% IS IN CONFLICT WITH THE OLD RULE~%
                         ~%~S~%" LHS (FIRST RULE)))
                (IF (Y-OR-N-P "ENTER ANYWAY?")
                    (RETURN-FROM COMPARE-LHS ())
                    (RETURN-FROM COMPARE-LHS T)))))))
```

9.8 PROBLEMS

9.1 Build an interface that allows the user to query the database as well as add items and rules.

9.2 Add a trace facility that allows the user to turn on and off a trace facility that traces entries into the database.

9.3 What efficiencies can you add to improve execution speed of PDI? These should not be at the expense of completeness.

9.4 Suppose that the assumption is made that, if something is not present in the database, then its negation can be inferred. What kind of impact would this have on the design and use of PDI?

9.5 Could the concept of *equality* be added to this prototype? How would you implement this?

9.6 Currently the only action in this prototype is that items are added to the database. Modify the system so that items can be deleted.

9.7 Modify the system so that the right-hand side of a rule can cause more than one thing to occur. For example, one item may be added to the database and another deleted.

9.8 Modify the right-hand side so that lambda forms may be used rather than simple insertions or deletions.

9.9 Is it possible to add rules about rules to PDI? These rules would look for certain conditions and modify the system accordingly.

9.10 Does the current system guard against rules that define cycles in the rulebase? If so, how is it done?

9.11 The function TEST allows rules to have multiple predicates on the left-hand side of the form (AND P1 P2 . . . Pn). It also can handle ORed predicates. *Fully test* the robustness of TEST to handle nested AND and ORed expressions.

9.12 Add the capability of TEST to handle NOT so that PDI can handle nested expressions with combinations of the boolean functions AND, OR, and NOT.

9.13 Change COMPARE-LHS so that subsumed rules are deleted and the new rule is placed in the rulebase.

10

Goal-Directed Inference and Uncertainty

10.1 INTRODUCTION

The final chapter of the book introduces the basics of goal directed inference. This is what most people refer to when they use the phrase *expert system*. An expert system can be designed to be data driven, goal driven, or both. The system designed in Chapter 9 was data driven. A goal directed system has the advantage that it pursues one line of reasoning at a time. For that reason, it can explain its own behavior in a straightforward way. The basic concept in goal directed inference is to state the problem to be solved in the form of a goal to be achieved. The solution process involves testing the goal against a data base of facts called *working memory* (WM). If the goal is in WM, then the problem is solved. If not, then the goal is broken down into subgoals. The idea is that, if each subgoal is solved, then the goal is solved. This decomposition of goals into subgoals continues until a subgoal is solved. This result is propagated back up the decomposition tree. If it propagates all the way to the initial goal, the problem is solved. If not, the process continues. If a subgoal proves to be unsolvable, this also propagates back up the goal tree. If it propagates all the way to the initial goal, the problem is unsolvable.

Figure 10.1 illustrates a simple goal tree, working memory, and the process that leads to both unsolvable and solvable goals. The goal stack is used to house subgoals that have not yet been solved as the tree is decomposed. The structure of the tree is shown visually, and it is also represented by the simple rules at the top of the figure. As the execution of the system starts, the goal, G is compared with the contents of WM. There is no match; so the subgoals that determine G, G1, and G2

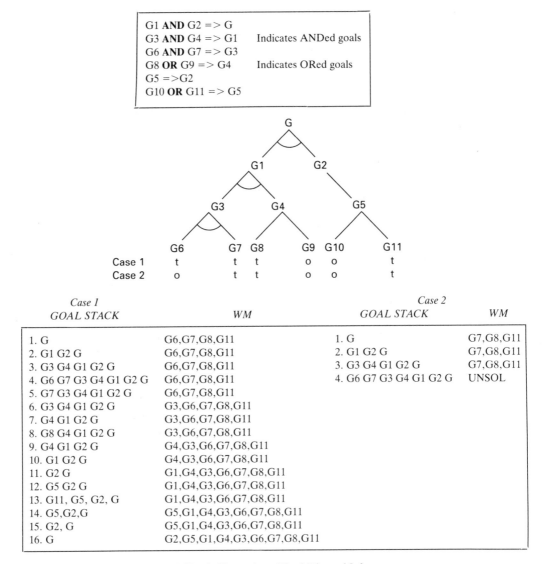

Figure 10.1 A Simple Illustration of Goal-Directed Inference.

are pushed onto the goal stack. Since neither of these is in WM, each becomes a subgoal to be solved. This continues until a match occurs in step 4. G6 in step 4 and G7 in step 5 are popped from the goal stack as solved. G3 is added to WM. This continues until G is solved. In the second case at step 4, there are no more subgoals to create and no matches with WM. The process ends with failure.

10.2 RULES AND KNOWLEDGE

The essence of an expert system is the rulebase. The rules are the program. When used in a *goal-directed inferencing* (GDI) system, the right-hand side (RHS) of each rule can be viewed as a goal and the left-hand side (LHS) conditions as the subgoals that must be solved for the goal or RHS to be solved. In Figure 10.1, for example, to solve G it is necessary to solve G1 and G2, and to solve G1, G3 and G4 must be solved.

Knowledge Acquisition

The first step in developing an application is choosing the right problem. A problem must be defined that is of reasonable size and that has a *realizable* knowledge base. The literature is replete with articles on how to make such a choice. Figure 10.2 lists several factors that are cited as important in selecting a problem. The most important single factor has to do with the knowledge itself. Can it be codified in a reasonable way? Can it be bounded using defaults so that the system can solve a reasonable range of problems? Can the system be developed over a long period with minimum modification to the existing knowledge base? Is the amount of knowledge required for a fully functioning system reasonable in size? Does the knowledge capture the heuristic quality or *expertness* of the problem?

The problem developed in this chapter is deciding *whether or not to buy a property,* a difficult decision making problem. The consequences are very expensive and a bad decision can be disastrous. Yet for most people the decision is forced after one or two days of house hunting. The decision is often based on a few surface factors or on hunches concerning the property. Since most people are not experts on property analysis, their knowledge is insufficient to truly establish the soundness of a property investment. A knowledge-based system in this area would ensure that a reasonable analysis of a potential property would be made and that alternative sources of information were explored to support the final decision. Since the knowledge sources for design of the knowledge base are experts at property analysis, the system also provides *expertise* at the business of property analysis.

---

1. Algorithmic approach will not work.
2. The knowledge domain contains heuristic knowledge.
3. There are recognized experts at this task.
4. The task requires symbolic reasoning.
5. The task is restricted in scope.
6. The task takes no more than several hours to do.
7. The task has a bounded number of concepts.
8. The task is decomposable.
9. The knowledge is not shallow.

Figure 10.2   Some Important Factors in Choosing an Application.

Structuring Knowledge

Structuring knowledge relies on the same principles as structuring computer programs. In particular, levels of abstraction and primitive definitions are the key ingredients. Sitting down at a computer and inputting rules using an expert system shell, or tool, is the worst way to design a knowledge-based system. The knowledge must be first studied independent of any symbol system such as Lisp. Once a means has been found to express the intrinsic structure in the knowledge, implementation languages can be considered.

The top level goal in this application is BUY-PROPERTY. The purpose of the system is to recommend whether or not a piece of property should be purchased. The assumption is made that the purchase decision is for personal residence, not for rental investment. Analysis of experts' house evaluation charts, going on assignment with experts, watching what they looked at and the kinds of data they created, discussing their decisions with them and reading books on the subject—all suggested that the decision to buy a property required the analysis of four separate subproblems:

1. COST OF PROPERTY
2. SOUNDNESS OF THE HOUSE
3. QUALITIES OF THE LOT
4. QUALITY OF THE NEIGHBORHOOD

All four of these factors still have an abstract quality about them because the analysis of the knowledge used in the application can be developed top down just like a program. In fact, development in this way allows the developer to build very early prototypes or preliminary versions of the application to provide a *base* for incremental development and testing. This first level breakdown can be translated into the first rule in the system.

```
IF      COST OF PROPERTY
        SOUNDNESS OF THE HOUSE
        QUALITIES OF THE LOT
        QUALITY OF THE NEIGHBORHOOD
THEN  BUY-PROPERTY
```

Now each of these abstract subgoals can be considered as a goal to be achieved, and the knowledge can be further analyzed, structured, and decomposed. At some point we must decide that problem decomposition should proceed no further. This defines the *grain* of the system and the primitive level. At this level, items are either known or can be decided upon.

COST is analyzed next. It turns out that cost is arrived at on a case-by-case basis. Factors include COMPARABLES, ASSESSMENTS, HISTORY, QUALIFI-

CATION, and PERSONAL. However, in terms of decision making, the experts use the following guidelines: If the buyer qualifies and is willing to pay a particular price, then the cost factor is satisfied and analysis can proceed. If the buyer qualifies but wants to pay the minimum price, then either comparables and history or an independent assessment will suffice to establish an acceptable cost. This factor is considered first because analysis can often stop at this point without expending additional effort. This last comment provides useful control knowledge—that is, knowledge that controls the use of knowledge, or knowledge about knowledge. Thus cost breaks down as follows;

> IF   QUALIFIED
>   ACCEPTABLE PRICE
> THEN   COST IS SATISFIED
>
> IF   QUALIFIED
>   COMPARABLES
>   HISTORY
> THEN   COST IS SATISFIED
>
> IF   QUALIFIED
>   ASSESSMENT
> THEN   COST IS SATISFIED

The HOUSE analysis includes both the INSIDE and the OUTSIDE of the house. If both of these are satisfactory, then the house is satisfactory. The INSIDE analysis breaks down, in turn, into three major factors: STRUCTURE, PLUMB-ING, and ELECTRICAL. The OUTSIDE analysis breaks down into three factors, FOUNDATION, ROOF, and SIDES. Figure 10.3 shows the general breakdown for all remaining subgoals. Figure 10.4 shows the detailed breakdowns for COST and HOUSE. The detailed breakdowns specify both the AND and OR relationships for the subgoals.

This process of analysis continues until the knowledge has been elaborated to the point where a prototype can be constructed. Figure 10.3 makes it clear that many new rules can be added at the leaves of the goal tree. However, for our purposes, the level of detail is sufficient to build a prototype. Values for leaf subgoals placed in the data base will be sufficient to activate the analysis. From the first prototyping point on, new knowledge can be incrementally added and tested using the developing prototype.

Implementing Rules

Now that the knowledge structure is clear, implementation can begin. The first item is to develop a data structure to define goal tree relations. Since during develop-ment, it might be desirable to add additional information about each goal or subgoal, a flexible structure that can be easily modified is desirable. Typically,

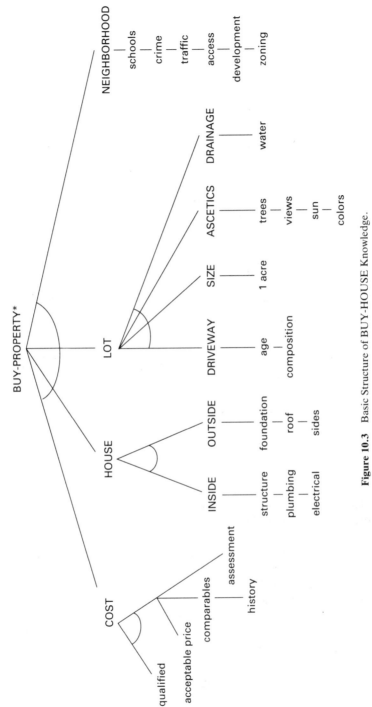

Figure 10.3 Basic Structure of BUY-HOUSE Knowledge.

*Vertically arranged factors are ANDed.

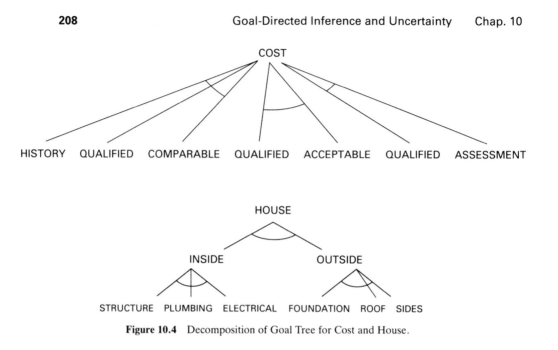

Figure 10.4 Decomposition of Goal Tree for Cost and House.

DEFSTRUCT is used to develop a frame-like structure for this purpose. In this application, a rule might be defined by the following DEFSTRUCT:

```
(DEFSTRUCT (RULE (:CONC-NAME NIL))
    LHS
    RHS
    (CFR 1.0))
```

The slot RHS has the goal as its value. The slot LHS has the subgoals that support the goal. LHS elements are considered ANDed together. ORed components will be written as separate rules. CFR refers to rule certainty. This may or may not be needed in a particular application. It will default to 1.0. Additional slots can be added at any time.

Since rules in such a system are almost always referred to in a sequential fashion, there is little need to provide a means for referring to individual rules by name. They can be placed directly into a hash table or list. Rules can then be accessed one at a time by walking down the list or table. In this application, reference can be accomplished both by name and through a hash table used to house the rulebase. The hash table is global and should be visible to the entire program. It will be initialized using DEFVAR.

```
(DEFVAR *RULEBASE* (MAKE-HASH-TABLE))
```

Rule Syntax

Rule syntax is a matter of taste, but it should make accessing rule components and instantiation as easy as possible. An important decision at the outset is to decide how context is to be controlled. Suppose I want to put data concerning three people into a *knowledge-based system* (KBS) that does loan processing. I then want to have the KBS provide an analysis for each person. It is important not to mix contexts when dealing with multiple cases in the same data base. It would be inconsistent if data from person 1 and data from person 2 satisfied different predicates on the LHS of a rule, and this activated the RHS. This would be incorrect because the LHS can only be satisfied properly if each part is satisfied by data from the same person. Each person is a *context*. Each solution must be based on a single context. We could choose to control context by building a GDI that could only solve one problem at a time. In the previous discussion, each person would have been run through the system separately. Three runs would have been required to process the loans for three people. The first version of GDI will control context explicitly using variable bindings. This allows multiple contexts represented as distinct bindings to be considered at one time. In a later version, context and bindings will be managed separated. The later version will demonstrate the additional power this separate management adds to the GDI system.

The basic syntax used for rules in GDI is ((LHS)(RHS)) where LHS takes the form (AND S1 S2 . . . Sn) and the RHS takes the form (G). The S's refer to subgoals and G is the GOAL that is ACHIEVEd when all S's are SOLVED. A robust system should be able to instantiate properly the RHS of rules that have properties such as the following.

```
((AND (TALL ?X)(SHORT ?Y)) (COMPLEMENTS ?X ?Y))
((AND (LIKES ?X TO DO ?Y TO ?Z))(?X SHOULD DO ?Y TO ?Z))
((AND (FOO ?X)(FOOY ?X))(BAR ?X))
((AND (FOO ?X BAR ?Y)(NOODLES ?Y))(FOOEY ?X ?Y)(HOOEY ?X))
```

The first case has different bindings occurring in each LHS component, but both are needed to instantiate the RHS. This can be difficult to implement since context can be a sticky problem. The second case has multiple variables on both the LHS and the RHS. The ability to handle and instantiate any permutation of variables and constants makes the system easy to use and understand. The cost is speed. In the third case, the predicates on the LHS have one variable that provides context control; that is, the RHS will not be solved unless the LHS predicates are both satisfied in the same context ?X. A simple macro called DEFRULE provides a means for the designer to define rules that abide by this syntax. Notice that the AND predicate is stripped off when the rule is entered into the rule base, *RULEBASE*.

```
(DEFMACRO DEFRULE (NAME LHS RHS &OPTIONAL (RULES *RULEBASE*))
   `(SETF (GETHASH ',NAME ',RULES)
       (MAKE-RULE :LHS ',(CDR LHS) :RHS ',RHS)))
```

In the BUY-PROPERTY application of GDI, the basic rules for the first prototype would be:

```
(DEFRULE R1 (AND (COST ?X) (HOUSE ?X) (LOT ?X) (NEIGHBORHOOD ?X))
    (BUY-PROPERTY ?X))
(DEFRULE R2 (AND (QUALIFIED ?X) (ACCEPTABLE ?X)) (COST ?X))
(DEFRULE R3 (AND (QUALIFIED ?X) (COMPARABLE ?X) (HISTORY ?X))
    (COST ?X))
(DEFRULE R4 (AND (QUALIFIED ?X) (ASSESSMENT ?X)) (COST ?X))
(DEFRULE R5 (AND (INSIDE ?X) (OUTSIDE ?X)) (HOUSE ?X))
(DEFRULE R6 (AND (DRIVEWAY ?X) (LOT-SIZE ?X) (ASCETICS ?X)
    (DRAINAGE ?X)) (LOT ?X))
(DEFRULE R7 (AND (TREES ?X) (VIEW ?X) (MORNING-SUN ?X))
    (ASCETICS ?X))
(DEFRULE R8 (AND (STRUCTURE ?X) (PLUMBING ?X) (ELECTRICAL ?X))
    (INSIDE ?X))
(DEFRULE R9 (AND (FOUNDATION ?X) (ROOF ?X) (SIDES ?X))
    (OUTSIDE ?X))
(DEFRULE R10 (AND (SCHOOLS ?X) (CRIME ?X) (TRAFFIC ?X) (ACCESS ?X)
    (DEVELOPMENT-PLANS ?X) (ZONING ?X)) (NEIGHBORHOOD ?X))
```

Implementing Fact Structures

Once the rule structure is decided upon, the structure of facts for working memory or the data base follows. Working memory (WM) defines the *STATE* of problem analysis as evaluation proceeds. Initially, it holds what is known about each context to be analyzed. It is used to determine which goals are satisfied, and it is updated when a new goal is satisfied. WM is global and can be managed in a global variable. WM can be structured in a variety of ways. The choice is a matter of efficiency. Typically, discrimination tree, hash table, or list structures are used. In this application, a simple list structure will suffice.

Context will be controlled during execution by having the GDI system operate with one set of bindings at a time. Whenever a set of bindings is established, those bindings will be maintained and passed to functions such that only solutions consistent with that set of bindings are considered. In this manner, one line of reasoning is considered at a time. This could be useful if an explanation facility was added to GDI. The globals now include the following:

```
(DEFVAR *RULEBASE* (MAKE-HASH-TABLE))
(DEFVAR *WM* ())
```

The basic structure of a fact in GDI has been determined by the rule syntax. A DEFSTRUCT will be used to provide the same flexibility in developing the concept of a fact as was provided for rules. The INFO slot of a fact would have rule syntax in it. The CF slot could contain certainty information.

```
(DEFSTRUCT (FACT (:CONC-NAME NIL))
  INFO
  CF)


(DEFUN DEFFACT (INFO &OPTIONAL (CF 1.0))
  (PUSHNEW (MAKE-FACT :INFO INFO :CF CF) *WM*
                       :TEST #'EQUAL :KEY #'INFO))
```

In the case of facts, it proved to be more natural to use a DEFUN to create a means of generating instances of facts. DEFFACT creates working memory elements. Context is taken as implicit in variable bindings. PUSHNEW ensures that duplication of facts does not occur.

```
(DEFFACT '(TREES HOUSE1))
(DEFFACT '(TREES HOUSE2))
(DEFFACT '(VIEW HOUSE1))
(DEFFACT '(VIEW HOUSE2))
(DEFFACT '(MORNING-SUN HOUSE2))
(DEFFACT '(MORNING-SUN HOUSE1))
(DEFFACT '(DRIVEWAY HOUSE1))
(DEFFACT '(DRIVEWAY HOUSE2))
(DEFFACT '(LOT-SIZE HOUSE1))
(DEFFACT '(LOT-SIZE HOUSE2))
(DEFFACT '(DRAINAGE HOUSE1))
(DEFFACT '(DRAINAGE HOUSE2))
(DEFFACT '(COST HOUSE1))
(DEFFACT '(COST HOUSE2))
(DEFFACT '(NEIGHBORHOOD HOUSE1))
(DEFFACT '(HOUSE HOUSE1))
(DEFFACT '(HOUSE HOUSE2))
```

10.3 THE BASIC ALGORITHM

A basic algorithm for GDI from Buchanan and Duda (1982) is shown next.

```
PROCEDURE ACHIEVE (G)
    Scan the knowledgebase for a set of rules S that determine G;
    If S is empty THEN ask the user about G
        ELSE
            WHILE G is unknown and rules remain in S DO
            BEGIN
                Call Choose-Rule (S) to choose a rule R from S;
                G' <-- condition (R);
                If G' is unknown THEN call ACHIEVE (G');
                If G' is true THEN apply R
    END.
```

This algorithm will provide a basic point of departure for developing the inference engine and control structures for GDI. The basic idea is to determine if any rules mention the goal G on their RHS. If so, they are added to the set S. While G is not solved (unknown) and rules remain in S, they are taken one at a time and a depth-first decomposition of the goal tree begins. Each item on the LHS becomes a subgoal to solve. The idea is to continue this process until solved subgoals are found or decomposition is complete. The recursive nature of ACHIEVE provides an implicit goal stack of unsolved subgoals. When one is solved, the recursion unwinds moving back up the goal stack. Eventually, G is solved or S becomes empty at the top level. In the absence of an internal solution, the user may also be queried for additional data. Two assumptions about G shape the implementation of ACHIEVE. First, goals will be entered without variables. Second, only top-level goals will be explicitly queried by the user. Since the top level is recursive, the recursive function ACHIEVE+ that contains the essential algorithm will be written first and then an initializing function ACHIEVE will be written that guards and uses ACHIEVE+.

```
(DEFUN ACHIEVE+ (G &OPTIONAL B)
   (MULTIPLE-VALUE-BIND (S B)
      (SCAN G B)
      (LET ((KNOWN (SOLVED G B)))
         (COND (KNOWN)
               (T (IF (EMPTY? S)
                  (QUERY-USER G)
                  (DO ()
                     ((OR KNOWN (EMPTY? S)) KNOWN)
                     (LET* ((RULE (POP S))
                           (BINDS
                              (DOLIST (GSUB (LHS RULE) B)
                                 (LET ((RES
                                       (ACHIEVE+ GSUB)))
                                    (IF RES RES
                                       (RETURN
                                          ()))))))
                        (IF BINDS
                           (REPORT-FACT
                           (DEFFACT
                              (INST (RHS RULE)
                                 BINDS)))
                        (SETF KNOWN BINDS)))))))))
```

ACHIEVE+ implements and expands the basic algorithm. The function SCAN takes a goal (G) and returns a list of rules (S) that mention G on their RHS. It also returns the bindings B that were gathered from the goal G and the RHS of unifying rules. The function SOLVED which is central to the effective operation of

ACHIEVE+, is used to determine if G is immediately solved. If it is then the value of KNOWN that would be a set of bindings is returned. If G is unknown and S is not empty, then a DO loop is entered. Choose-rule is simply (POP S) in this implementation. It could be made much more powerful using meta-knowledge or other rule management concepts, such as specificity, to determine which rule to look at next. The recursive call to ACHIEVE+ is embedded within a DOLIST. This is very important because it provides a means of managing the implicit goal stack discussed earlier. When the DOLIST function is completed for all elements on LHS, the result is given to the variable BINDINGS. Each call to ACHIEVE+ within the DOLIST will eventually return either bindings or NIL to DOLIST. Within DOLIST if any recursive call to ACHIEVE+ results in failure (NIL is returned), the DOLIST is terminated by RETURN. This is an important efficiency since a failure means the RHS cannot be established. It would be fruitless to continue to pursue LHS elements in this case. If bindings are found for all elements, all LHS subgoals have been solved so the RHS has been solved. The RHS is then INSTantiated with the new bindings and added to WM. The SETF at the end returns the bindings from the DO loop. The function REPORT-FACT provides some feedback to the user as processing is occurring.

The function ACHIEVE, both guards ACHIEVE+ and initializes the problem. It also controls the reporting function. If G contains variables this implies that it is in error. The assumption was made that a goal would be entered without variables. A specific goal should be specified for GDI. If it is, the specific case is evaluated. Otherwise, ACHIEVE calls REPORT with NIL as the first argument to report that the goal G (containing variables) cannot be achieved.

```
(DEFUN ACHIEVE (G)
  (ASSERT (NOT (CONTAINS-VAR? G)) (G)
    "STATEMENT OF GOAL CANNOT CONTAIN VARIABLES")
  (LET ((B (ACHIEVE+ G ()))))
    (IF
       B
       (REPORT B G)
       (REPORT NIL G))))
```

The SOLVED function is of central importance in GDI. In this version it is redundant of TEST. However, it is conceptually distinct and will be further developed in the final version of GDI. SOLVED calls TEST with a goal G and bindings B. TEST returns bindings consistent with B or NIL. TEST is a simplified version of the version used in PDI. It is less general than that version. It assumes all tests will be ANDed predicates. It is faster than the general version.

```
(DEFUN SOLVED (G B)
  (TEST G B))

(DEFUN TEST (PAT B)
"TEST(PAT)-->BINDINGS|T|NIL
```

```
TEST RETURNS A LIST OF BINDINGS THAT MATCHED ALL PREDICATES
A NIL RETURNS INDICATES NO LHS MATCH. T indicates a match."
   (ASSERT (CONSP PAT))
   (LET ((STK ()))
      (LABELS ((AND+ (PAT B)
                     (COND ((NULL PAT) (PUSH B STK))
                           (T
                            (LET ((P (FIRST PAT)))
                               (DOLIST (ELE *WM*)
                                  (LET ((B (MATCH-UNIFY P
                                                   (INFO ELE) B)))
                                     (AND+ (REST PAT) B)))))))))
         (IF (EQ (CAR PAT) 'AND)
             (AND+ (REST PAT) B)
             (AND+ (LIST PAT) B)))
       STK))
```

The function SCAN walks through the rulebase collecting rules that unify the RHS and the GOAL. It also collects bindings from the unification process that represent the variable values in G. MAPHASH provides a fast accessing function for this purpose.

```
(DEFUN SCAN (GOAL B &OPTIONAL (RULES *RULEBASE*))
   (LET ((S ()))
      (MAPHASH
         #'(LAMBDA (NAME RULE)
               (LET ((BINDING (MATCH-UNIFY (RHS RULE) GOAL B)))
                  (IF BINDING
                      (PROGN
                         (SETF B BINDING)
                         (PUSH RULE S))))) RULES)
       (VALUES S B)))
```

The rest of the utilities and reporting functions as well as *reused* components from PDI in the last chapter are shown in the final version of the program in the summary section of the chapter.

Testing GDI

The GDI program is actually three components managed by means of DEFSYS:

- The first component, called RULESTR.LSP, contains the defstructs, macros, and global variables.
- The second component, called GDIBODY.LSP, houses the inference engine.
- The third component, called GDIDATA.LSP, contains rules and working memory elements for testing.

```
(DEFSYS :NAME GDI
        :FILES ("RULESTR" "GDIBODY" "GDIDATA"))
```

The first test was to compile the components. This revealed no fatal errors, but it pointed out that SCAN, QUERY-USER, and SHOW-RULE named variables that were never referenced. These were compiled out using (DECLARE (IGNORE <variable>)). Test runs showed that GDI was able to handle all the cases discussed earlier. It also suggested that maintaining context was critical to the proper functioning of the GDI system. Figure 10.5 shows some test results. Notice also that GDIDATA.LSP is not part of the COMPILE-FILES file list. The rules would not be compiled.

Remember GDI is a prototype, as development proceeds, many efficiencies can be added by shaping code to fit the problem. A good example is the function TEST. It really does more work than necessary, as was evident when timing various functions during testing. A new version of the TEST function is shown below. As soon as a binding is found, control is returned to the calling function. The previous version continued on even though this was unnecessary.

```
(DEFUN TEST (PAT B)
"TEST(PAT)-->BINDINGS|T|NIL
RETURNS A LIST OF BINDINGS THAT MATCHED ALL PREDICATES
NIL RETURNS MEANS NO LHS MATCH IN DB. T is a match."
  (ASSERT (CONSP PAT))
  (DOLIST (ELE *WM* NIL)
    (LET ((B (MATCH-UNIFY PAT (INFO ELE) B)))
      (IF B
          (RETURN-FROM TEST B))))))
```

```
WELCOME TO PDI
CHOOSE ONE OF THE FOLLOWING:

CHOICE-->2
GOAL-->(BUY-PROPERTY HOUSE1)
ESTABLISHED: (ASCETICS HOUSE1)
ESTABLISHED: (LOT HOUSE1)
ESTABLISHED: (BUY-PROPERTY HOUSE1)
ESTABLISHED BUY-PROPERTY FOR THE CONTEXT HOUSE 1

WELCOME TO PDI
CHOICE-->2
GOAL-->(BUY-HOUSE ?X)
ESTABLISHED: (ASCETICS HOUSE2)
ESTABLISHED: (LOT HOUSE2)
UNABLE TO ESTABLISH BUY-PROPERTY FOR CONTEXT HOUSE2
SOLVED THE GOAL BUY-PROPERTY FOR HOUSE1
```

Figure 10.5   Sample Run Using GDI.*

*Note that cost, house, and neighborhood were already in *WM* for HOUSE 1.

10.4 UNCERTAINTY

It could be that a simple solution to a goal directed problem is not sufficient. It might be assumed that, in most real world problems, information is ambiguous and incomplete. There may also be information from multiple sources that, when taken together, strengthens our belief in the information. For these reasons, it would be desirable to modify GDI so that it might consider CERTAINTY in the solution process. This could mean that a goal is not solved until it is satisfied above a certain threshold of certainty, or it could mean that, when a solution is reported, the certainty of the asserted solution should be reported also.

A simple MYCIN like certainty management scheme will be added to GDI. This approach is sufficient to illustrate the basic concepts. The goal will be to keep track of certainty as the solution is formed and to report it with any solution. No attempt will be made to use it to decide when a goal is solved, though that would require only trivial changes to the modified program. The student is directed to Shortliffe and Buchanan (1975) for the detailed rationale and critique of this approach to certainty.

Calculating a Certainty Factor

The range of values for certainty calculations is arbitrary. In this example, the range of values could be between -1.00 and $+1.00$ though practically they will be between 0 and 1. Associated with each rule in GDI is a certainty factor called CFR. This is the intrinsic certainty associated with the rule and usually defaulted to 1.0. Each fact in the rule base also has a certainty, called CF, associated with it. A true assertion or fact has a CF = 1.0 and a false assertion in WM has a CF = -1.0.

Suppose we have the following situation. WM contains the facts;

```
((SMART STUDENT 0.4) (LIBRARY STUDENT 0.5)
 (BOOKS STUDENT 0.6))
```

The system also contains the rules:

```
R1 ((AND (STUDIES ?X)) -> (SMART ?X) 1.0)
R2 ((AND (LIBRARY ?X)(BOOKS ?X))->(SMART ?X) 0.9)
```

The subgoal (STUDIES ?X) has already been satisfied and thus SMART has been solved and placed in working memory. Since multiple sources of information may improve the quality of the solution, analysis continues using the second rule (R2). This was not done in the old version of GDI. The only change required to change this in GDI is to change the test for termination of the DO loop in ACHIEVE+ from (OR KNOWN (EMPTY? S)) to (EMPTY? S). This forces the system to consider *all* rules that solve a particular goal.

There are two components to the calculation of certainty for the second solution to the goal SMART. The first component involves calculating the certainty

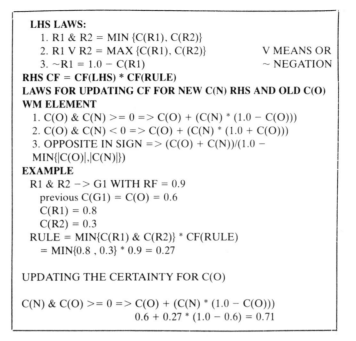

Figure 10.6   Formula for Certainty Calculations.

for the rule R2. The formula in Figure 10.6 describes the calculation for various cases. For this example, the LHS part would be $MIN\{0.5\ 0.6\} = 0.5$. This is then multiplied by the intrinsic certainty for the rule. In this case, the value would be 0.9. So the certainty value for the assertion of SMART from the new solved rule would be $0.9 * 0.5 = 0.45$. Call this value NEW.

The second component requires that the certainty factor of the *previous* working memory assertion of SMART be updated for this additional solution. As shown in Figure 10.6, when both the old and new values are greater than or equal to zero, the calculation is:

$$OLD + (NEW * (1.0 - OLD))$$
$$0.4 + (0.45 * (1.0 - 0.4)) = 0.67$$

The certainty value for SMART in WM would be changed from 0.4 to 0.67.

The second component brings up an interesting problem in implementation. If a fact immediately solves a goal, does the system still collect all rules whose RHS unifies with the goal and then combine *all* the certainty factors? The answer is *NO*. In this implementation, if a goal or subgoal is immediately solved, the element in working memory is treated as if it had the status of an assumption or a premise. That is, no additional solutions would be considered. On the other hand, if the goal is not immediately solved then all solutions are collected and the certainty updated accordingly.

Modifying GDI for Certainty Calculations

The most pervasive change to GDI to handle certainty is that both binding information and certainty data must be propagated by the ACHIEVE, ACHIEVE+, SOLVED, and TEST functions. This turns out to rather minor since the basic design was sound. The first change is to TEST; it has been modified so that it returns multiple values. The first is the binding or NIL. The second is the CF value or NIL. This change requires that the function SOLVED, which receives the TEST results, be changed to accommodate multiple values. Changes are highlighted in italics.

```
(DEFUN TEST (PAT B)
 "TEST(PAT)-->BINDINGS|T|NIL
 RETURNS A LIST OF BINDINGS THAT MATCHED ALL PREDICATES
 A NIL RETURNS INDICATES NO LHS MATCH IN DB.T is a match."
   (ASSERT (CONSP PAT))
   (DOLIST (ELE *WM* (VALUES NIL NIL))
      (LET ((B (MATCH-UNIFY PAT (INFO ELE) B)))
         (IF B
             (RETURN-FROM TEST (VALUES B (CF ELE)))))))))
```

SOLVED has undergone revision. It must return both bindings and certainty data to ACHIEVE+.

```
(DEFUN SOLVED (G B)
   (MULTIPLE-VALUE-BIND (BINDINGS UCF)
      (TEST G B)
      (VALUES BINDINGS UCF)))
```

The new functions CFACTOR (which calculates rule certainty for ANDed LHS components) and UPDATE-CF (which adjusts the CF for previous CF values in WM) are shown below. UPDATE-CF only takes care of the case in which both the RULE and OLD values are greater than or equal to zero. DEFFACT has been modified to automatically update the CF of existing WM elements using UPDATE-CF. This update is shown in the boldface part of the code.

```
(DEFUN CFACTOR (R L)
   (* (CFR R) (APPLY #'MIN L)))

(DEFUN UPDATE-CF (RULE OLD)
   (+ OLD (* RULE (- 1.0 OLD))))

(DEFUN DEFFACT (INFO &OPTIONAL (CF 1.0))
   (LET ((OLD (FIRST (MEMBER INFO *WM*
                  :TEST #'EQUAL :KEY #'INFO))))
```

```
(COND (OLD
       (SETF (CF OLD) CF)
       OLD)
      (T (PUSH (MAKE-FACT :INFO INFO :CF CF *WM*)
         (FIRST *WM*))))))
```

The fundamental changes were to ACHIEVE+. This function had to be modified to handle multiple values throughout. In particular, every return point had to be re-worked. The main changes are highlighted in the function. The idea is to propagate the certainty data. If all the subgoals that support the goal are satisfied in the DOLIST, a stack CERT of certainty coefficients that have been pushed as each subgoal was satisfied, (COND (RES (PUSH CET CERT), is given to CFACTOR along with RULE for calculating rule certainty. When the RHS is instantiated and added to WM as a solved goal, DEFFACT calculates UPDATE-CF *if the goal has a previous solution.* We will just note that ACHIEVE had to undergo cosmetic changes to accommodate the new reporting requirements. Figure 10.7 shows the contents of working memory. Figure 10.8 shows the contents of the current rulebase.

```
(DEFUN ACHIEVE+ (G &OPTIONAL B)
   (MULTIPLE-VALUE-BIND (S B)
      (SCAN G B)
      (MULTIPLE-VALUE-BIND (KNOWN CERTAINTY)
         (SOLVED G B)
         (COND (KNOWN (VALUES KNOWN CERTAINTY))
               (T (IF (EMPTY? S)
                      (QUERY-USER G)
                      (DO ((PREVIOUS NIL))
                          ((EMPTY? S)) (VALUES KNOWN CERTAINTY))
                         (LET* ((RULE (POP S))
                                (CERT ())
                                (BINDS
                                    (DOLIST (GSUB (LHS RULE) B)
                                        (MULTIPLE-VALUE-BIND (RES CET)
                                            (ACHIEVE+ GSUB B)
                                            (COND (RES
                                                    (PUSH CET CERT)
                                                    (SETF B RES))
                                                  (T (RETURN
                                                        (VALUES
                                                           RES CET))
         ))))))
                         (IF BINDS
                            (LET ((ELE
                                    (CREATE-NEW-FACT
                                       RULE BINDS CERT PREVIOUS)))
                               (UPDATE-SOLUTION BINDS ELE)))))))))))
```

```
CHOICE-->3
FACT: (BUY-PROPERTY HOUSE1) CF= 0.8
FACT: (LOT HOUSE1) CF= 0.8
FACT: (ASCETICS HOUSE1) CF= 0.8
FACT: (SHORT HOUSE1) CF= 0.4
FACT: (HOUSE HOUSE1) CF= 0.8
FACT: (NEIGHBORHOOD HOUSE1) CF= 0.8
FACT: (COST HOUSE1) CF= 0.8
FACT: (DRAINAGE HOUSE1) CF= 0.8
FACT: (LOT-SIZE HOUSE1) CF= 0.8
FACT: (DRIVEWAY HOUSE1) CF= 0.8
FACT: (MORNING-SUN HOUSE1) CF= 0.8
FACT: (VIEW HOUSE1) CF= 0.8
FACT: (TREES HOUSE1) CF= 0.8
FACT: (BOOKS LES) CF= 0.6
FACT: (LIBRARY LES) CF= 0.4
FACT: (STUDIES LES) CF= 0.3
```

Figure 10.7   Working Memory with CF Values.

```
LHS:((SCHOOLS ?X) (CRIME ?X) (TRAFFIC ?X) (ACCESS ?X)
     (DEVELOPMENT-PLANS ?X) (ZONING ?X))
RHS:(NEIGHBORHOOD? X)

LHS:((DRIVEWAY ?X) (LOT-SIZE ?X) (ASCETICS ?X) (DRAINAGE ?X))
RHS:(LOT ?X)

LHS:((TREES ?X) (VIEW ?X) (MORNING-SUN ?X))
RHS:(ASCETICS ?X)

LHS:((COST ?X) (HOUSE ?X) (LOT ?X) (NEIGHBORHOOD ?X))
RHS:(BUY-PROPERTY ?X)

LHS:((STRUCTURE ?X) (PLUMBINB ?X) (ELECTRICAL ?X))
RHS:(INSIDE ?X)

LHS:((PRICE ?X))
RHS:(COST ?X)

LHS:((FOUNDATION ?X) (ROOF ?X) (SIDES ?X))
RHS:(OUTSIDE ?X)

LHS:((INSIDE ?X) (OUTSIDE ?X))
RHS:(HOUSE ?X)

LHS:((STUDIES ?X))
RHS:(SMART ?X)

LHS:((LIBRARY ?X))
RHS:(SMART ?X)

LHS:((BOOKS ?X))
RHS:(SMART ?X)
```

Figure 10.8   Internal Representation of Rules.

CREATE-NEW-FACT instantiates a new fact using DEFFACT. It also performs a critical function with regard to certainty management. Suppose S contains more than one rule whose RHS unifies with the goal to be achieved. The certainty value from the first solution is stored in the variable PREVIOUS. If another solution is found both the new certainty value CERT and the value of PREVIOUS are used to adjust the certainty factor for the fact. This will work for any number of additional solutions.

```
(DEFUN CREATE-NEW-FACT (RULE BINDS CERT PREVIOUS)
   (DEFFACT
      (INST (RHS RULE) BINDS)
      (IF PREVIOUS
          (UPDATE-CF (CFACTOR RULE CERT) PREVIOUS)
          (CFACTOR RULE CERT))
   ))
```

UPDATE-SOLUTION removes clutter from ACHIEVE+. It creates local side-effects to the variables KNOWN, PREVIOUS and CERTAINTY.

```
(DEFMACRO UPDATE-SOLUTION (BINDS NEW-WM-ELE)
   `(PROGN
       (SETF KNOWN ,BINDS)
       (SETF PREVIOUS (CF ,NEW-WM-ELE))
       (SETF CERTAINTY PREVIOUS)))
```

10.5 MANAGING CONTEXT

The current version of GDI manages context by assuming that the variable bindings of an input fact is the context in which the fact is meaningful. For the fact (TALL PAT) with the goal (TALL ?X), for example, the context would be PAT. This, however, limits the generality of GDI. It may be the case that for a single context several different sets of bindings might be appropriate. For example, the context might be HOUSE1 and the names of several different EVALUATORS or PROPERTY ACCESSORS might be represented as variable values for data elements. Maintaining context explicitly and allowing multiple bindings makes the system much more powerful and flexible.

Two new system variables will be added to GDI called *CONTEXT* and *CURRENT-CONTEXT*. *CURRENT-CONTEXT* will be initialized to the context value DEFAULT. This will also be installed on the system context list, *CONTEXT*. When a new fact is added to the system during run time; context must be input explicitly. When added using DEFFACT, context is either explicitly stated or defaults to the value of *CURRENT-CONTEXT*.

```
(DEFVAR *CONTEXT* '(DEFAULT))
(DEFVAR *CURRENT-CONTEXT* 'DEFAULT)
```

Changes are required to DEFFACT to support this stronger context control. The changes are noted in italics. CREATE-NEW-FACT must also be modified to provide DEFFACT with the CONTEXT information.

```
(DEFUN DEFFACT (INFO &OPTIONAL (CF 1.0)
                     (CONTEXT *CURRENT-CONTEXT*))
  (LET ((OLD (FIRST (MEMBER INFO *WM*
                        :TEST #'EQUAL :KEY #'INFO))))
      (COND ((AND OLD (EQ (CONTEXT OLD) CONTEXT))
             (SETF (CF OLD) CF)
             OLD)
            (T (PUSHNEW CONTEXT *CONTEXT* :TEST #'EQ)
               (PUSH (MAKE-FACT :INFO INFO
                                :CF CF :CONTEXT CONTEXT)
                 *WM*)
               (FIRST *WM*)))))

(DEFUN CREATE-NEW-FACT (RULE BINDS CERT PREVIOUS
                        CONTEXT)
  (DEFFACT
    (INST (RHS RULE) BINDS)
    (IF PREVIOUS
        (UPDATE-CF (CFACTOR RULE CERT) PREVIOUS)
        (CFACTOR RULE CERT))
    CONTEXT))
```

The top level user interface function called GDI modeled after the PDI interface used in the last chapter with prompts for ACHIEVE and DEFFACT would be:

```
(DEFUN GDI ()
  "GDI()-->
  TOPLEVEL CONTROL AND USER INTERFACE FOR GDI"
  (LOOP
    (CASE (MENU)
      ((1) (DEFFACT (PROMPT 'FACT)(PROMPT 'CF=)
                    (PROMPT 'CONTEXT)))
      ((2) (ACHIEVE (PROMPT 'GOAL) (PROMPT 'CONTEXT)))
      ((3) (SHOW-WM))
      ((4) (SHOW-RULE))
      ((5) (CLEAR-WM))
      (OTHERWISE (RETURN-FROM GDI 'DONE)))
    (PAUSE-UNTIL-KEYPRESSED)))
```

ACHIEVE needs modification to control context. Every GOAL sent to ACHIEVE is evaluated in one explicit context. The only changes to ACHIEVE+ are to modify CREATE-NEW-FACT and DEFFACT to include CONTEXT.

```
(DEFUN ACHIEVE (G CONTEXT)
    (ASSERT (NOT (CONTAINS-VAR? G)) (G)
    "STATEMENT OF GOAL CANNOT CONTAIN VARIABLES")
    (IF (MEMBER CONTEXT *CONTEXT*)
        (MULTIPLE-VALUE-BIND (RES CERT)
            (ACHIEVE+ G CONTEXT)
            (REPORT RES CERT G CONTEXT))
        (REPORT NIL 0 G CONTEXT)))
```

TEST must now find bindings B *in context.*

```
(DEFUN TEST (PAT CONTEXT B)
"TEST(PAT)-->BINDINGS|T|NIL
RETURNS A LIST OF BINDINGS THAT MATCHED ALL PREDICATES
NIL RETURN INDICATES NO LHS MATCH. T is a match."
    (ASSERT (CONSP PAT))
    (DOLIST (ELE *WM* (VALUES NIL NIL))
        (LET ((B (MATCH-UNIFY PAT (INFO ELE) ())))
            (IF (AND B (EQ (CONTEXT ELE) CONTEXT))
                (RETURN-FROM TEST (VALUES B (CF ELE)))))))
```

REPORT has an improved syntax as well. Figures 10.9 to 10.11 show sample runs using the final version of GDI with both uncertainty and better context control.

CHOICE-->2

GOAL-->(BUY-PROPERTY HOUSE1)

CONTEXT-->HOUSE

WORKING . . . NO SOLUTION IN CONTEXT HOUSE

CHOICE-->2

GOAL-->(BUY-PROPERTY PAT)

CONTEXT-->HOUSE

SOLVED THE GOAL: (BUY-PROPERTY PAT)

FOR CONTEXT: HOUSE

AND CF = 0.6

Figure 10.9 Run of BUY-PROPERTY with Uncertainty.

```
CHOICE-->2
GOAL-->(SMART LES)

CONTEXT-->SCHOOL
SOLVED THE GOAL: (SMART LES)
FOR CONTEXT: SCHOOL
AND CF = 0.832
```

Figure 10.10   Second Sample Run of GDI with Uncertainty.

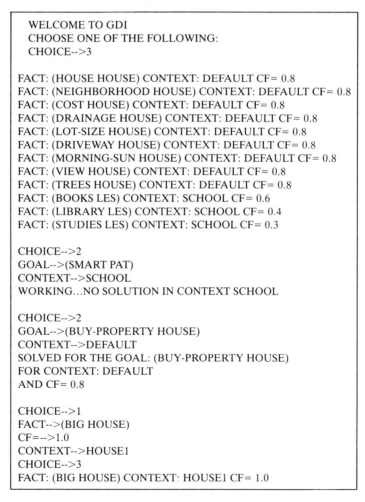

```
WELCOME TO GDI
CHOOSE ONE OF THE FOLLOWING:
CHOICE-->3

FACT: (HOUSE HOUSE) CONTEXT: DEFAULT CF= 0.8
FACT: (NEIGHBORHOOD HOUSE) CONTEXT: DEFAULT CF= 0.8
FACT: (COST HOUSE) CONTEXT: DEFAULT CF= 0.8
FACT: (DRAINAGE HOUSE) CONTEXT: DEFAULT CF= 0.8
FACT: (LOT-SIZE HOUSE) CONTEXT: DEFAULT CF= 0.8
FACT: (DRIVEWAY HOUSE) CONTEXT: DEFAULT CF= 0.8
FACT: (MORNING-SUN HOUSE) CONTEXT: DEFAULT CF= 0.8
FACT: (VIEW HOUSE) CONTEXT: DEFAULT CF= 0.8
FACT: (TREES HOUSE) CONTEXT: DEFAULT CF= 0.8
FACT: (BOOKS LES) CONTEXT: SCHOOL CF= 0.6
FACT: (LIBRARY LES) CONTEXT: SCHOOL CF= 0.4
FACT: (STUDIES LES) CONTEXT: SCHOOL CF= 0.3

CHOICE-->2
GOAL-->(SMART PAT)
CONTEXT-->SCHOOL
WORKING...NO SOLUTION IN CONTEXT SCHOOL

CHOICE-->2
GOAL-->(BUY-PROPERTY HOUSE)
CONTEXT-->DEFAULT
SOLVED FOR THE GOAL: (BUY-PROPERTY HOUSE)
FOR CONTEXT: DEFAULT
AND CF= 0.8

CHOICE-->1
FACT-->(BIG HOUSE)
CF=-->1.0
CONTEXT-->HOUSE1
CHOICE-->3
FACT: (BIG HOUSE) CONTEXT: HOUSE1 CF= 1.0
```

Figure 10.11   Sample Run of GDI Final.

```
(DEFUN REPORT (RES CERT G CONTEXT)
   (IF RES
       (PRINC
           (FORMAT () "~%~5TSOLVED THE GOAL: ~S
             ~%~20TFOR CONTEXT: ~S
             ~%~20TAND CF= ~S~%"
             G CONTEXT CERT))
         (PRINC (FORMAT ()
                   "~3%~20TWORKING...NO SOLUTION IN CONTEXT ~S"
                   CONTEXT)))))

(DEFUN SHOW-WM ()
   (DOLIST (ELE *WM*)
       (PRINC (FORMAT ()
                   "~10TFACT: ~S CONTEXT: ~S CF= ~F~%" (INFO ELE)
                   (CONTEXT ELE)(CF ELE)))))
```

10.6 SUMMARY

This chapter discussed the development of rule bases and goal directed expert systems. Two versions of a goal directed system called GDI were presented. The first can provide a basic solution to goal directed problems. The second incorporates certainty into the process. The entire GDI prototype with certainty and improved context control is shown below. This includes functions from chapter nine.

```
;;; IF AN IMMEDIATE SOLUTION IS FOUND THEN RETURN IT
;;; ELSE COLLECT ALL RULES WHOSE RHS UNIFIES WITH THE
;;; GOAL. COMBINE THE CERTAINTY FOR ALL SOLUTIONS FOUND.
;;;
;;;-----------------------------------------------------
;;; GLOBALS
;;;-----------------------------------------------------

;;; Note: May want to change DEFVAR to SETF when testing

(DEFVAR *RULEBASE* (MAKE-HASH-TABLE))
(DEFVAR *WM* ())
(DEFVAR *CONTEXT* '(DEFAULT))
(DEFVAR *CURRENT-CONTEXT* 'DEFAULT)

;;;-----------------------------------------------------
;;; DATA STRUCTURES
;;;-----------------------------------------------------
```

```lisp
(DEFSTRUCT (RULE (:CONC-NAME NIL))
   LHS
   RHS
   (CFR 1.0))

(DEFSTRUCT (FACT (:CONC-NAME NIL))
   INFO
   CF
   CONTEXT)

;;;-------------------------------------------------
;;; MACROS THAT SUPPORT DATA STRUCTURES
;;;-------------------------------------------------

(DEFMACRO DEFRULE (NAME LHS RHS &OPTIONAL (RULES *RULEBASE*))
   `(SETF (GETHASH ',NAME ',RULES)
       (MAKE-RULE :LHS ',(CDR LHS) :RHS ',RHS)))

;;; REMOVES SOME CLUTTER FROM THE INFERENCE ENGINE

(DEFMACRO UPDATE-SOLUTION (BINDS NEW-WM-ELE)
   `(PROGN
       (SETF KNOWN ,BINDS)
       (SETF PREVIOUS (CF ,NEW-WM-ELE))
       (SETF CERTAINTY PREVIOUS)))

;;;-------------------------------------------------
;;; TOP LEVEL CONTROL
;;;-------------------------------------------------

(DEFUN GDI ()
 "GDI()-->
 TOPLEVEL CONTROL FOR GOAL DIRECTED INFERENCE"
   (LOOP
      (CASE (MENU)
         ((1) (DEFFACT (PROMPT 'FACT) (PROMPT 'CF=) (PROMPT 'CONTEXT)))
         ((2) (ACHIEVE (PROMPT 'GOAL) (PROMPT 'CONTEXT)))
         ((3) (SHOW-WM))
         ((4) (SHOW-RULE))
         ((5) (CLEAR-WM))
         (OTHERWISE (RETURN-FROM GDI 'DONE)))
      (PAUSE-UNTIL-KEYPRESSED)))

;;;-------------------------------------------------
;;; THE INFERENCE ENGINE
;;;-------------------------------------------------
```

```
(DEFUN ACHIEVE (G CONTEXT)
   (ASSERT (NOT(CONTAINS-VAR? G)) (G)
      "STATEMENT OF GOAL CANNOT CONTAIN VARIABLES")
   (IF (MEMBER CONTEXT *CONTEXT*)
       (MULTIPLE-VALUE-BIND (RES CERT)
          (ACHIEVE+ G CONTEXT)
          (REPORT RES CERT G CONTEXT))
       (REPORT NIL 0 G CONTEXT)))

(DEFUN ACHIEVE+ (G CONTEXT &OPTIONAL B)
  (MULTIPLE-VALUE-BIND (S B)
     (SCAN G B)
     (MULTIPLE-VALUE-BIND (KNOWN CERTAINTY)
        (SOLVED G CONTEXT B)
        (COND (KNOWN (VALUES KNOWN CERTAINTY))
              (T (IF (EMPTY? S)
                     (QUERY-USER G)
                 (DO ((PREVIOUS NIL))
                     ((EMPTY? S) (VALUES KNOWN CERTAINTY))
                    (LET*
                        ((RULE (POP S))
                         (CERT NIL)
                         (BINDS
                            (DOLIST (GSUB (LHS RULE) B)
                               (MULTIPLE-VALUE-BIND (RES CET)
                                  (ACHIEVE+ GSUB CONTEXT B)
                                  (COND (RES
                                           (PUSH CET CERT)
                                           (SETF B RES))
                                        (T (RETURN
                                              (VALUES RES CET))))))))
                       (IF BINDS
                           (LET ((ELE
                                  (CREATE-NEW-FACT RULE BINDS
                                     CERT PREVIOUS CONTEXT)))
                             (UPDATE-SOLUTION BINDS ELE)))))))))))

(DEFUN DEFFACT (INFO &OPTIONAL (CF 1.0)(CONTEXT *CURRENT-CONTEXT*))
   (LET ((OLD (FIRST (MEMBER INFO *WM* :TEST #'EQUAL :KEY #'INFO))))
      (COND ((AND OLD
                 (EQ (CONTEXT OLD) CONTEXT))
            (SETF (CF OLD) CF)
            OLD)
           (T (PUSHNEW CONTEXT *CONTEXT* :TEST #'EQ)
              (PUSH
```

```
                  (MAKE-FACT :INFO INFO :CF CF :CONTEXT CONTEXT) *WM*)
            (FIRST *WM*)))))

(DEFUN CREATE-NEW-FACT (RULE BINDS CERT PREVIOUS CONTEXT)
   (DEFFACT
      (INST (RHS RULE) BINDS)
      (IF PREVIOUS
          (UPDATE-CF (CFACTOR RULE CERT) PREVIOUS)
          (CFACTOR RULE CERT))
      CONTEXT))

(DEFUN SCAN (GOAL B  &OPTIONAL (RULES *RULEBASE*))
   (LET ((S NIL))
      (MAPHASH #'(LAMBDA (NAME RULE)
                    (DECLARE (IGNORE NAME))
                    (LET ((BINDING (MATCH-UNIFY (RHS RULE) GOAL B)))
                       (IF BINDING
                           (PROGN
                              (SETF B BINDING)
                              (PUSH RULE S)))))
            RULES)
      (VALUES S B)))
   (DEFUN SOLVED (G CONTEXT B)
      (MULTIPLE-VALUE-BIND (BINDINGS UCF)
          (TEST G CONTEXT B)
          (VALUES BINDINGS UCF)))

   (DEFUN TEST (PAT CONTEXT B)
   "TEST(PAT)-->BINDINGS|T|NIL
   RETURNS A LIST OF BINDINGS THAT MATCHED ALL PREDICATES
   NIL RETURN INDICATES NO LHS MATCH. T is a match."
      (ASSERT (CONSP PAT))
      (DOLIST (ELE *WM* (VALUES NIL NIL))
          (LET ((B (MATCH-UNIFY PAT (INFO ELE) B)))
             (IF (AND B
                    (EQ (CONTEXT ELE) CONTEXT))
                 (RETURN-FROM TEST (VALUES B (CF ELE)))))))

   (DEFUN EMPTY? (S)
      (NULL S))

   (DEFUN QUERY-USER (G)    ;CURRENTLY A DUMMY
      (DECLARE (IGNORE G))
      (VALUES))
```

```lisp
;;;----------------------------------------------------
;;; UNCERTAINTY CALCULATIONS FOR REDUNDANT ENTRIES
;;;----------------------------------------------------

(DEFUN UPDATE-CF (RULE OLD)
   (+ OLD (* RULE (- 1.0 OLD))))

(DEFUN CFACTOR (R L)
   (* (CFR R) (APPLY #'MIN L)))


;;;----------------------------------------------------
;;; REPORTING UTILITIES
;;;----------------------------------------------------

(DEFUN REPORT (RES CERT G CONTEXT)
   (IF RES
       (PRINC
          (FORMAT () "~2%~5TSOLVED THE GOAL: ~S
            ~%~20TFOR CONTEXT: ~S
            ~%~20TAND CF= ~S~%"
            G
            CONTEXT
            CERT))
       (PRINC
          (FORMAT () "~3%~20TWORKING...NO SOLUTION IN CONTEXT ~S"
            CONTEXT)))
   (VALUES))


;;;----------------------------------------------------
;;; LOW LEVEL UTILITIES
;;;----------------------------------------------------

(DEFUN SHOW-RULE (&OPTIONAL (RULES *RULEBASE*))
   (MAPHASH #'(LAMBDA (KEY VAL)
                (DECLARE (IGNORE KEY))
                (PRINC (FORMAT () "~% LHS:~S~% RHS:~S~2%"
                         (LHS VAL) (RHS VAL))))
       RULES))

(DEFUN SHOW-WM ()
   (DOLIST (ELE *WM*)
       (PRINC (FORMAT () "~10TFACT: ~S CONTEXT: ~S CF= ~F~%" (INFO ELE)
                (CONTEXT ELE) (CF ELE)))))

(DEFUN CLEAR-WM ()
   (SETF *WM* ())
   (SETF *CONTEXT* ()))
```

```
;;;------------------------------------------------
;;; REUSABLE COMPONENTS FROM PDI
;;;------------------------------------------------

(DEFUN MATCH-UNIFY (P TE B)
"MATCH-UNIFY(P TE B)-->BINDINGS|T|FAILURE
BINDINGS INDICATE UNIFICATION. T INDICATES MATCHING CONSTANTS.
NIL INDICATES FAILURE. NON-STANDARD EXIT ON FAILURE TO MATCH AT ATOMIC
LEVEL"
    (CATCH 'FAILURE
        (LET ((RES (MATCH+ P TE B)))
          (IF RES RES T))))

(DEFUN MATCH+ (P TE B)
"MATCH+(P TE B)-->BINDINGS|NIL
SHOULD ONLY BE USED thru MATCH-UNIFY WHICH CONTROLS CATCHER"
    (LABELS ((VAR? (EXP)
                (AND (SYMBOLP EXP)
                     (EQ #\? (SCHAR (STRING EXP) 0))))
             (CONST? (EXP)
                (OR (NUMBERP EXP)
                    (AND (SYMBOLP EXP) (NOT (VAR? EXP)))))
             (PATTERN? (EXP)
                (CONSP EXP))
             (VALUE-OCCURS? (TE BIND)
                (EQUAL TE (SECOND BIND)))
             ;INST was made external for this program
             (VAR-OCCURS-IN (P TE)
                (COND ((ATOM TE)
                       (IF (EQ P TE) (THROW 'FAILURE ())))
                      (T (VAR-OCCURS-IN P (FIRST TE))
                         (VAR-OCCURS-IN P (REST TE))))))
    ;BODY OF MATCH+
    ;PROPAGATE-BINDINGS FIRST
    (IF B (SETF P (INST P B) TE (INST TE B)))
    ;NOW CHECK ATTRIBUTES OF P AND TE
    (COND ((EQUAL P TE) B)
          ((VAR? P)
           (LET ((BINDING (FIND P B :KEY #'FIRST)))
             (COND ((VAR-OCCURS-IN P TE) (THROW 'FAILURE ()))
                   ((NULL BINDING) (PUSH (LIST P TE) B) B)
                   ((VALUE-OCCURS? TE BINDING) B)
                   (T (THROW 'FAILURE '())))))
          ((VAR? TE) (MATCH+ TE P B))
```

```
        ((AND (PATTERN? P) (PATTERN? TE)
              (= (LENGTH P) (LENGTH TE)))
           (DO ((PATS P (CDR PATS))
                (TES TE (CDR TES)))
               ((NULL PATS) B)
               (SETF B (MATCH+ (FIRST PATS) (FIRST TES) B))))
        ((OR (CONST? P) (CONST? TE))
           (IF (EQUAL P TE) B (THROW 'FAILURE ())))
        (T (THROW 'FAILURE ())))))

;;; THE INST FUNCTION IS USED BY MATCH-UNIFY AND GDI

(DEFUN INST (PAT BINDINGS)
"INST(PAT BINDINGS)-->INSTANTIATED PATTERN"
   (IF (CONSP PAT)
       (DOLIST (BINDING BINDINGS PAT)
          (SETF PAT
             (SUBST (SECOND BINDING)
                    (FIRST BINDING)
               PAT)))
       (DOLIST (BINDING BINDINGS PAT)
          (IF (EQ PAT (FIRST BINDING))
              (RETURN-FROM INST (SECOND BINDING)))))))

(DEFUN CONTAINS-VAR? (TERM)
   (DOLIST (ELE TERM ())
      (IF (VAR? ELE) (RETURN-FROM CONTAINS-VAR? T))))

(DEFUN VAR? (EXP)
   (AND (SYMBOLP EXP)
        (EQ #\? (SCHAR (STRING EXP) 0))))


;;;------------------------------------------------
;;; MENU INTERFACE SUPPORT
;;;------------------------------------------------

(DEFUN MENU ()
   (PRINC (FORMAT () "~%~20T WELCOME TO GDI~%"))
   (PRINC (FORMAT () "~2%~10T CHOOSE ONE OF THE FOLLOWING:~2%"))
   (MAPCAR #'(LAMBDA (MENU-ITEM)
               (PRINC (FORMAT () "~%~10T~A" MENU-ITEM)))
     '("1. ADD A FACT"
       "2. ACHIEVE A GOAL"
       "3. SHOW WORKING MEMORY"
```

```
        "4. SHOW RULEBASE"
        "5. CLEAR WORKING MEMORY"
        "6. QUIT"))
    (LET ((N (PROMPT 'CHOICE)))
        (IF (INTEGERP N) N (MENU)))))

(DEFUN PROMPT (CATEGORY)
    (PRINC (FORMAT () "~4%~10T~A-->" CATEGORY))
    (READ))

(DEFUN PAUSE-UNTIL-KEYPRESSED ()
    (PRINC (FORMAT () "~%~% ANY KEY TO CONTINUE~%"))
    (READ-CHAR))

;;;------------------------------------------------
;;; RULEBASE
;;;------------------------------------------------

(DEFRULE R1 (AND (COST ?X)(HOUSE ?X)(LOT ?X)(NEIGHBORHOOD ?X))
    (BUY-PROPERTY ?X))
(DEFRULE R2 (AND (PRICE ?X))(COST ?X))
(DEFRULE R3 (AND (INSIDE ?X)(OUTSIDE ?X))(HOUSE ?X))
(DEFRULE R4 (AND (DRIVEWAY ?X)(LOT-SIZE ?X)(ASCETICS ?X)(DRAINAGE ?X))
    (LOT ?X))
(DEFRULE R5 (AND (TREES ?X)(VIEW ?X)(MORNING-SUN ?X))(ASCETICS ?X))
(DEFRULE R6 (AND (STRUCTURE ?X)(PLUMBING ?X)(ELECTRICAL ?X))
    (INSIDE ?X))
(DEFRULE R7 (AND (FOUNDATION ?X)(ROOF ?X)(SIDES ?X))  (OUTSIDE ?X))
(DEFRULE R8 (AND (SCHOOLS ?X)(CRIME ?X)(TRAFFIC ?X)(ACCESS ?X)
    (DEVELOPMENT-PLANS ?X)(ZONING ?X))  (NEIGHBORHOOD ?X))
(DEFRULE R9 (AND (STUDIES ?X))(SMART ?X))
(DEFRULE R10 (AND (LIBRARY ?X))(SMART ?X))
(DEFRULE R11 (AND (BOOKS ?X))(SMART ?X))

;;;------------------------------------------------
;;; FACT BASE
;;;------------------------------------------------

(DEFFACT '(NEIGHBORHOOD PAT) 1.0 'HOUSE)
(DEFFACT '(STUDIES LES) 0.3 'SCHOOL)
(DEFFACT '(LIBRARY LES) 0.4 'SCHOOL)
(DEFFACT '(BOOKS LES) 0.6 'SCHOOL)
(DEFFACT '(TREES FRED) 0.8 'HOUSE)
(DEFFACT '(VIEW FRED) 0.8 'HOUSE)
```

```
(DEFFACT ' (MORNING-SUN FRED) 0.8 'HOUSE)
(DEFFACT ' (TREES PAT) 0.8 'HOUSE)
(DEFFACT ' (VIEW PAT) 0.6 'HOUSE)
(DEFFACT ' (MORNING-SUN PAT) 0.8 'HOUSE)
(DEFFACT ' (DRIVEWAY PAT) 0.8 'HOUSE)
(DEFFACT ' (LOT-SIZE PAT) 0.8 'HOUSE)
(DEFFACT ' (DRAINAGE PAT)0.8 'HOUSE)
(DEFFACT ' (COST PAT)0.8 'HOUSE)
(DEFFACT ' (NEIGHBORHOOD PAT) 0.8 'HOUSE)
(DEFFACT ' (INSIDE FRED) 0.4 'BAR)
(DEFFACT ' (OUTSIDE NED) 0.3 'BAR)


;;;------------------------------------------------
;;; END OF FILE
;;;------------------------------------------------
```

10.6 PROBLEMS

10.1. Improve the user interface. This should include activating the QUERY-USER facility so the user can add facts to WM during program execution.

10.2. Add a save facility so that working memory can be saved to a file.

10.3. Write a rule compiler that verifies rules for rule redundancy, cycles, contradictions, and rule subsumption.

Redundancy	P(x) & Q(x)−>S(x)
	Q(y) & P(y)−>S(y)
Cycles	P−>Q, Q−>R, R−>S, S−>P
Contradictions	P−>S & P−> ~S
Subsumption	P−>S subsumes P & Q−> S

10.4. Add a dictionary facility to the rule definition system that automatically checks the syntax of a rule. Is the format correct? Are the terms in the rule in the dictionary? If not, should they be added?

10.5. Is there any advantage to changing POP S to CHOOSE-RULE with a more powerful means of choosing which rule to look at next.

10.6. Index the rules and working memory elements to make access more efficient. Use hash tables.

10.7. Modify GDI so that variables can be used in queries. Assume that variables in queries means that the user is requesting all solutions in the specified CONTEXT.

10.8. Add an explanation facility and a trace facility that keeps track of the solution steps and subgoal solutions for queried goals. This facility should be available after each query is processed.

10.9. Modify CFACTOR and UPDATE-CF to take care of all the cases mentioned in Figure 10.6.

10.10. Modify GDI so that OR and NOT predicates can be used in the LHS of GDI rules.

Appendix

Alphabetical Listing of Primitives Defined in Text

Primitive	Chapter in Harrison	Page in Steele
*	1	199
+	1	199
−	1	199
/	1	200
/=	2	196
1+	2	200
1−	2*	200
<	2*	196
<=	2*	196
=	2	196
>	2*	196
>=	2*	196
ABS	2	205
ACONS	3	279
AND	4	82
APPEND	3	268
APPLY	4	107
APROPOS	1	443
AREF	6	290
ASSERT	4	434
ASSOC	3	280
ATOM	2	73
BIT	6	293
BIT-AND	6	294
BIT-EQV	6	294
BIT-IOR	6	294

Primitive	Chapter in Harrison	Page in Steele
BIT-NOT	6	295
BIT-XOR	6	294
BLOCK	4	119
BOUNDP	2	90
BUTLAST	3	271
CAR	3	262
CASE	7	117
CATCH	7	139
CDR	3	262
CEILING	2	215
CHAR	6	300
CLOSE	6	332
CLRHASH	6	285
COERCE	2	51
COMPILE	4	438
COMPILE-FILE	7	439
COND	4	116
CONS	3	266
CONSP	3	74
COPY-LIST	3	268
COPY-TREE	3	269
COS	2	207
DECF	4	201
DECLARE	4	153
DEFCONSTANT	4	68
DEFMACRO	5	145
DEFPARAMETER	4	68
DEFSTRUCT	6	307
DEFUN	4	57
DEFVAR	4	68
DELETE-IF	3	254
DESCRIBE	1	441
DIRECTORY	6	427
DO	4	122
DOCUMENTATION	1	440
DOLIST	4	126
DOTIMES	4	126
DRIBBLE	1	443
ED	1	442
ENDP	3	264
EQ	3	77
EQL	3	78
EQUAL	3	80
ERROR	5	429
EVAL	1	321
EVENP	2	196
EXP	2	203
EXPT	2	203
FBOUNDP	2	90
FILE-NAMESTRING	6	417

Primitive	Chapter in Harrison	Page in Steele
MAPHASH	6	285
MAPLIST	4	128
MAX	2	198
MEMBER	3	275
MERGE-PATHNAMES	7	415
MIN	2	198
MINUSP	2	196
MOD	2	217
MULTIPLE-VALUE-BIND	6	136
NCONC	3	269
NOT	4	82
NREVERSE	8	248
NSUBST	9	274
NTH	3	265
NTHCDR	3	267
NULL	3	73
NUMBERP	2	74
ODDP	2	196
OPEN	6	418
OR	4	83
PLUSP	2	196
POP	3	271
PRIN1	1	383
PRINC	1	383
PRINT	1	383
PROBE-FILE	6	424
PROCLAIM	4	156
PROG1	4	109
PROG2	4	109
PROGN	4	109
PSETF	5	97
PUSH	3	269
PUSHNEW	3	270
QUOTE	1	86
QUOTE	2	86
READ	1	375
READ-CHAR	7	379
READ-LINE	1	378
REM	2	217
REMHASH	6	284
REMOVE	3	253
REMOVE-DUPLICATES	8	254
REMOVE-IF	3	253
REST	3	266
RETURN	4	120
RETURN-FROM	4	120
REVERSE	3	248
ROUND	2	215
RPLACA	3	272
RPLACD	3	272

Primitive	Chapter in Harrison	Page in Steele
SBIT	6	293
SCHAR	6	300
SECOND	3	266
SET	2	92
SET-DIFFERENCE	3	278
SET-DISPATCH-MACRO-CHARACTER	5	364
SET-MACRO-CHARACTER	5	362
SETF	2	94
SETQ	2	91
SIN	2	207
SORT	3	258
SPECIAL	4	157
SQRT	2	205
STEP	1	441
STRING	6	304
SUBSEQ	3	248
SUBST	9	273
SUBSTITUTE	9	255
SVREF	6	291
SXHASH	6	285
SYMBOL-FUNCTION	2	90
SYMBOL-NAME	2	168
SYMBOL-PACKAGE	2	170
SYMBOL-PLIST	2	166
SYMBOL-VALUE	2	90
TAGBODY	5	130
TERPRI	1	384
THIRD	3	266
THROW	7	142
TIME	1	441
TRACE	1	440
TRUNCATE	2	215
TYPE	4*	158
UNION	3	276
UNLESS	8	115
UNTRACE	1	440
UNWIND-PROTECT	6	140
VALUES	2	134
VECTOR	6	290
VECTOR-POP	6	296
VECTOR-PUSH	6	296
VECTOR-PUSH-EXTEND	6	296
WITH-OPEN-FILE	6	422
Y-OR-N-P	1	407
YES-OR-NO-P	1	408
ZEROP	2	195

*No formal definition.

Bibliography

ABELSON, H., SUSSMAN, G. J., AND SUSSMAN, J. *Structure and Interpretation of Computer Programs.* Cambridge, MA: The MIT Press, 1985.

BUCHANAN, B. G. AND DUDA, R. O. "Principles of Rule-Based Expert Systems." Stanford University, Heuristic Programming Project, *Report HPP-82–14*, August 1982.

BUCHANAN, B. G. AND SHORTLIFFE, E. H. *Rule-based Expert Systems.* Reading, MA: Addison-Wesley, 1984.

CARLSSON, M. "On Implementing Prolog In Functional Programming." *IEEE*, 1984, 154–159.

CHANG, C. L. AND LEE R. C. *Symbolic Logic and Mechanical Theorem Proving.* New York, Academic Press, 1973.

CHARNIAK, E. AND McDERMOTT, D. *Introduction to Artificial Intelligence.* Reading, MA: Addison-Wesley, 1985.

CHARNIAK, E., RIESBECK, C. K., McDERMOTT, D. V. AND MEEHAN, J. R. *Artificial Intelligence Programming,* 2nd ed. Hillsdale, NJ: Lawrence Erlbaum Associates, 1987.

FELDMAN, Y. A. AND RICH, C. "Pattern-Directed Invocation with Changing Equalities." *AI Memo No. 1017.* Cambridge, MA: MIT, AI Laboratory, 1988.

GENESERETH, M. R. AND NILSSON, N. J. *Logical Foundations of Artificial Intelligence.* Los Altos, CA: Morgan Kaufmann Publishers, 1987.

LISKOV, B. AND GUTTAG, J. *Abstraction and Specification in Program Development.* Cambridge, MA: The MIT Press, 1986.

MANNA, Z. AND WALDINGER, R. *Studies in Automatic Programming Logic.* Amsterdam, Netherlands, Elsevier North-Holland, 1977.

MASON, I. A. *The Semantics of Destructive Lisp*, CSLI/SPI International, Stanford, CA, 1986.

Nilsson, N. J. *Principles of Artificial Intelligence*. Palo Alto, CA: Tioga Publishing, 1980.

Pearl, J. *Heuristics*. Reading, MA: Addison-Wesley, 1984.

Steele, G. *Common Lisp*. Palo Alto, CA: Digital, 1984.

van Melle, W. J. *Systems Aids in Constructing Consultation Programs*. Ann Arbor, MI: UMI Research Press, 1981.

Winston, P.H. *Artificial Intelligence*, 2nd ed. Reading, MA: Addison-Wesley, 1984.

Index